Management of Foreign Exchange Risk

This book provides a technical and specialised discussion of contemporary and emerging issues in foreign exchange and financial markets by addressing the issues of risk management and theory and hypothesis development, which have general implications for finance theory and foreign exchange market management. It offers an in-depth, comprehensive analysis of the issues concerning the volatility of exchange rates.

The book has three main objectives. First, it applies the integrated study of exchange rate volatility in terms of depth and breadth. Second, it applies the integrated study of exchange rate volatility in Malaysia, as a case study of a developing country. Malaysia had imposed capital control measures in the past and has now liberalised its exchange rate market and will continue to liberalise it further in the long run. Hence, the need to understand exchange rate volatility measurement and management will be even more important in the future. Third, the book highlights new conditional volatility models for a developing country, such as Malaysia, and develops advanced econometric models which have produced results for sound risk management strategies and for achieving risk management in the financial market and the economy. Additionally, the authors recommend risk management themes which may be of relevance to other developing countries.

This work can be used as a reference book by fund managers, financial market analysts, researchers, academics, practitioners, policy makers and postgraduate students in the areas of finance, accounting, business and financial economics. It can also be a supplementary text for Ph.D. and Masters' students in these areas.

Yew C. Lum is a Senior Lecturer in Finance and Coordinator of Faculty and Student Services Committee at Xiamen University Malaysia.

Sardar M. N. Islam is currently a Professor of Economic Studies, and has also been a Professor of Business, Economics and Finance (2007–2017) at Victoria University, Melbourne, Australia.

Banking, Money and International Finance

French Banking and Entrepreneurialism in China and Hong Kong
From the 1850s to 1980s
Hubert Bonin

Banking, Lending and Real Estate
Claudio Scardovi and Alessia Bezzecchi

The Regulation of Financial Planning in Australia
Current Practice, Issues and Empirical Analysis
Angelique Nadia Sweetman McInnes

Financial Risk Management in Banking
Evidence from Asia Pacific
Shahsuzan Zakaria and Sardar M. N. Islam

The Economics of Financial Cooperatives
Income Distribution, Political Economy and Regulation
Amr Khafagy

Financial Integration in the European Monetary Union
Sławomir Ireneusz Bukowski

Banking in China 1890s–1940s
Business in the French Concessions
Hubert Bonin

Management of Foreign Exchange Risk
Evidence from Developing Economies
Yew C. Lum and Sardar M. N. Islam

For more information about this the series, please visit: www.routedge.com/
series/BMIF

Management of Foreign Exchange Risk

Evidence from Developing Economies

Yew C. Lum and Sardar M. N. Islam

Routledge
Taylor & Francis Group

LONDON AND NEW YORK

First published 2021
by Routledge
2 Park Square, Milton Park, Abingdon, Oxon OX14 4RN

and by Routledge
605 Third Avenue, New York, NY 10017

First issued in paperback 2022

Routledge is an imprint of the Taylor & Francis Group, an informa business

© 2021 Yew C. Lum and Sardar M. N. Islam

Publisher's Note
The publisher has gone to great lengths to ensure the quality of this
reprint but points out that some imperfections in the original copies may
be apparent.

British Library Cataloguing-in-Publication Data
A catalogue record for this book is available from the British Library

Library of Congress Cataloging-in-Publication Data
Names: Lum, Y. C., author. | Islam, Sardar M. N., 1950– author.
Title: Management of foreign exchange risk: evidence from developing
economies / Y.C. Lum and Sardar M.N. Islam.
Description: Abingdon, Oxon; New York, NY: Routledge, 2021. |
Series: Banking, money and international finance |
Includes bibliographical references and index.
Identifiers: LCCN 2020014339 (print) | LCCN 2020014340 (ebook)
Subjects: LCSH: Foreign exchange market—Developing countries. |
Foreign exchange market—Malaysia. | Financial risk
management—Mathematical models.
Classification: LCC HG3877 .L86 2021 (print) |
LCC HG3877 (ebook) | DDC 332.4/5091724—dc23
LC record available at https://lccn.loc.gov/2020014339
LC ebook record available at https://lccn.loc.gov/2020014340

ISBN 13: 978-0-367-41857-1 (hbk)
ISBN 13: 978-0-367-54259-7 (pbk)
ISBN 13: 978-0-367-81659-9 (ebk)

DOI: 10.4324/9780367816599

Typeset in Times New Roman
by codeMantra

Contents

Figures

Tables

Foreword

This is an interesting and useful book in the area of financial risk management, foreign exchange and financial economics. It has provided a comprehensive analysis of the issues of time-varying volatility of exchange rates. The incorporation of asymmetric effects and non-Gaussian distribution in stochastic volatility models led to better modelling and measurement of exchange rate risks. Several important implications of the results provide strategic options for foreign exchange rate risk analysis and management. It develops advanced econometric models which have produced results for sound risk management strategies for achieving risk management in the financial market and the economy. This book is technical and specialised to focus on contemporary and emerging issues in foreign exchange and financial markets, in addressing the issues of risk management and for theory and hypothesis development, which will have general implications for finance theory in all economies for economic management and financial risk control.

The book can be used as a reference book by researchers, academics, practitioners, policy makers and postgraduate students in the areas of risk management, business, finance, applied econometrics and financial economics. It can also be a supplementary text for Ph.D. and Masters' students in these areas.

Professor Allan Manning
DBA, B.Com, MBA, FCPA, ANZIIF (Fellow)
(HM, CIP), FCII, FIICP, FCILA, FUEDI ELAE
Executive Chairman
The LMI Group
Melbourne
Australia
President of the International Institute
of Claims Professionals
31/09/2019

Summary and preface

Introduction

The last few decades have seen a tremendous increase in the risk levels of the foreign exchange market with large fluctuations due to the liberalisation of policies in developed and especially developing markets with trillions of daily trade and capital flows, as well as numerous financial and currency crises. There is, hence, an intense aspiration for systematic and structured foreign exchange risk management resolutions which involved three main tasks: risk management modelling, risk measurement and analysis, and formulation of risk management policies and strategies. Most empirical studies documented in the literature have applied univariate standardised discrete stochastic volatility models, assuming normal density functions and symmetric effects, and proceeded with other regression analysis, including causal relationships and cointegration testing. Implications are derived based on the usage of simple risk models. There is a need to test the sensitivity of the assumptions of the basic risk models and the comprehensive and systematic risk management framework, and to complement the lack of in-depth studies of exchange rate risks for developing countries. There are, hence, many gaps in the current literature in the area of exchange rate risk management, especially in developing countries.

Objectives

The main objective of this book is to carry out financial engineering approaches to bridge some gaps by focusing on three main tasks in a developing market, such as that of Malaysia. The challenge is to discover new findings in terms of better risk management models, more effective risk measurements and, finally, implications of risk management of developing markets. Recommendations are made for policies and strategies to provide for a more effective risk management of the foreign exchange market for developing countries. The book attempts to ask questions in relation to three separate but inter-related areas: (1) risk models, (2) risk measurements and (3) risk management issues. The focus of the book is on developing markets such as that of Malaysia, as there are relatively few studies that have investigated exchange rate volatilities in developing markets. An effort is made in this book to compare the exchange rate volatility analysis of a developing market in Malaysia with that of Thomas and Shah (1999), where exchange rate volatility of India was studied.

Critical literature review

The standard time series analysis rests on important concepts such as stationarity, autocorrelation, white noise, innovation and the autoregressive moving average models. Volatility modelling like Autoregressive Conditionally Heteroscedastic (ARCH) models introduced by Engle (1982) will take centre stage in stochastic modelling used for exchange rate volatility in this book. The ARCH model is a better risk management model for exchange rates compared to standard time series modelling. These generalised ARCH (GARCH)-type models of Bollerslev (1986), through an efficient modelling of volatility and variability of the prices of financial assets, led to a fundamental change in the approaches used in international economics and finance. Professors Robert F. Engle and Clive W. J. Granger were jointly awarded the Nobel Prize for Economics in 2003 for analysing economic time series with time-varying volatility.

The many empirical findings of the standard time series do not support the assumptions of standard linear time series models and hence there is a need to introduce the nonlinear time series models of GARCH. GARCH models are simple to be used in practice as well as sufficiently complex to capture various main stylised facts of financial data series: unpredictability of data, volatility clustering, leptokurticity of the marginal distributions and asymmetries.

Most empirical studies have applied standard GARCH models with normal density functions and assume symmetric effects. There are many exchange rate volatility studies in developed countries but few exchange rate volatility studies applied to developing economies. One example of such studies that applied to developing countries includes Tan and Chong (2008), where macroeconomic variables were analysed in Malaysia, Indonesia and Thailand. Chong and Tan (2007) analysed exchange rate volatility by using an exponential GARCH models for Malaysia, Indonesia, Thailand and Singapore. Thomas and Shah (1999) extended the analysis of volatility issues in three financial markets (stocks, exchange rates and money markets) in India.

Methodology

The discrete stochastic volatility models or better known as GARCH-type models are estimated by the G@RCH module (details can be found in Laurent, 2006) as part of the OxMetric software (Doornik, 2009), and applied to the daily series of five major currency pairs with respect to the Malaysian ringgit. The full daily data period runs from 1 January 1997 to 15 January 2014 and is split into two exchange rate eras, stripping away data around the Asian financial crisis: (1) from 1 October 1998 to 30 December 2005; and (2) 1 January 2006 to 15 January 2014. In Malaysia, the first exchange rate era is when the central bank of Malaysia imposed capital control, while the second era is when the capital control was relaxed and managed float was implemented.

The rigidity of the popular GARCH models applied by most studies in the exchange rate documented in literature is being investigated. Three extensions focused on these GARCH models are identified: (1) non-Gaussian density functions (Jondeau *et al.*, 2007), (2) asymmetric effects (Pagan and Schwert, 1990, Brailsford and Faff, 1996 and Loudon *et al.*, 2000) and (3) multivariate approaches (Bauwens *et al.*, 2006). Once the appropriate risk models for the underlying exchange rate have been identified, the risk measurements for analysis are calculated using: (1) volatility persistency (Ding and Granger, 1996) over different exchange rate era, (2) risk premium (Engle *et al.*, 1987) and (3) Value-at-Risk (Jorion, 2000).

Finally, the findings on the risk models and risk measurements are linked to the implications of risk management in a developing country such as Malaysia. The findings are compared with those in India (Thomas and Shah, 1999), given the similarity of the exchange rate liberalisation experience. The book discusses four perspectives of risk management: (1) government stabilisation policies, (2) individuals and institutions, (3) education on risk management and (4) efficient market hypothesis first proposed by Fama (1970).

Results, discussion and implications

This book has three main areas of focus. First, the book applies the integrated study of exchange rate volatility in terms of depth and breadth. Second, it applies the integrated study of exchange rate volatility in Malaysia as a case study of a developing country. Malaysia had imposed capital control measures in the past and has now liberalised its exchange rate market and will continue to liberalise it further in the long run. Hence, the need to understand exchange rate volatility measurement and management will be even more important in the future. Third, the book highlights new conditional volatility models for a developing country and recommends some risk management issues which may be of relevance to other developing countries.

An in-depth analysis is provided to answer questions pertaining to risk modelling, risk measurement and risk management, focusing on the Malaysian exchange rate markets. For risk modelling, both hypotheses of normal density functions and symmetric effects have been rejected by the findings. Chong and Tan (2007) used Exponential GARCH (EGARCH) models to estimate the conditional standard deviation for Malaysia and it was found that the leverage tests failed for most of the currency pairs. Next, GARCH models with skewed Student density function to address these two issues were utilised and they performed relatively better than the standardised GARCH models with normal density function and symmetric effects. It was also found that the tail parameters under the skewed Student distribution are statistically significant, implying that important information is captured in the tail parameters of the skewed Student distribution. The asymmetric parameters of the skewed distribution, however, provided mixed results for the different currency pairs. Finally, diagnostic tests of these skewed Student distribution, however, did not improve significantly the normality tests, implying that skewed Student density functions did not address the non-Gaussian issues. Multivariate GARCH (MGARCH) model in Chapter 5 was more restrictive in terms of flexibility and restrictions. Only DCC models of Tse and Tshui (2002) and Engle (2002) were able to withstand the sensitivity of density functions in both cases. Both the scalar and diagonal BEKK MGARCH models were also mildly sensitive to the change in density functions. In conclusion, MGARCH models were unable to provide risk measurements in terms of volatility persistency, risk premium and VaR except for the conditional correlations between the different currency pairs. The better MGARCH models could, however, generate these conditional correlations, as correlations between the different exchange rate pairs changed over time. Univariate GARCH models do not explicitly model these inter-relationships between different currency pairs. These conditional correlations would be important for investment portfolio in different exchange rate pairs.

The findings of this book are different from those of Thomas and Shah (1999). This study in Malaysia yields mixed findings in terms of change in exchange rate volatility during capital control, whereas Thomas and Shah (1999) found that India yielded greater exchange rate risk through a combination of months of fixed prices, followed by very large adjustments. Malaysia did not adjust the pegging of the MYR/USD during the capital control, resulting in all exchange rate pairs exhibiting changes in volatilities under different exchange rate regimes. The American dollar, British pound and Japanese yen all exhibited greater volatilities while the euro and Swiss franc demonstrated reduction in volatilities post exchange rate liberalisation.

It was found that skewed Student density functions perform better than Gaussian distribution, as the former distribution captures asymmetric and tail parameters. Tail parameters are significant across all currency pairs and across both exchange rate regimes, implying that important information is captured in the tail parameters. Hence, it is fruitful to focus on the tail distribution such as that of the extreme value theory. Asymmetric effects were not significant for all five currency pairs during the peg period while asymmetric effects were found in three currency pairs (MYR/EUR, MYR/JPY and MYR/CHF) post exchange rate liberalisation. This book also did not find any significant relationships between the conditional risk and conditional return under the conditional Capital Asset Pricing Model (CAPM).

RiskMetrics models, under managed float era for Malaysia, performed well under controlled exchange rate environment but relatively badly with more rejections of the null hypothesis that the failure rate is equal to the chosen level of confidence level. This is even more relevant for short positions than for long positions when Bank Negara Malaysia (BNM) abolished capital control. Following Giot and Laurent (2003), Asymmetric Power GARCH (APARCH) models with skewed Student density functions were applied. APARCH models perform relatively better than the RiskMetrics models. VaR performance under APARCH models improved for long positions even after BNM relaxed capital control and is also relatively better than RiskMetrics for short positions for both exchange rate eras.

The empirical findings of this book are also influenced by the characteristics of the developing Malaysian market, which can be classified under three major headings: (1) characteristics specific to the Malaysian ringgit such as relatively low trading volume and restrictive trading by central banks in the international foreign exchange markets, (2) general market-related characteristics and (3) underdeveloped financial systems.

There are three new academic contributions from this book. The first contribution is in terms of modelling exchange rate volatility, it can be generalised that developing countries with the above three characteristics, is that the popular and simplistic RiskMetrics models are not suitable especially during post exchange rate liberalisation. The Asymmetric Power ARCH model, introduced by Ding *et al.* (1993), performs better regardless of exchange rate eras. Another new contribution: GARCH models with skewed Student density, rather than Gaussian density, are more suitable for developing countries which had liberalised their exchange rate market post capital control, as in the case of Malaysia. Finally, we found that there are no significant relationships between conditional mean and conditional risk for the Malaysian exchange rate market.

The analysis is concluded by relating the implications discussed above to risk management from four different perspectives, namely, government stabilisation policies, individuals and institutions, education on risk management and implications for efficient market hypothesis. This approach of linking risk management to risk measurement is new compared to the traditional approach of risk management by financial products and provides a more strategic view of risk management for different stakeholders from the risk modelling and measurement process.

Acknowledgements

The authors would like to acknowledge the generous financial support from Xiamen University Malaysia Research Fund under grant number XMUMRF/ 2018-C2/ISEM/0006 to support the completion of this book. They are very grateful for the constructive comments provided by anonymous reviewers for the manuscript of the book to further enhance the quality of the book. Finally, they are appreciative of Kristina Abbotts and Christiana Mandizha of Routledge who have been very professional and efficient in the handling of the publication process of this book.

Abbreviations

ADF	Augmented Dickey Fuller
AIC	Akaike Information Criteria
APARCH	Asymmetric Power ARCH
AR	Auto-Regressive or Autoregressive
ARCH	Auto-Regressive Conditional Heteroskedasticity
ARDL	Autoregressive Distributed Lag
ARFIMA	Fractionally Integrated ARMA
ARMA	Auto-Regressive and Moving Average
ASEAN	Association of Southeast Asian Nations
BEKK	Baba, Engle, Kraft and Kroner
BFGS	Broyden, Fletcher, Goldfarb and Shanno
BNM	Bank Negara Malaysia/Central Bank of Malaysia
CAPM	Capital Asset Pricing Model
CCC	Constant Conditional Correlation
cDCC	Corrected DCC
CHF	Swiss Franc
DECO	Dynamic Equicorrelation
DCC	Dynamic Conditional Correlation
DGP	Data Generating Process
Diag-BEKK	Diagonal-BEKK
DM	Deutsche Mark
ECU	European Currency Unit
EGARCH	Exponential GARCH
EWMA	Exponentially Weighted Moving Average
FIGARCH	Fractional Integrated GARCH
FSA	Financial Services Act
GARCH	Generalised Autoregressive Conditional Heteroskedasticity
GARCH-M	GARCH in Mean
GARP	Global Association of Risk Professionals
GBP	Great Britain Pound
GED	Generalised Error Distribution
GJR GARCH	Glosten, Jagannathan, Runkle GARCH

GLCs	Government-Linked Corporations
GO-GARCH	Generalised Orthogonal GARCH
HKD	Hong Kong Dollar
IFSA	Islamic Financial System Act
IGARCH	Integrated GARCH
IMF	International Monetary Fund
i.i.d.	Independent and Identically Distributed
JPY	Japanese Yen
LM	Lagrange Multiplier
MA	Moving Average
MGARCH	Multivariate GARCH
ML	Maximum Likelihood
MYR	Malaysian Ringgit
NARCH	Nonlinear ARCH
NLS GO-GARCH	Nonlinear Least Squares Generalised Orthogonal GARCH
NSBT	Negative Sign Bias Test
O-GARCH	Orthogonal GARCH
PGARCH	Power GARCH
PSBT	Positive Sign Bias Test
QML	Quasi-Maximum Likelihood
QMLE	Quasi-Maximum Likelihood Estimator
SBT	Sign Bias Test
SDR	Special Drawing Rights
SGD	Singapore Dollar
SIC	Schwartz Information Criteria
SV	Stochastic Volatility
TGARCH	Threshold GARCH
USD	US Dollar
VaR	Value-at-Risk
VARMA	Vector ARMA

1 Strategic overview

Background of the study

Every economy in the world experiences change. Changes in technology, tastes of individuals, institutions, law, economic policies and regulations have effects on resource allocation in the economy. Changes outside a country have impacts through trade and capital interactions. These changes generate a variety of risks for all individuals and companies. In this book, "risk" is defined as exposure to an uncertain event and also the movements of the underlying fundamentals.

Risk measurement is becoming increasingly important in financial risk management of banks and other institutions associated with the financial markets. The need to quantify risk typically arises when a financial institution has to determine the amount of capital to hold as protection against unexpected losses. In fact, risk measurement is concerned with all types of risks encountered in finance. Some major forms of risk are as follows. Credit risk is the risk of not receiving repayments on outstanding loans as a result of borrower's default. Operational risk is the risk of losses resulting from failed internal processes, people and systems or external events. Liquidity risk occurs when, due to a lack of marketability, an investment cannot be bought or sold quickly enough to prevent a loss. Model risk can be defined as the risk due to the use of a misspecified model for risk measurement. Market risk is the risk of change in the value of a financial position. This book focuses on market risk and model risk as discussed above.

Foreign exchange markets are extremely interesting for statistical studies because of the vast number and quality of data they produce. The markets have no business-hour limitations. They are open worldwide, 24 hours a day including weekends, except perhaps a few worldwide holidays. Trading is essentially continuous, the markets (at least for the most traded currencies) are extremely liquid and the trading volumes are huge. Daily volumes are in the order of $USD10^{12}$, approximately the gross national product of Italy. Typical sizes are deals in the order of $USD10^{6}–10^{7}$ and most of the deals are speculative in origin. As a consequence of the liquidity, good databases contain about 1.5 million data points per year and data have been collected from over many years. Relevant statistics on the global foreign exchange rates are summarised in the Bank for International Settlements (BIS) Triennial Central Bank Survey.

Many empirical studies have examined the movements of exchange rate markets. For instance, Mun (2007) applied Exponential GARCH (EGARCH) by Nelson (1991) to the dynamic movements of both stock market and exchange rate volatility. He found that exchange rate movements have a significant influence on equity market volatility but have no measurable influence on the US/local market correlation for most cases. Tai (2004) examined four Asian foreign exchange markets, namely Japan, Hong Kong, Singapore and Taiwan, during the 1997 Asian financial crisis and found that the time-varying risk premium is a very strong candidate in explaining the predictable excess return puzzle (proposed by Lewis, 1994) as the risk premiums are both statistically and economically significant. Hurley and Santos (2001) found that for ASEAN currencies prior to the financial crisis in 1997, the Indonesian rupiah was the most volatile, followed by the Philippine peso, while the Singapore dollar was the least variable. They also found that the switch to *de facto* pegging against the US dollar in the mid-1980s was found to stabilise the variability in the currencies of all ASEAN nations, with the exception of the Malaysian Ringgit. Gan and Soon (2003) found that Malaysia has the largest current account reversal among the four East Asian economies; the other three economies were Indonesia, Thailand and South Korea, suggesting that Malaysia had managed to achieve reduction in domestic absorption due to the transfer of resources overseas. The expansionary macroeconomic policies in combination with the expenditure-switching effect of a large real exchange rate depreciation and favourable international demand for Malaysian exports had allowed the current account surplus to be maintained and the economic activity to recover rather quickly.

This book looks at the unique natures of foreign exchange markets of developing countries. There are different definitions of developing countries classified by different organisations – examples include the United Nations Development Programme, the World Bank and the International Monetary Fund which have different classification systems based on countries' development attainment. Nielsen (2011) did however propose a trichotomous taxonomy that would better capture the observed diversity between developing and developed countries as well as within developing countries. Many developing countries did not and do not have the resources to stimulate the economy and protect their socially disadvantaged populations to the same extent as the industrialised countries. The experiences of several emerging market economies suggest that the sustainability of exchange rate policy depends both on adequate policy responses to the shocks to the economy and on the fragility of the economic, financial and political system. Many developing countries did not have the resources to stimulate the economy and protect their socially disadvantaged populations to the same extent as the industrialised countries. The experiences of several emerging market economies suggested that the sustainability of exchange rate policy depends both on adequate policy responses to the shocks to the economy and on the fragility of the economic, financial and political system. Some pieces of research that looked at these exchange rate policies of developing countries that were hot by currency crisis include Frankel and Rose (1996), Chang and Velasco (2000) and Frankel (2005). Prasad *et al.* (2005) suggested that financial integration should be approached cautiously, with good institutions and macroeconomic frameworks being viewed as important. The review of the available evidence does not, however, provide a clear road map for the optimal pace and sequencing of integration. For instance, there is an unresolved tension between having good institutions in place before undertaking capital market liberalisation and the notion that such liberalisation can, itself, help a country import best practices and provide an impetus to improve domestic institutions.

Given that many issues can be found in foreign exchange markets, this book focuses on the unique features of Malaysia, a developing country, and examines various aspects of foreign exchange risk in Malaysia so that one can have a clearer understanding of the movements of the exchange rate market. Malaysia's economy has been experiencing liberalisation of the foreign exchange market since 2005. Liberalisation has helped convert the steady stream of change in the real economy into a steady stream of price changes. This has yielded a changed environment of price volatility in the economy. In this new environment, we need to improve our understanding of risk in order to measure it more effectively and create new kinds of financial instruments which allow for risk reduction through hedging.

In 2013, the Central Bank of Malaysia (Bank Negara Malaysia) further liberalised the foreign exchange administration rules to enhance the economy's competitiveness and further develop the domestic financial market. The liberalisation measures were driven by the introduction of the Financial Services Act (FSA) and the Islamic Financial System Act (IFSA). The measures include allowing residents to freely invest in onshore foreign currency-denominated assets to spur the domestic foreign exchange market through greater demand for foreign currency products and services. Another measure allows resident *takaful* operators to undertake investments abroad of any amount of their resident clients. This measure would further promote the development of the Islamic financial markets through an increased flow of cross-border Islamic financial activities and greater use of Islamic financial intermediaries. The liberalisation measures would also enhance regulatory efficiency, as resident *takaful* operators and resident insurers would only be subject to their risk-based capital framework when undertaking investment abroad for their own accounts.

To further promote a risk-management culture and support the development of the foreign exchange market, residents and non-residents would now be permitted to undertake anticipatory hedging involving the ringgit for financial account transactions with onshore banks. Furthermore, non-residents would be permitted to hedge ringgit exposure arising from the ringgit investments acquired prior to 1 April 2005 with onshore banks, in addition to the current flexibility, to hedge the ringgit investments acquired from 1 April 2005.

The main objective of this book is to concentrate on risk measurement and risk management of the foreign exchange market in developing countries, using Malaysia as a case study. There have been many recent developments in the area of volatility modelling, especially time-varying volatility for explaining the behaviour of nominal spot exchange rate movements (see Baillie and McMahon (1989), Campbell *et al.* (1997), Verbeek (2000) and Knight and Satchell (2002)). The book shows the analysis of exchange rate volatility through standard methods like variance-covariance and standard deviations of past exchange rate movements are limited in terms of risk management implications.

This book will analyse five main trading currencies with respect to Malaysian ringgit to provide breadth of study in terms of risk modelling, measurement and management. The depth of this book is achieved through three ways of extending the standard time-varying approach of the stochastic modelling of exchange rate volatility. The first approach is the application and analysis of a non-Gaussian approach due to non-Gaussian density functions of the volatility exhibited in most empirical exchange rate studies. The second way is to extend the asymmetric and leverage effects (see Black, 1976) of the exchange rate volatility. The third approach to increase the depth of research for this book is to extend the above univariate analysis to multivariate approaches. This multivariate approach gives rise to better tools for decision making in various areas such as asset pricing models, portfolio selection and hedging decisions. Through these different approaches of breadth and depth of analysis to various risk measurement of Malaysia' foreign exchange markets, we are able to understand the important issues in relation to how quickly exchange rate volatility information flows in the market.

Contribution to knowledge

By focusing on the measurement and management of foreign exchange volatility from the perspective of public and private entities, it is hoped that a better understanding of the underlying volatility structure will help academics, investors and regulators to predict and simulate foreign exchange volatility more effectively in the future. The importance of this book lies in its attempt to improve current financial econometric modelling, particularly in analysing and forecasting volatility of exchange rates, which originated from Engle (1982) and Bollerslev (1986). The extremely low statistical explanatory power of these time-varying volatility models requires more research in this area and this book aims to improve on these models by calibrating new ones that perform better, especially for model fitting, so that better risk management techniques can be applied. Risk measurement is essentially a statistical issue based on historical observations and given a specific model, a statistical estimate of the distribution of the change in value of the exchange rate is calculated.

Another contribution of this book is its focus on an appropriate methodology for simulating the behaviour of the foreign exchange markets, which is the application of non-Gaussian density functions. Summarised in Jondeau *et al.* (2007), the violations of normality distribution and asymmetric effects of the volatility density functions are common among financial data found in foreign exchange markets.

A comprehensive study of exchange rate volatility provides in-depth analysis not only of the univariate properties of exchange rate volatility between Malaysia and five major trading economies (the USA, the UK, European Union, Japan and Switzerland), but also of the multivariate properties between those five different economies. The extension of univariate to multivariate analysis is important to understand not only individual currency pairs but also dynamics between different currency pairs which would help investors and managers to apply the portfolio investment more accurately through a more precise risk measurement.

Finally, this book focuses on the issues of volatility of developing foreign exchange markets instead of advanced economies since there is relatively limited research carried out on the former. There are many studies that focused on impact of exchange rate volatilities on developed countries compared to developing countries. Aghion *et al.* (2009) found significant impact effects of exchange rate volatility on long-term rate of productivity growth, but the effect depends critically on a country's level of financial development. For countries with relatively low levels of financial development, exchange rate volatility generally reduces growth, whereas for financially advanced countries, there is no significant effect. Levy-Yeyati and Sturzenegger (2003) found that, for developing countries, less flexible exchange rate regimes are associated with slower growth, as well as with greater output volatility. For industrial countries, regimes do not appear to have any significant impact on growth. Panel estimations by Schnabl (2008) revealed a robust negative relationship between exchange rate volatility and growth for countries in the economic catch-up process with open capital accounts. Husain *et al.* (2005) found that for developing countries with little exposure to international capital markets, pegs are notable for their durability and relatively low inflation. In contrast, for advanced economies, floats are distinctly more durable and also appear to be associated with higher growth.

Malaysia is used as a case study due to the recent liberalisation of its foreign exchange markets as well as its controversial decision to impose capital control. This book follows Thomas (1995) and Thomas and Shah (1999) in terms of providing a starting platform for analysing volatility issues. Both studies analysed the volatility issues of financial markets in India. India is a good, comparative benchmark for Malaysia as India experienced economic liberalisation in 1995 and Malaysia followed suit in 2005 by removing capital control in the exchange rate market. Thomas (1995) found that there was volatility clustering over time and stock market volatility increased after economic liberalisation, but risk was not priced in the stock market return in the Bombay Stock Exchange. Thomas and Shah (1999) then extended the analysis of volatility issues in three financial markets (stocks, exchange rates and money markets) in India. They found that for the dollar-rupee exchange rate, institutional details and regime shifts had a major impact upon the models and parameter estimates for the risk measurement. They also found that greater government controls (1990–1995) can yield greater price risk through a combination of months of fixed prices followed by very large adjustments. These two studies thus provide a good foundation for building further knowledge to better understand the economics of developing countries and finance in developing markets which are discussed further in the next section.

This book differs in a few ways from the above two studies in that it focuses on the study of exchange rate volatility, provides appropriate methodologies in developing the appropriate volatility model of foreign exchange markets as well as links various economic theories in explaining those exchange rate volatility movements. Finally, a more in-depth study of the previously regulated and recently liberalised foreign exchange markets in Malaysia is conducted and some policy implications are provided and compared with the Indian case study in Thomas and Shah (1999) for regulators to apply in the context of other developing markets in the future. A comparable study in this area of exchange rate volatility issues in Malaysia is discussed further in section "Geographical location of the topic".

This book does not analyse the level of exchange rate, as was done by many researchers, but rather analyses Malaysia's exchange rate risk measurement and risk management issues under different exchange rate era and links those risk management issues to economic policy implications for both public and private sectors. An in-depth analysis is first applied to exchange rate risk modelling, followed by risk measurement; univariate stochastic volatility modelling is introduced to capture the volatility clustering over time. Finally, extension to multivariate stochastic volatility modelling provides the relationships of co-movements of exchange rate volatility of five different major trading economies.

There are three new academic contributions from this book. There are strong pieces of evidence to support the popular and simplistic RiskMetrics models which are not suitable especially during post exchange rate liberalisation. The Asymmetric Power ARCH model, introduced by Ding *et al.* (1993), performs better regardless of exchange rate eras. It is also found in this study that exchange rate volatility models with skewed Student density, rather than Gaussian density, are more suitable for developing countries. Finally, there are no significant relationships between the conditional mean and conditional risk for the developing countries' exchange rate market.

To summarise, the main objective of this book is to determine whether the integrated approach of studying exchange rate risk management in a developing country, such as Malaysia, would reveal some policy implications on risk management of the exchange rate of a developing country that had imposed capital control, followed by economic liberalisation. To provide readers with a better understanding of the issues of exchange rate volatility, section "History of the topic" provides an overall summary of the exchange rate behaviour, including volatility issues. Section "Geographical location of the topic" discusses the comparison of different empirical studies, including that of the Malaysian exchange rate markets.

History of the topic

There are two main areas of research in the field of exchange rate behaviour. On the one hand, there are theoretical (structural) models of exchange rate behaviour including Purchasing Power Parity (PPP) and other macroeconomic models. On the other hand, there is the statistical analysis of exchange rates, including testing of efficiency and distribution of changes in the exchange rate as well as the volatility. One particular growing area of empirical research is the measurement of asset return volatility and an examination of the economic variables that might influence it. Microstructural issues such as bid-ask spreads and trading variables (e.g. order flow, size of trades) are another important area for exploration.

Volatility modelling has been a growing area of research in recent years. This interest is largely motivated by the importance of volatility in financial markets. Volatility estimates are also widely used as simple risk measures in many asset-pricing models. Analysis of volatility enters option-pricing formulae derived from models such as the Black-Scholes model and its various extensions. The types of methodology used by agents to forecast volatility includes historic volatility using concepts of moving averages but they still cannot explain various stylised facts (see Chapter 2, section "Classical time series models and financial series", for more information regarding these stylised facts, found in the volatility of exchange rate).

For hedging against risk and portfolio management, reliable volatility estimates are very crucial. If volatility fluctuates in a forecastable manner, then volatility forecasts are useful for risk management. Volatility forecastability, however, varies with horizon and different horizons are relevant to different applications. The assumed model, together with the horizons, forms the joint assessments of volatility forecastability. Christoffersen and Diebold (2000), however, developed a model-free procedure for assessing volatility forecastability across horizons and concluded that volatility forecasting is still relevant at short horizons. Most studies have focused on a narrow aspect of volatility modelling, while this book covers a comprehensive analysis of exchange rate volatility using Malaysia as a case study.

There are many empirical studies that analyse the volatility of spot exchange rate markets using discrete stochastic volatility models like ARCH and GARCH models. An in-depth literature review of these discrete stochastic volatility or conditional variance models is provided in Chapter 2, while the technical representations are elaborated in Chapters 4 and 5 for univariate and multivariate models, respectively. Early work using univariate models (e.g. Diebold, 1986; Engle and Bollerslev, 1986; Baillie and Bollerslev, 1989; Bollerslev *et al.*, 1992) established strong ARCH effects using intraday, daily and weekly data with much weaker effects at a monthly horizon and with ARCH effects largely disappearing at horizons over one month.

In the literature that examines persistence in volatility, the idea that news or new information in one market can affect volatility in another market is prevalent. Engle *et al.* (1990) and Ito *et al.* (1992) used the analogy of a meteor shower vs a heat wave. A hot day in New York may be followed by another hot day in New York, but not usually by a hot day in Tokyo – this is the idea of "news" as a heat wave. Alternatively, a meteor shower in New York will almost certainly be followed by a meteor shower in Tokyo – that is, news in one market "spills over" into other markets (after a short lag). Using intraday data in the USD-yen exchange rate, Engle *et al.* (1990) found that news is like a meteor shower and moves across different markets as they open around the world.

There are also studies that investigate exchange rate volatilities in developing countries. Many researchers analysed various factors driving the exchange rate volatilities for developing countries; see Calvo *et al.* (1996), Eichengreen and Hausmann (1999), Eichengreen *et al.* (2003b) and Fraga *et al.* (2003) for detailed discussion. There are another group of researchers focusing on the impact of exchange rate regime on the exchange rate volatilities of developing countries; some notable studies including Frankel (1999), Fischer (2001), Bleaney and Fielding (2002), Calvo and Reinhart (2002), Calvo and Mishkin (2003), Frankel (2003), Arize *et al.* (2000) and Aghion *et al.* (2009) considered the relationship between exchange rate volatility and economic growth and found that exchange rate volatility reduced growth for developing countries. Schnabl (2008) applied panel estimations and revealed a robust negative relationship between exchange rate volatility and growth for developing countries with open capital account. Devereux and Lane (2003) found through empirical research that the standard optimal currency area variables were more important in explaining bilateral exchange rate volatility.

Longmore and Robinson (2004) and Olowe (2009) modelled exchange rate volatility for developing countries and recently more studies have been increasingly carried out on the exchange rate volatility modelling and forecasting including Kamal *et al.* (2012), Abdalla (2012), Antonakakis and Darby (2013) and Thorlie *et al.* (2014). Miletić (2015) compared exchange rate volatility modelling of developing countries and developed countries.

There are also many research works on the exchange rate volatility modelling of specific developing countries including Abdalla (2012) on Arab countries, Bala and Asemota (2013) on Nigeria, Ramzan *et al.* (2012) on Pakistan and Murari (2015) on India. Asymmetric exchange rate volatility modelling included Longmore and Robinson (2004), Olowe (2009), Thorlie *et al.* (2014) and Epaphra (2017). Thomas and Shah (1999) investigated the relationships between risks in three financial markets in India: stock markets, exchange rate markets and money markets. They found that India's economy had experienced liberalisation of many markets and the steady stream of changes in the real economy had helped yield an altered environment of price volatility in the economy. They tried to answer two key volatility issues in the Indian markets: is volatility in Indian markets constant and is volatility clustering present? They then applied GARCH models to model the volatility of dollar-Indian rupee exchange rate and found two key ideas in understanding risk. The first was a reminder that institutional details and exchange rate regime shifts have a major impact upon the models and parameter estimates that go into the calculation of risk measures. The second is that greater government controls (1990–1995) can yield greater price risk through a combination of months of fixed prices followed by very large adjustments. The following section focuses on the empirical work that has been conducted on Malaysia and the reasons for choosing Malaysia as a case study for this book.

Geographical location of the topic

This section highlights many important and unique reasons for choosing Malaysia as a case study to analyse, in depth, the volatility of developing foreign exchange markets.

Malaysia is chosen as a case study in this book as it is the only developing country during the Asian financial crisis that did not follow the conventional restrictive monetary policy to stabilise the exchange rate and bring about improvement in the external balance. Instead, the authorities chose to peg the exchange rate with the US dollar and impose capital control followed by moderate expansionary policies. The Malaysian government decided to let the Malaysian ringgit currency floated again in 2005, implying that volatility would be an important factor to consider in the future. These unique policies pose interesting research questions and warrant a more in-depth analysis of the behaviour and performance of the risk dimension of foreign exchange rates especially when developing economies may face external shocks in the future. Exchange rate issues dominate public debates in developing financial markets. Devereux (2003) deliberated on the Asian financial crisis, while Dixon (1999) discussed about the controversy between exchange rates and economic fundamentals among many others. McKenzie (1999) provided a comprehensive survey of the impact of exchange rates volatility on international trade flows, while Crosby and Voss (1999) put forward some theoretical issues in exchange rate determination. The latter argued that there are no agreed theoretical economic models that can provide sufficient explanation to the unique structure of developing economies especially for higher frequency data.

There are limited empirical studies that have analysed the exchange rate volatility issues in Malaysia. Chong and Tan (2007) examined the factors affecting exchange rate volatility from a macroeconomic perspective for Malaysia, Thailand, Indonesia and Singapore. They found that there are links between macroeconomic factors and exchange rate volatility in both the short run and the long run. Their empirical results indicated that a set of common factors did influence exchange rate volatility, whereby the stock market is a great influence commonly found across the four ASEAN countries. Tan and Chong (2008), however, found that amplified instability of macro-variables in Thailand and Indonesia due to financial crisis was not stabilised by switching the exchange rate system to a flexible regime. For Malaysia, a switch from the managed float to the pegged system successfully reduced any volatility. Their empirical findings strongly suggest that central banks of small open developing economies adopt a more fixed rather than a more flexible system.

We have now provided the summary of the exchange rate volatility issues in section "History of the topic" and also the reasons for analysing the Malaysian exchange rate markets in section "Geographical location of the topic". The next three sections elaborate on the benefits of this study (section "Benefits to the community") and address the questions of why it is significant (section "Why is it significant?") and to whom it is significant (section "Who is it significant to?").

Benefits to the community

Exchange rate volatility measurement and management are important in today's globalised market as countries are more interconnected than ever before due to technological advancements and involved many stakeholders. Different stakeholders will want to manage exchange rate risks differently. Stakeholders include customers of financial institutions, shareholders of institutions, management, board of directors, regulators, politicians or the public at large.

Shiller (2003) argued that the proliferation of risk management thinking coupled with technological sophistication of the 21st century will allow any agent in the society, from an individual to a company to a country, to apply the scientific and systematic risk management methodology to the risks they faced. In the face of the spillover scenarios, such as the Asian financial crisis, society views risk management positively and entrusts regulators with the task of forging the framework that will safeguard its interests. Consider the debate surrounding the use and misuse of financial derivatives – regulation serves to reduce the risk of the misuse of these products, but at the same time recognises their societal value in the global financial system.

Foreign exchange markets are generally very volatile, especially for developing economies. Hence, by focusing on the concept of time-varying volatility, one will hopefully understand better the underlying dynamics, thereby contributing to better forecast and decision management. The needs for accurate volatility forecasts are driven, first, by the increased usage of derivatives (thus determining the appropriate hedge ratios) and, second, by the recent implementation of risk-based capital requirements by financial institutions worldwide under the Basel III framework proposed by the Basel Committee based in Switzerland.

The concepts and theories developed from the case of Malaysia in this book can also be applied later to other financial markets within Malaysia and also to different developing economies. It is hoped that the work on the above gaps not only adds depth to the existing academic research on time-varying volatility models but also complements the risk management practices that are currently in use by practitioners in foreign exchange markets. A better understanding of the dynamics of volatility for developing countries should also shed more light for regulators (central bankers) instead of relying on generic foreign exchange theories/policies that are normally applied in developed countries to help better manage their respective economies.

Why is it significant?

In terms of outside-sample (*ex ante*) forecasting performance, many authors like Day and Lewis (1992) found that GARCH models perform badly in predicting volatility. One of the reasons for this unsatisfactory performance is that the statistical significance of risk premium is not particularly robust across alternative currencies and time periods. The imperfection of the forecasting power of GARCH models requires more in-depth research to enhance the usefulness and economic interpretations of GARCH models. Extension to the GARCH models includes developing leverage/asymmetric effects, incorporating various non-Gaussian density functions, allowing for time-varying parametric estimations for the conditional first moment and the interactions between the first and second moments of exchange rate movements. All these extensions further help in improving the forecasting power of the current GARCH models as well as in explaining the current shortcomings. This book provides a wholesome analysis of Malaysia's foreign exchange market risk in relation to economic and financial liberalisation, an in-depth analysis of the stochastic volatility of the exchange rate incorporating asymmetric and leverage effects using non-Gaussian density functions and an analysis of extension to multivariate modelling to capture interdependence of exchange rate volatility between the five different economies (the USA, the UK, Europe, Japan and Switzerland) that are major trading partners with Malaysia.

There are limited studies on Malaysia's exchange rate volatility risk management issues. While Tan and Chong (2008) and Chong and Tan (2007) attempted to analyse the exchange rate volatility issues by applying the standard volatility models, this book tries to answer the important questions of how the deviation of normal distribution and asymmetric effects in relatively less matured exchange rate markets affect the empirical results and, hence, the implications of the empirical work (see also Lum and Islam 2016a, 2016a, 2016c, and 2016d).

Attempts are made to answer some simple but important issues in three different areas of exchange rate risk in this book after reviewing the literature gaps in these areas.

1   Risk modelling:

    a   Can the exchange rate volatility or movements be modelled?
    b   If so, which models are appropriate especially for Malaysia?
    c   Will the exchange rate volatility models of a developing country such as Malaysia differ from those of other developing countries such as India that had experienced capital control in the past and liberalised the exchange rate market later?
    d   Will the liberalisation of the exchange rate market affect the risk models?
    e   Will models in multivariate dimensions outperform those under univariate dimensions?

2   Risk measuring:

    a   Does the exchange rate volatility change over different regimes or are they persistent?
    b   If the exchange rate volatility is not persistent over different regimes, does the volatility increase or decrease post liberalisation of the exchange rate market?
    c   Is there a risk premium in the exchange rate market?
    d   Will multivariate models provide different results to univariate models?

3   Risk management (which is addressed in more detail in section "Who is it significant to?"):

    a   What are the implications on public institutions especially the central bank?
    b   What are the implications on private institutions and individuals?
    c   What are the implications on educational institutions and professional bodies?
    d   What are the implications on the efficient market hypothesis?

Chapter 3 investigates questions 1a and 1b, while Chapters 4 and 5 mainly address questions 1c, 1d, 1e and 2. Chapter 6 draws on the empirical results of Chapters 4 and 5 to make some concluding remarks on question 3.

Who is it significant to?

Modern society relies on the smooth functioning of banking and insurance systems and has a collective interest in the stability of such systems. The regulatory process culminating in Basel III has been strongly motivated by the fear of systemic risk, i.e. the danger that problems in a single financial institution may spill over and, in extreme situations, disrupt the normal functioning of the entire financial system. Good risk measurement is a must as banking clients demand objective and detailed information on exchange rate-related products and banks can face legal action when this information is found wanting. For any product sold, a proper quantification of the underlying risks needs to be explicitly made, allowing the client to decide whether or not the product on offer corresponds to his or her risk appetite.

A bank's attitude to risk is not passive and defensive as it actively and willingly takes on risk, because it seeks a return and this return does not come without risk. Indeed, risk management can be seen as the core competence of an insurance company or a bank. By using its expertise, market position and capital structure, a financial institution can manage risks by re-packaging and transferring them to markets in customised ways. Managing risk is, therefore, related to preserving the flow of profit and to techniques like asset liability management which might be defined as managing a financial institution so as to earn an adequate return on funds invested and to maintain a comfortable surplus of assets beyond liabilities.

This study is significant to traders and investors who are engaged in the foreign exchange markets for hedging against risk and investment portfolio management. It can provide a comprehensive understanding of the behaviour of foreign exchange markets for speculators in such markets. This study can also help academics and students pursuing research degrees to better understand the dynamics of return and volatility structure in foreign exchange markets. Regulatory bodies, especially in developing economies (since their exchange rate markets are affected by external factors and, hence, are very volatile), are also interested in better understanding the behaviour of foreign exchange markets using the stochastic approach and multivariate modelling to capture interdependence of exchange rate volatility across different countries. Managing exchange rate risk exposure has gained prominence in the last decade, as a result of the unusual occurrence of a large number of currency crises.

The overall view of the background (section "Background of the study") and the history (section "History of the topic") of the exchange rate volatility issues including risk modelling, risk measuring and, finally, risk management issues have been presented. The importance of this research has also been outlined and justified. The contribution of this book is highlighted in section "Contribution to knowledge", where this study aims to investigate the feasibility of a new volatility model for a developing country such as Malaysia (section "Geographical location of the topic"), taking into account issues not addressed by the literature to date and the implications on risk measurement and, hence, risk management policies. The last three sections cover the elaborations on the benefits of this study (section "Benefits to the community") and address the question of why this study is significant (section "Why is it significant?") and to whom it is significant (section "Who is it significant to?"). The next and last section of this chapter provides an overall road map for readers to navigate on.

Organisation of book

Chapter 2 reviews the literature on exchange rate risk modelling, risk measurement and risk management, especially the impact of economic liberalisation and the background behind stochastic volatility modelling. This chapter also provides the motivations behind modern risk management, particularly relating to foreign exchange volatility. In this chapter, one is introduced to the literature on classical time series models and financial series as well as volatility models and their structures.

Chapter 3 focuses on the discussions of exchange rate risks in Malaysia and investigates the exchange rate risk issues from three different angles: historical events, present developments and future developments, including economic liberalisation which is expected to increase the volatility of exchange rates. This chapter also analyses various basic statistical properties of the daily exchange rate data of five major currency pairs and sets the foundations for the next two chapters that analyse the structures, statistical inference and financial applications of stochastic modelling of exchange rate volatility.

Chapter 4 analyses the different exchange rate risk modelling and measurement issues including various econometric and empirical results and analysis including the validation of stochastic volatility models used for the Malaysian exchange rate markets. This chapter also extends the standard analysis of exchange rate volatility by relaxing the Gaussian or normal distribution of exchange rate volatility as well as addresses the asymmetric or leverage effects of exchange rate volatility.

Chapter 5 extends the analysis of Chapter 4 to a multivariate approach to capture the inter-relationship of exchange rate volatility between different countries. To conclude this book, Chapter 6 provides a summary of the results, implications and limitations of the study as well as some recommendations for future studies pertaining to exchange rate volatility of a developing country.

2 Exchange rate risk management and modelling

Introduction

A comprehensive literature review of key areas of interest to this study is presented in this chapter, which begins with the examination of many documented studies on exchange rate markets especially exchange rate volatility, and follows by various volatility models that are used in financial markets, particularly exchange rate markets. The next three chapters analyse in greater depth the risk measurement and risk management of the exchange rates using Malaysia as a case study. The next chapter focuses on a basic analysis of exchange rate volatility in Malaysia, including background developments and some time series and statistical analysis on the exchange rate data.

Exchange rate risk and economic liberalisation

Exchange rate risk management is an integral part of every firm's decisions about foreign currency exposure (Allayannis et al., 2001). Currency risk hedging strategies entail eliminating or reducing this risk, and require understanding of both the ways that the exchange rate risk could affect the operations of economic agents and techniques to deal with the consequent risk implications (Barton et al., 2002). Dornbusch (1976) provided a solid foundation on modelling exchange rate dynamics using expectations. Selecting the appropriate hedging strategy is often a daunting task due to the complexities involved in measuring accurately current risk exposure and deciding on the appropriate degree of risk exposure that ought to be covered. The need for currency risk management started to arise after the breakdown of the Bretton Woods system and the end of the US dollar peg to gold in 1973 (Papaioannou, 2006). Most multinational firms have risk committees to oversee the corporate treasury's strategy in managing the exchange rate (and interest rate) risk (Lam, 2003). This shows the importance firms attach to risk management issues and techniques. International investors also manage their exchange rate risk independently from the underlying assets and/or liabilities.

A common definition of exchange rate risk relates to the effect of unexpected exchange rate changes on the value of a firm (Madura, 2016). To manage the exchange rate risk inherent in every multinational firm's operations, a firm needed to determine the specific types of current risk exposure, the hedging strategy and the available instruments to deal with these currency risks.

The issues of exchange rate behaviour have been a subject of research and policy making, especially since the collapse of the Bretton Woods arrangement on 15 August 1971. Today, foreign exchange markets are extremely unpredictable and susceptible to fundamental economic factors and market sentiments (see Hansanti *et al.* (2007) for the study of the international financial economics). The high degree of unpredictability and uncertainty of exchange rate movements since the introduction of the flexible exchange rate in 1973 has led policy makers and researchers to investigate the nature and degree of the impact of such movements on exchange rate behaviour, see Baillie and McMahon (1989), Marsh and McDonald (1999) and Sarno and Taylor (2002) for excellent theoretical and empirical work in this area while Knight and Satchell (2002) and Taylor (2005) provided in-depth discussion on forecasting volatility. The unique nature of developing countries which have different structures compared to developed countries allows researchers to test the rigidity of most exchange rate theories which are normally derived from developed countries.

There are many empirical studies that have focused on exchange rate of developing countries. Edwards (1989) studied the exchange rate misalignment among developing economies, Hinkle and Monteil (1999) included the effects of the Asian financial crisis on Asian economies while Rusydi and Islam (2006) focused their examination of exchange rate determination in Indonesia. Ho and Ariff (2009) studied the foreign exchange behaviour in the Asia Pacific and Eastern European developing countries by dividing the driving factors into parity factors and non-parity determinants, while Ho and Ariff (2011) applied the sticky price hypothesis to the Asia Pacific countries. Tan and Chong (2008) highlighted the importance of choice of exchange rate system to macroeconomic stability of small open developing economies of Indonesia, Malaysia and Thailand. Chong and Tan (2007) examined the factors of exchange rate volatility from a macroeconomic perspective for Malaysia, Indonesia, Thailand and Singapore.

Before proceeding to analyse the exchange rate volatility modelling and measurement, the various developmental economic theories in the literature are reviewed in order to facilitate the attempt to link the empirical findings of this study to some theoretical framework and to devise some risk management policies and implications.

First is the discussion on the exchange rate regimes used by various developing countries and some of the reasons for making these choices. Exchange rate regimes are important part of this book as they will affect the currency volatilities and hence implications. Weil (1987), Hellar (1976) and

Savvides (1993) found the country characteristics and exchange rate regime to be closely related, while Honkapohja and Pikkarainen (1992) did not find evidence to support this conclusion. The latter argued that it is inappropriate to include the inflation differential among the explanatory variables as it might be the effect of the exchange rate regime rather than a cause; they also use per capita income as a proxy for Mundell's criterion of economic flexibility. They found that small countries tend to peg their currency, as do those with low commodity diversifications while the remaining factors have, in practice, hardly any power in explaining the choice of a country's exchange rate system.

The discussion then flows to the effects of liberalisation and economic policies adopted by various developing countries since the 1970s. Developing countries then faced difficulties when attempting to borrow overseas in their own currency, reflecting the idea of innate weakness that is not due to past behaviour but instead limits what developing countries can achieve on their own merits. Finally, the IMF and its respective roles in affecting the exchange rate markets in these developing countries are examined.

Developing country members of the IMF are easily the most frequent users of IMF conditional loans. However, the terms and conditions attached to these loans are sometimes regarded by them as being too harsh and imposing unacceptable economic and political costs. At times, potential borrowers would not accept the IMF's conditions and would turn down a loan. Some borrowers failed to abide by the loan conditions and had their loan withdrawn. However, most developing countries would adjust their balance of payments to the sustainable levels so as to accept and abide by the IMF's conditionality clauses. According to Hallwood and MacDonald (2000), there are five factors that could determine whether a country should peg or manage-float its exchange rate:

- Size of the country;
- Degree of openness;
- Degree of financial integration;
- Inflation rate relative to the world average;
- Trade patterns.

Frankel (2006) put forward the notion that a large country like China should support the view that the *de facto* dollar peg may now have outlived its usefulness for China due to the following reasons: (i) although foreign exchange reserves are a useful shield against currency crises, China's current level is fully adequate and US treasury securities do not pay a high return; (ii) it may become increasingly difficult to sterilise the inflow over time; (iii) although external balance could be achieved by expenditure reduction, e.g. by raising interest rates, the existence of two policy goals (external balance and internal balance), in general, requires the use of two independent policy instruments (e.g. the real exchange rate and the interest rate); (iv) a large economy like China can achieve adjustment in the real exchange rate more easily via flexibility in the nominal exchange rate than via price flexibility; (v) the experience of other developing markets points towards exiting from a peg when times are good and the currency is strong, rather than waiting until times are bad and the currency is under attack; (vi) from a long-run perspective, prices of goods and services in China are low – not just low relative to the USA (0.23) but also low by the standards of a Balassa-Samuelson relationship estimated across countries (which predicts 0.36). In this specific sense, the yuan was undervalued by 35% in 2000, and still is by at least as much as that figure today. The study finds that, typically across countries, such gaps are corrected halfway, on average, over the subsequent decade. These six arguments for increased exchange rate flexibility need not imply a free float. China is a good counter-example to the popular "corners hypothesis" prohibition on intermediate exchange rate regimes. However, the specific changes announced by the Chinese authorities in July 2005 have not yet resulted in a *de facto* abandonment of the dollar peg.

Economic liberalisation philosophy began sweeping across developing countries in the late 1970s. The level of the real exchange rate (nominal exchange rate deflated by some chosen price index) affects a country's current account, resource allocation and internal balance. Economic liberalisation philosophy includes a cut in import tariffs and reduced government spending as a share of GDP. Edwards (1989), Le Fort (1988) and Tokarick (1995) found that trade liberalisation causes real depreciation.

Edwards (1989) noted that issues are more complicated in a dynamic framework. For example, if a shock depreciates the equilibrium real exchange rate, the actual exchange rate may fail to quickly depreciate sufficiently and will give rise to a trade deficit. This deficit may be financed by borrowing from overseas. Thus, the rate of depreciation of the real exchange rate is slowed down by the foreign borrowing, but it ends up having to depreciate even more than if there had not been any foreign borrowing because of the need to generate a trade surplus.

The shock causes a country's real exchange rate to take on some trajectory over time. It will be very difficult for a government to know exactly what the shock is as it depends on the nature of the shock, amount and terms of foreign borrowing, substitutability in production and consumption, the relative strength of income effects, rates of preference and whether shocks are temporary or permanent.

This is a point of great practical importance for a developing country's government concerned with exchange rate policy. It means that it is difficult to know whether a real exchange rate is adjusting close to its equilibrium path and hence no policy action needs to be taken or whether policy action is required because it is well off its equilibrium path and is causing resource misallocation and macroeconomic disequilibrium. Suppose that a government attempts to maintain international competitiveness by following a policy of nominal exchange rate depreciation at the same rate as the domestic inflation differential over the world average rate of inflation. This policy is in fact equivalent to a policy of targeting the real exchange rate. One potential problem with this policy is that if the real exchange rate is shocked, say by a sharp improvement in a country's international terms of trade (see Montiel and Ostry 1991, 1992), the real exchange rate would need to appreciate to reflect the increased demand for non-traded goods. If there is no nominal exchange rate variability, all shocks to the real exchange rate will show up as a variation in the rate of inflation.

There are many empirical studies on the linkages of exchange rate and the real economy. Stiglitz (2002) examined the consequences of capital market liberalisation, with special reference to its effects under different exchange rate regimes. Capital market liberalisation has not led to faster growth in developing countries, but instead has created greater risks. He described how IMF policies have exacerbated the risks, as a result of the macro-economic response to crises, with bail-out packages that have intensified moral hazard problems. He also provided a critique of the arguments for capital market liberalisation. He argued that capital flows give rise to larger externalities, which affect others, rather than simply the borrower and lender, and whenever there are larger externalities, there is potential scope for government interventions, some of which are welfare increasing.

Barkoulas *et al.* (2002) meanwhile investigated the effects of exchange rate uncertainty on the volume and variability of trade flows. Employing a signal extraction framework, they showed that the direction and magnitude of importers' and exporters' optimal trading activities depend upon the source of the uncertainty (general microstructure shocks, fundamental factors driving the exchange rate process or a noisy signal of policy innovations), providing a rationale for the contradictory empirical evidence in the literature. They also showed that exchange rate uncertainty emanating from general microstructure shocks and the fundamental factors reduced the variability of trade flows, while uncertainty relating to a noisy signal of policy innovations increased variability.

While Stiglitz (2002) explained how IMF policies have exacerbated the risks as a result of the macroeconomic response to crises, with bail-out packages that have intensified moral hazard problems, Barkoulas *et al.* (2002) provided a rationale for the contradictory empirical evidence in the literature. Thus, the question as to where Malaysia stands in terms of the exchange rate policy in these two contradictory views needs to be addressed. The Malaysian ringgit exchange rate was a controversy, particularly after the Asian financial crisis in 1997–1998. In the period from September 1998 to July 2005, the Malaysian ringgit was pegged to the United States (US) dollar at 3.8 Malaysian ringgit for one US dollar. During the pegged period, the current account was continuously in surplus and foreign reserves had been rising steadily, reflecting exchange rate intervention by the authorities to prevent real appreciation of the Malaysian ringgit (Koske, 2008). In 2002, the overall balance of payments was US dollar 3,657 million. In 2005 and 2006, the overall balance of payments was US dollar 3,620 million and

6,864 million, respectively. In 2008, according to IMF, the overall balance of payments was a deficit of US dollar 3,450 million. One explanation for the deficit balance of payments was the relatively strong Malaysian ringgit. In addition, the world economy was in recession and Malaysia adopted a managed floating exchange rate regime (Fischer, 2008). A managed floating exchange rate regime is argued to have led to less real exchange rate misalignment than a floating exchange rate regime. Nonetheless, a fixed exchange rate regime is believed to limit real exchange rate misalignment the most (Dubas, 2009).

The above literature reviews covered the economic liberalisation effects on the exchange rates of developing countries. Next, we will look at the recent work on exchange rate volatilities especially for developing economies.

Arize *et al.* (2000) empirically investigated the impact of real exchange rate volatility on the export flows of 13 less developed countries (LDCs) over the quarterly period of 1973–1996. Estimates of the cointegrating relations are obtained using Johansen's multivariate procedure, while estimates of the short-run dynamics are obtained for each country using the error-correction technique. The major results showed that increases in the volatility of the real effective exchange rate, approximating exchange rate uncertainty, exert a significant negative effect on export demand in both the short run and the long run in each of the 13 LDCs. These effects may result in significant reallocation of resources by market participants.

Bartram and Bodnar (2012) examined the importance of exchange rate risk in the return-generating process for a large sample of non-financial firms from 37 countries. They argued that the effect of exchange rate exposure on stock returns should be conditional and showed evidence of a significant return premium to firm-level currency exposures when conditioning on the exchange rate change. The return premium was directly related to the size and sign of the subsequent exchange rate change, suggesting fluctuations in exchange rates as a source of time variation in currency risk premia. For the entire sample, the return premium ranged from 1.2% to 3.3% per unit of currency exposure. The premium was larger for firms in developing markets, while in developed markets it was statistically significant only for local currency depreciations. Overall, the results indicated that exchange rate exposure plays an important role in generating cross-sectional return variation. Moreover, they showed that the impact of exchange rate risk on stock returns was predominantly a cash flow effect as opposed to a discount rate effect. Other researchers include Abbott *et al.* (2012) who studied exchange rate regimes and foreign direct investment in developing countries.

Finally, Poon *et al.* (2005) found that there was a stable long-run relationship between exports and the exchange rate of five selected East Asian economies, namely Indonesia, Japan, South Korea, Singapore and Thailand. The exchange rate volatility had significantly impacted the volume of exports of the economies concerned and they also found that the innovations of exchange rate volatility had a minor impact on the export patterns.

There have been many studies conducted on Malaysian exchange rate markets, including Wong (2013) who investigated real exchange rate misalignment and economic growth in Malaysia. The results of the ARDL approach show that an increase in real exchange rate misalignment will lead to a decrease in economic growth. Exchange rate devaluation can stimulate economic growth. In the short run, government intervention is important, not only to smoothen fluctuations in the exchange rate, but also to minimise real exchange rate misalignment. In the long run, financial institutions and markets should be strengthened. Real exchange rate misalignment should be avoided to enable the allocation of resources in the economy according to fundamentals. A managed floating exchange rate regime can be a choice of exchange rate regime in other developing countries to achieve rapid economic growth.

There are specific theoretical frameworks that can be applied to developing countries. Eichengreen and Hausmann (1999, 2003a–c), Eichengreen *et al.* (2002, 2003a–e) and Hausmann and Panizza (2003) first coined the concept of "original sin" for developing countries when they face difficulties when attempting to borrow overseas in their own currencies. The "original sin" captures the idea of the innate weakness that is not due to past behaviour but limits what developing countries can achieve on their own merits.

Eichengreen *et al.* (2002) measured the degree to which original sin affects a country by one minus the percentage of its international bonds and cross-border bank loans that are denominated in the domestic currency. Their findings revealed that most developing countries suffer from high levels of original sin and that it changes little over time. In their empirical work, they reported that higher levels of original sin are associated with higher volatility of real output and international capital flows, with greater management of exchange rates and with lower creditworthiness. They also argued that an effort to build deep and liquid domestic financial markets in developing countries would take too long and would be increasingly difficult to be achieved in a world of liberalised financial markets and floating exchange rates. There are many studies that criticise the original sin concept as being too pessimistic, including those of Goldstein and Turner (2004) and Reinhart *et al.* (2003). Eichengreen *et al.* (2003e) and Eichengreen and Hausmann (2003b) appeared to have modified their earlier views significantly in at least three areas according to Goldstein and Turner (2004). First, Eichengreen *et al.* (2003e) and Eichengreen and Hausmann (2003b) acknowledged explicitly that aggregate currency mismatch is not necessarily a consequence of original sin (since a net debtor country may respond to original sin with a large reserve accumulation) and that original sin is not the only thing that matters for currency mismatches. Currency mismatch, according to Goldstein and Turner (2004), is defined as when an entity's net worth or net income (or both) is sensitive to changes in the exchange rate. This definition is also close to the one that the Financial Stability Forum (2000) has proposed. Currency mismatches pose a serious threat to financial stability and sustainable economic growth in developing economies. The implicit notion is that if an entity's balance sheet and net income statement are fully hedged against exchange rate changes, then those changes could have little impact.

Second, Eichengreen and Hausmann (2003b) recognised the fact that a growing number of developing countries are demonstrating the ability to overcome the difficulties of developing domestic bond markets. Third, they acknowledged that domestic policies and institutions are important for the ability of the countries not only to borrow in their own currency domestically but also to borrow from abroad. They still maintained that original sin is at the heart of financial vulnerability in developing countries and that good domestic policies and institutions are not sufficient to overcome original sin. They also emphasised that building up international reserves or limiting international capital flows to reduce or eliminate currency mismatch is costly.

In making the case for controlling currency mismatches, Goldstein and Turner (2004) noted that countries that have experienced the largest currency mismatches have typically been the ones that have suffered the largest output losses during crises. They also explained how currency mismatches can adversely constrain the scope for cuts in interest rates during a crisis and can contribute to a "fear of floating" in the conduct of exchange rate policy. They found evidence that there is a significant differentiation among developing countries in their capacity to cope with potential currency mismatches, as revealed in the liquidity and maturity of their foreign exchange, bond and derivative markets.

In contrast to some earlier studies (see Rogoff (1999), Fischer (1999) and other related studies) which concluded that the origins of currency mismatch lie primarily in imperfections in international capital markets and network externalities, Goldstein and Turner (2004) highlighted past and present weaknesses in economic policies and institutions in developing countries themselves. Their action plan to control currency mismatches in those developing countries includes (1) a managed floating currency regime to produce an awareness of currency risk and incentive to control it; (2) an inflation target regime for monetary policy to produce the stability in long-term inflation expectations which is very important in building a healthy domestic bond market; (3) regular publication of data to enhance market discipline; (4) enhanced supervision and monitoring of currency mismatches in banks and in their loan customers; (5) changes in official safety nets and in IMF policy conditionality to produce greater incentives to limit bailout of losses stemming from currency mismatches and to reduce the size of mismatches; (6) implementation of more prudent debt and reserve management policies in developing economies and (7) higher priority given in developing countries to develop domestic bond markets, encouraging the availability of hedging instruments and reducing barriers to entry of foreign-owned banks.

The next aspect of the review is to look at IMF focusing on macroeconomic issues and its major influence on global exchange rate policies and developments. One of the IMF's main objectives, when a member country seeks to raise funds to finance a balance of payment deficit, is to ensure payment equilibrium as soon as possible. Dale (1983) described IMF's unique function as to promote the adjustment process, while Guitian (1976) was of the opinion that the ultimate aim of the IMF is to restore viability to the balance of payments in the context of price stability and sustained economic growth, without resorting to measures that impair the freedom of trade and payments. Polak (1991) argued that these objectives are not necessarily consistent with each other. In the late 1980s, the IMF had begun to place greater emphasis on the objectives of structural adjustment and economic growth. This emphasis is demonstrated by the introduction of the Structural Adjustment Facility in 1986 and the Enhanced Structural Adjustment Facility in 1988 for the use of low-income countries. Tanzi (1987) commented that the IMF has shifted its interpretation of the "Guidelines on Conditionality" from the emphasis on the aggregate budget deficit and its rapid reduction to a greater consideration for the specific content of government expenditure and tax programmes. The IMF, hence, recognises that the targets for the fiscal deficit should include measures to reduce price distortions in order to promote economic growth in the medium term and to reduce poverty in the long term.

In 1990, the Managing Director, Michel Camdessus, stated that "growth" was IMF's main objective. He argued that a balance of payment equilibrium was consistent with "high-quality growth", while disequilibriums were associated with unsustainable "flash-in-the-pan growth", financed by running down international reserves. In the early days, the IMF sought a robust theory of the balance of payments upon which a consistent set of adjustment policies could be based, which was provided by Polak (1957). Empirical evidence showed that the demand for money was a stable function of a few economic variables. The velocity of circulation of money was stable, at least in the long run. Thus, changes in the money supply should have had predictable effects on nominal national income. According to Jonston and Brekk (1989), the monetary policy of many developing countries is secondary to fiscal policy. As a result, in many cases, exchange rates were depreciating and the current account was in chronic deficit despite the use of import controls and official currency inconvertibility.

IMF's policy measures, however, are not universally accepted as ideal; some of the critics include certain recipients of IMF conditional loans and a group of economic theorists known as the new structuralist school (Taylor, 1983; Van Wijnbergen, 1983a, b; Buffie, 1984; Kohsaka, 1984). According to the new structuralist scenario, the IMF's view of benefits of financial liberalisation is flawed because they failed to model financial institutions in developing countries correctly. The economic structures of developing countries are quite different from those of developed countries. Taylor (1983) also noted that developing countries are structurally diversed and pointed out that no single set of institutions or equations can capture all of this variety. Spraos (1986) argued that the demand for money function is not necessarily stable and payment deficits may have non-monetary causes. Hence, monetary targeting by the IMF as part of conditional loan packages may not be appropriate.

Stiglitz (2003) attempted to explain why the IMF has pursued policies that in many cases not only failed to promote the stated objectives of enhancing growth and stability but were probably counterproductive and even flew in the face of a considerable body of theoretical and empirical work, which suggested that these policies would be counterproductive. He argued that the root of the problem lies with the IMF's system of governance. He concluded by proposing reforms required by the IMF to mitigate some of the problems it has encountered in the past.

By understanding how economic liberalisation affected the exchange rate volatility of developing economies in the literature, the next step is to build appropriate models to capture the dynamics of the exchange rate volatility.

Classical time series models and financial series

Time series analysis, both theoretical and empirical, has been, for many years, an integral part of the study of financial markets, with empirical research beginning with the papers by Working (1934), Cowles (1933) and Cowles and Jones (1937). The predictability of price changes has since become a major theme of financial research but, surprisingly, little progress was made in this field until Kendall (1953) found that the weekly changes in a variety of financial prices could not be predicted from either past changes in the series or past changes in other price series.

The standard time series analysis rests on important concepts such as stationarity, autocorrelation, white noise and innovation, and on a central family of models, the autoregressive moving average (ARMA) models. These concepts are insufficient for the analysis of financial time series due to many stylised facts found in the studies (see Mandelbrot, 1963; Fama, 1965), and subsequent empirical studies, which are of crucial importance in finance. The main stylised facts include unpredictability of returns and volatility clustering and, hence, predictability of squared returns, leptokurticity of the marginal density functions and asymmetries effects. For statistical convenience, ARMA (an Integrated ARMA or ARIMA) models are generally used under stronger assumptions on the noise than on weak white noise.

Classical formulations such as ARIMA models centred on the second-order structure are inappropriate. Indeed, the second-order structure of most financial time series is close to that of white noise. The fact that large absolute returns tend to be followed by large absolute returns (for both positive and negative price variations) is hardly compatible with the assumption of constant conditional variance, which is also commonly known as conditional heteroscedasticity. Conditional variance is the variance conditional on past information. Conditional heteroscedasticity is perfectly compatible with stationarity, just as the existence of a non-constant conditional mean is compatible with stationarity. The following section discusses these types of conditional volatility models in more detail.

Exchange rate volatility modelling in a univariate framework

Volatility modelling in financial markets has attracted growing attention by academics, mainly due to its rigidity in establishing volatility measures and conflicting results (Hallwood and MacDonald, 2000). Volatility modelling is used as a floating exchange measure in assessing volatility of exchange rates relative to some benchmark, whether it is volatile against a historical measure or relative to fundamental determinants. The study of volatility in the exchange rate markets is also crucial for a number of reasons: it can affect a country's international competitiveness; central banks can use foreign exchange policy to insulate an economy from shocks from overseas and finally exchange rate stability allows countries to pursue independent monetary policy as well as to control their balance of payments. Volatility of exchange rates could mean extraordinary gains or losses and, hence, greater uncertainty for businesses and policy makers.

This issue is particularly relevant for the Malaysian exchange rate market since it has shown considerable volatility during the pre- and post-economic crisis periods of the late 1990s. Good macroeconomic and financial theorists want to get the facts straight before theorising, thereby resulting in the explosive growth in the methodology and application of time series econometrics in the last 40 years. Many factors have fuelled that growth, ranging from important developments in related fields (see Box and Jenkins, 1970) to dissatisfaction with the "incredible identifying restrictions" associated with traditional macroeconometric models (Sims, 1980) and the associated recognition that many tasks of interest, such as forecasting, simply do not require a structural model (see Granger and Newbold, 1977). A short list of active subfields includes vector autoregressions, index and dynamic factor models, causality, integration and persistence, cointegration, seasonality, unobserved-components models, state-space representations and the Kalman filter, regime-switching models, nonlinear dynamics and optimal nonlinear filtering. Any such list must also include models of volatility dynamics.

Models of autoregressive conditional heteroskedasticity (ARCH), in particular, provide parsimonious approximations to volatility dynamics and have been widely used in macroeconomics and finance. Economists are typically introduced to heteroskedasticity in cross-sectional contexts, such as when the variance of a cross-sectional regression disturbance depends on one or more of the regressors. A classic example is the estimation of Engel curves by weighted least squares, in light of the fact that the variance of the disturbance in an expenditure equation may depend on income. Heteroskedasticity is equally pervasive in time series contexts prevalent in macroeconomics and finance. ARCH models assume the variance of the current error term or innovation to be a function of the actual sizes of the previous time periods' error terms, which are able to model the time-varying volatility clustering of financial data. At the same time, ARCH models are simple enough to allow for a complete study of the solutions as the linear structure of these models can be displayed through several representations.

Exhaustive surveys of the ARCH literature already exist, including the studies by Engle and Bollerslev (1986), Bollerslev et al. (1992), Bera and Higgins (1995) and Bollerslev *et al.* (1994). Francq and Zakoïan (2010) discussed GARCH models in detail. Reference shall be made below to those studies that are particularly relevant to the foreign exchange market.

The original work on price changes in speculative markets generally assumed normally distributed errors, so the basic model applied was Gaussian random walk model (see Kendall (1953) and Osborne (1959)). Many empirical studies on foreign exchange markets have, however, cast doubts on this assumption (see Cornell and Dietrich (1978) and McFarland *et al.* (1982)). There are also many stylised facts concerning return volatility for foreign exchange markets in the short term. Return volatility appears to go through periods where changes (in either positive or negative directions) are large and other periods when changes are small leading to wide volatility fluctuations across time. The changes in returns also tend to exhibit clustering behaviour. There are also outliers that occur more frequently and result in fat tails (compared with normal distribution). These reported phenomena in the unconditional density functions can be explained as the conditional density functions with finite moments, where Mussa (1979) described this time-varying volatility as an empirical regularity of exchange rate behaviour.

There are many recent studies on model time-varying volatility of foreign exchange markets (see Engle *et al.* (1990), Diebold and Nason (1990) and an excellent survey by Bollerslev *et al.* (1992)). These models are now commonly used to empirically describe the stylised facts found in foreign exchange rates while researchers are still trying to find economically based models to explain the nature of kurtosis and time-dependent heteroskedasticity.

One breakthrough that links empirical modelling to economic theory is the risk premium, where the time-varying volatility or risk premium is considered an important factor in explaining exchange rate movements. The relationship is a positive one that reflects the first rule in finance: high risk will result in high return. This relationship is also an attempt to link the risk and return rather than model them in isolation. Poterba and Summers (1988) were among the first to investigate whether changes in investors' perceptions of risk are large enough to account for the very sharp movements in stock prices that are actually observed. Their findings revealed that persistence in volatility is too low to explain the observed sharp movement in stock prices. Chou (1988) repeated Poterba and Summers' (1988) analysis using a time-varying risk premium concept and found that the latter's method might have incorrectly captured the true degree of persistence. Baillie and Bollerslev (1989) and Bollerslev (1990) applied similar work to the spot foreign exchange market and concluded that time-varying risk premiums explain the exchange rates well in higher frequency data.

Since exchange rate risk can affect cash flows and stock prices of firms, the exposure to this risk is a key concern for investors, analysts and managers. As a result, there have been tremendous efforts over the past 20 years to quantify the impact of fluctuating exchange rates. Floating the exchange rate has resulted in increased observed volatility relative to some form of benchmark.

Exchange rates have been volatile on a historical basis. MacDonald (1999) showed that the volatility of the Group of Seven bilateral US dollar currencies increased on a monthly basis, from 0.2% in 1961–1970 (part of the Bretton Woods period) to 1.18% in 1974–1983. There are also many other researchers who have applied time-varying models in the exchange rate markets. Mun (2007) applied exponential GARCH (EGARCH), proposed by Nelson (1991), to both the dynamic movements of stock market and exchange rate volatility. He found that exchange rate movements have a significant influence on the equity market volatility but have no measurable influence on the US/local market correlation for most cases.

The literature review of univariate GARCH models for financial markets like exchange rate markets is huge – most applied research work however used basic GARCH or specific extension of GARCH like asymmetry GARCH models without justifying the choices. This book tries to close the gaps in these area by focusing on three main areas: (1) justify the choices of the use of GARCH models or their extension, (2) compare their differences with the basic benchmark by computing various risk measures (3) and finally linking them to various views of the risk management of the foreign-exchange markets.

Exchange rate volatility modelling in a multivariate framework

Multivariate GARCH (MGARCH) models were initially developed in the late 1980s and the first half of the 1990s, and after a period of tranquility in the second half of the 1990s, these models seem to be experiencing again a quick expansion phase. The MGARCH literature is extensive, including, among others, Bollerslev *et al.* (1988), Engle *et al.* (1990), Engle and Kroner (1995), Kroner and Ng (1998), Hafner and Herwartz (1998), Van der Weide (2002), Tse and Tsui (2002), Engle (2002) and Kawakatsu (2006). Estimation issues are discussed by Jeantheau (1998), Van der Weide (2002) and Comte and Lieberman (2003). Bauwens *et al.* (2006) provided a review of the whole MGARCH literature, including model specifications and inference methods. Gouriéroux (1997), Campbell *et al.* (1997), Franses and Van Dijk (2000) are books that include multivariate GARCH models.

One of the practical problems is that the univariate time series always delivers weak evidence against the hypothesis that all autocorrelations are zero. This is because one loses power by forecasting returns using only past returns, ignoring all the other possible information variables. The autocorrelations of *ex post* returns can be very small even when expected returns are variable and highly persistent. The reason is that innovations in the expected returns cause movements in *ex post* returns in the opposite direction; the resulting negative serial correlation in *ex post* returns tends to offset the positive serial correlation arising from persistent expected returns. It is possible to construct an example in which expected returns are variable and persistent, but *ex post* returns are white noise. One difficulty that arises is that a strong assumption on the covariance of the two components is needed to identify the parameters of the model from the autocorrelations of returns. A multivariate approach is thus preferable to the exclusive focus on univariate autocorrelations based on the two reasons presented above.

There are many applications of MGARCH in the literature; Kearney and Patton (2000) and Karolyi (1995) studied the volatilities and co-volatilities of several markets. Bollerslev (1990) and Longin and Solnik (1995) investigated whether the correlations between asset returns change over time. Another application of MGARCH models is the computation of time-varying hedge ratios; see Lien and Tse (2002) for a survey on hedging and additional references. Asset pricing models relate returns to "factors", such as the market return in the capital asset pricing model. A specific asset excess return (in excess of the risk-free return) may be expressed as a linear function of the market return. Assuming its constancy, the slope, or β coefficient, may be estimated by ordinary least squares estimation. For portfolio analysis, since β is the ratio of a covariance to a variance, an MGARCH model can be used to estimate time-varying β coefficients. Bollerslev *et al.* (1988), De Santis and Gerard (1998) and Hafner and Herwartz (1988) provided examples on estimation of these time-varying coefficients.

The management and monitoring of very large portfolios of financial assets are routine for many individuals and organisations. The two most widely used models of conditional covariances and correlations in the class of multivariate GARCH models are BEKK and DCC. It is well known that BEKK suffers from the archetypal "curse of dimensionality", while DCC does not. Caporin and McAleer (2012) provided the comparisons between these two classes of MGARCH models and guide to discriminate them in practical applications.

Bautista (2006) examined six countries by tracking the correlation of the real exchange rate and the real interest differential from 1986 to 2004 and noting the shifts in the nominal exchange rate regime. The analysis used the dynamic conditional correlation multivariate DCC model. For each country, a DCC model is estimated to determine the correlation of the two variables over time. These countries are Indonesia, Korea, Malaysia, the Philippines, Singapore and Thailand. They found that positive time-varying correlations characterise the relation during pegged regimes while correlations are negative during freely managed regimes.

This book will bridge the gaps of the literature in one key way: by comparing the univariate GARCH models with multivariate GARCH models instead of just choosing one over the other models. The extensions of the univariate GARCH models will be utilised in MGRCH models for comparison purpose.

Risk management of exchange rate volatility

The rapid expansion in risk management interest and capability is driven by several factors. One obvious factor is the growth in financial derivative markets and products, and the exciting capabilities for risk management that they provide. A second key factor is the revolution in modelling and forecasting volatility that began in academics in the last 30 years (Engle, 1982). The key insight is that if volatility fluctuates in a forecastable way, then good volatility forecasts can improve financial risk management, which is forecasting the risk associated with holding potentially complicated nonlinear portfolios at various horizons. Christoffersen and Diebold (2000) found that volatility forecastability decays quickly with horizon. Volatility forecastability, although clearly of relevance for risk management at the very short horizons relevant for trading desk management, may not be important for risk management in general.

One of the primary restrictions of generalised autoregressive conditional heteroscedasticity (GARCH) is that it enforces symmetric responses of volatility to positive and negative shocks, while many previous studies used asymmetric volatility in their estimations. Black (1976), Campbell and Hentschel (1992) and Christie (1982) reported a larger increase of volatility in response to negative shocks than positive shocks in the share market. This asymmetry in the reaction to shock is explained with the leverage of firms and volatility feedback effect. Ghazali and Lean (2015) however found that the local gold returns demonstrated an inverted asymmetric reaction to positive and negative innovations respectively. Positive shock increased the gold returns' volatility more than the negative shock in full sample as well as the stock market downside, thus supporting the hedge and safe haven properties of gold investment in Malaysia.

This book will not just focus on the forecastability of exchange rate volatility but also try to link risk management to the exchange rate volatility in various angles, which has not been done comprehensively in the literature of exchange rate volatility, especially for developing countries.

Conclusion

The review of literature pertaining to various exchange rate issues, particularly in relation to the Malaysian exchange rate market, is presented in this chapter. The review covers issues that are associated with economic liberalisation and exchange rate risks, including different exchange rate regimes of developing economies, the relationship between liberalisation and exchange rate volatility, the original sin hypothesis that applies to a developing country such as Malaysia and also the roles of IMF that will affect exchange rate risks.

The review also covers the concepts of conditional and unconditional moments as part of the risk measurement. Volatility modelling in a univariate case is discussed and a critical analysis of the literature is conducted to provide a broad overview of what has been done in this volatility modelling area. Finally, the discussion of the multivariate case provides the breadth of volatility modelling in recent times to investigate the possible interdependence of various exchange rate volatilities.

The gaps of the existing literature review of the exchange rate volatility reflected that there is insufficient comprehensive analysis of exchange rate volatility of developing countries. Most of the studies will model exchange rate volatility in very simplistic form in terms of using historical and static data – an example is standard deviation. The main motive of this book is that if the model for the exchange rate volatility is incorrect, then the measurement of the exchange rate volatility will not be accurate and hence will not provide proper risk management implications for stakeholders.

The next chapter provides a more in-depth discussion and details of exchange rate volatility in Malaysia, especially in terms of risk and economic liberalisation. The challenge is to determine whether basic time series statistical measurement of exchange rate risk is sufficient to model and measure exchange rate risk from a risk management perspective.

3 Exchange rate risk and economic liberalisation

Introduction

The first part of the discussion in section "Developments in the Malaysian exchange rate market" covers the developments in the Malaysia exchange rate market, which is followed by an in-depth analysis of the exchange rates of five different major currency pairs with the Malaysian ringgit to provide an overall view of the movements of the exchange rates, particularly relating to the exchange rate volatility, in section "Data analysis of Malaysia's exchange rate". Section "Implications" concludes this chapter and provides the motivation for Chapters 4 and 5 on univariate stochastic volatility modelling of exchange rates in Chapter 4 and on an extension to multivariate stochastic volatility modelling of exchange rates, respectively, to capture the inter-relationships of the five different trading countries with Malaysia.

Developments in the Malaysian exchange rate market

Gan and Soon (2003) noted that Malaysia has the largest current account reversal among the four East Asian economies, suggesting that Malaysia had managed to achieve reduction in domestic absorption due to the transfer of resources overseas. The expansionary macroeconomic policies in combination with the expenditure-switching effect of a large real exchange rate depreciation and favourable international demand for Malaysian exports had allowed the current account surplus to be maintained and economic activity to recover rather quickly. Doraisami (2004) discussed the motivations and effects of Malaysian capital control in details.

There are also many other studies that focused on Malaysian foreign exchange markets; Tse and Tsui (1997) compared the Malaysian ringgit with the Singapore dollar, while Mahmood and Ahmad (2006) compared the two different regimes, the pre- and post-pegging, to the US dollar of the Malaysian foreign exchange markets.

The history and development of the foreign exchange markets in Malaysia may be divided into three main periods: before and during the Asian financial crises in 1998 when pegging of the ringgit to the US dollar had not taken place; start of ringgit pegging to the US dollar from 1 September 1998 until 1 April 2005 and, finally, de-pegging from the US dollar after 1 April 2005.

Asian financial crises period

Radelet and Sachs (1998), and many others, provided a comprehensive review of the Asian financial crises. Gan and Soon (2003) discussed some effects of the Asian financial crises on the Malaysian economy. Before 1997-Q4, Malaysia's current account deficit was 7.1% (relative to GDP) in each quarter, mainly due to the high investment ratio and substantial financing through capital inflows. After 1997-Q4, the current account surplus for the next 12 months averaged 12.9% of GDP with RM12.9 billion net outflow of debt-creating and equity capital in 1997 compared to RM21.7 billion outflow in 1998.

Malaysia's stock market capitalisation stood at RM888 billion at the beginning of the year 1997 but it had declined to RM200 billion by September 1998. The yield of one-year Malaysian government securities rose from an average of 6.5% at the beginning of 1997 to a peak of 10.1% in June 1998. Aggregate investment to GDP ratio fell sharply from 53% before 1997-Q4 to 30% afterwards. Retrenchment in the private sector was most severe in services and construction sectors where large infrastructure projects with high import content were either deferred or cancelled. Investment in the manufacturing sector, which typically accounted for 34% of private investment, declined by 38% in 1998.

The average consumption to GDP ratio fell to 53.6% compared to 60% before 1997-Q4. The moderate drop most likely reflected the consumption-smoothing behaviour following the slowdown in income growth.

The import to GDP ratio declined from 1997-Q4 to 1998-Q4, while exports increased from 86% to 112% in 1999-Q4. The increase in exports was, however, unable to offset the decline in real investment and consumption in 1998 for three consecutive quarters. Nevertheless, exports outgrew imports ever since, mainly due to the valuation effect from the depreciation of the ringgit. The expansion in export volume was the result of an increase in manufactured and mineral exports. The manufactured items were electronic goods and electrical products together with wood-based products.

The exchange rate depreciation raised the domestic price of tradable goods relative to the price of non-tradable goods produced in the economy, thereby changing the incentive for the production and consumption of these goods. An exchange rate-induced increase in the price of tradable goods made its production more profitable, causing resources to shift out of the non-tradable sector into the tradable sector. The reverse is true for consumption where consumers preferred non-tradable goods due to the relative increase in the price of the tradable goods. This combined effect resulted in an improvement in Malaysia's current account position.

The supply side of manufacturing showed much resilience and flexibility, which enabled the sector to take advantage of the enhanced international competitiveness brought about by the depreciation of the ringgit. Approximately half of the manufacturing outputs were produced by foreign majority-owned firms, where their balance sheets remained relatively intact by the financial crisis. Large-scale capacity was under way in 2000 due to rising capacity utilisation. Import of capital goods in 2000 rose by 48% compared to 13% in 1999.

On the demand side, the USA and the EU had rising import demand during the period, 1998–2000, while Japan witnessed an increase in 1999–2000. Singapore and the three economies mentioned above accounted for two-thirds of Malaysian manufactured goods exports. These adjustments in the negative output gap brought about by the contraction in economic activity, complemented by the adjustment in domestic relative prices, resulted in an easing of inflationary pressure from 1998-Q4 due to the depreciation of the ringgit.

Bank Negara Malaysia (BNM) reversed its earlier policy of easing the increase in the interest rate by using sterilised foreign exchange market intervention, and aggressively pursued a tighter monetary policy to stabilise the exchange rate, thus reducing inflationary pressure and slowing down domestic credit demand. The actions taken by BNM also contributed to the reversal of Malaysia's current account position.

On 1 September 1998, BNM announced the following conditions to be imposed:

- Fixed exchange rate of 3.8 Malaysian ringgit to one USD in order to ease monetary policy;
- Capital control;
- Moderate expansionary policy.

The initial fiscal response was aimed at restraining aggregate demand and reducing current account deficit, which was to be achieved through cutback in government current expenditure, privatisation and deferring the implementation of selective infrastructure projects. In March 1998, the government cut back on its original fiscal surplus of 2.7%, outlined in the 1998 budget which was announced in October 1997, to 0.5% of GNP. In July 1998, the government announced a fiscal stimulus package and projected a budget deficit of 3.7% for 1998. The 1999 Budget, which was announced in October 1998, targeted 6.1% of GNP. The Federal Government budget was in deficit for 9 out of 11 quarters from 1998-Q2 to 2000-Q4.

Post-Asian financial crises

As part of the financial sector master plan, the foreign exchange market is one area that BNM has been looking to further liberalise since 2000. Several major foreign exchange administration policies were liberalised on 1 April 2004 to promote the efficiency of business operations in Malaysia and better risk management of investments. One year later, further relaxations to the foreign exchange administration rules took place as part of BNM's ongoing initiatives towards reducing cost of doing business, improving regulatory delivery system and encouraging better risk management activities by residents and non-residents as well as promoting the development of domestic foreign exchange market, in order to promote stability in the financial system and economy of the country (see Appendix 1 for further details).

The liberalisation of foreign exchange administration rules of 23 March 2004 announced by BNM also eliminated remnants of the restrictions on investors. The Malaysian foreign exchange environment was then, by far, much more liberal than that existing prior to September 1998. Bank Negara Malaysia had announced in January 2005 the usage of repurchase agreements as a monetary policy instrument, introduced the Institutional Custodian Programme to enable borrowing and lending of securities and provided a securities lending facility for principal dealers.

The implementation of these measures was aimed at improving the price discovery process and increasing the efficiency of capital allocation within the financial system. The aggressive sterilisation operations carried out by Bank Negara Malaysia which had resulted in a rise in monetary aggregates (M3 grew by 12.4% in December 2004) were sustained at a level consistent with the pace of real economic activity.

Preventing an excessive build-up in liquidity remains the key challenge for the central bank. The strong current account position, the inflow of foreign direct and portfolio investment and strong tourist receipts have sharply pushed up foreign reserves. Most of these inflows have been sterilised, as indicated by the limited rise in base money relative to the upsurge in reserves. As of mid-December 2004, the central bank had absorbed an estimated RM130.6 billion from the banking system, mainly through interbank borrowings.

On the exchange rate front, strong economic fundamentals, marginal misalignment against regional currencies and narrowing interest rate differentials between domestic and US interest rates suggest little pressure on the ringgit peg. Despite that, and while the ringgit peg arguably offers an environment of stability against the background of volatile global foreign exchange markets, a shift to a basket peg with a more flexible rate may put the economy in a better position in the event of serious exchange rate corrections and could help manage excess liquidity. The next sub-section outlines the developments of de-pegging the ringgit.

Morgan Stanley Capital International reinstated Malaysia into its key developing market indices at full weightings from 31 May 2000. All leading international credit rating agencies also restated Malaysia's sovereign debt rating as investment grade. The IMF papers by Ostry *et al.* (2011) as well as by Habermeier *et al.* (2011) concluded that capital controls may prove useful in managing specific risks associated with international flows. With the banking system having recovered from the Asian financial crisis, Danamodal, the agency established during the crisis to recapitalise financial institutions, was closed in early 2004. The Corporate Debt Restructuring Committee, established to help corporate debt resolution, had already been closed in late 2002. Danaharta, the national asset management agency, was on track to cease operations by the end of 2005.

Signalling a shift to a more market-driven approach to interest rate determination, a new interest rate framework was introduced with the overnight policy rate replacing the three-month intervention rate as the policy benchmark. Legislation was amended to allow mergers of commercial banks and finance companies within the same banking group in order to improve operational efficiencies. This amendment cleared the way for five such mergers in 2004. Another significant development was the acquisition by Temasek Holdings, Singapore's state-owned investment company, of a substantial stake in Alliance Bank – evidence that Malaysia was gradually opening its financial services to foreign participation. Taking a step towards greater bilateral trade and economic cooperation, the Singapore and Malaysia securities exchanges agreed to jointly develop a cross-trading link, which would increase liquidity and access to capital.

According to research conducted by the Asian Development Bank, Malaysia's inflation rate in 2004 – an average of 1.4% over the year – was the lowest in Southeast Asia, although it was constrained by fuel price subsidies and price controls. Demand pressures were generally benign, but cost pressures, reflected in higher food prices and transport charges, nudged up inflation from 1.2% in May 2004 to a five-year high of 2.1% in December 2004. Job creation outstripped additions to the workforce and the unemployment rate remained stable over time.

The major challenge for fiscal policy is to rein in the deficit in the medium term without derailing economic growth, through a focus on projects with high returns, low-import content and strong industrial linkages. This strategy would involve small projects being awarded to Malaysians in areas such as agriculture and rural development. Deficit reduction was carried out on two fronts, by cutting spending and by improving revenue collection efforts through improved compliance. Other steps included a gradual reduction of subsidies on gasoline and diesel fuels, and, in the longer term, changes to the tax structure. A goods and services tax was proposed to be implemented starting 1 January 2007 to broaden the tax base, but it was later decided to be deferred due to the political election that was to be held on 18 March 2008, as well as ironing out the technicalities of the execution process. The Malaysian government has since implemented the broad-based goods and services tax, at 6%, on 1 April 2015 to replace the consumption tax, and the sales and services tax.

To improve their efficiency and profitability, the Government-Linked Corporations (GLCs) were put under the oversight of Khazanah, the government's investment corporation, which would revamp their operations so as to turn them ultimately into market-driven entities. This would involve further board and management changes and the introduction of key performance indicators, such as fixed-term contracts and performance-linked compensation for management. Privatisation, another strategy aimed at improving economic efficiency, has slowed down, but the reforms of the GLCs may be the initial steps in preparing some for divestment in the future.

There are various propositions of an alternative currency unit rather than relying on the traditional US dollar, and following the concept of European Currency Unit (ECU). According to Google, Asian Monetary Unit is a basket of currencies proposed by the Research Institute of Economy, Trade and Industry, and is conceptually similar to the ECU. The ASEAN 10+3 currencies are the component currencies of the AMU. The ASEAN 10+3 is composed of Brunei, Cambodia, Indonesia, Laos, Malaysia, Myanmar, the Philippines, Singapore, Thailand, Vietnam, Japan, South Korea and China.

It was recently reported that the Asian Development Bank would formulate a conceptual currency unit based on a package of Asian currencies in order to promote regional economic cooperation and development. This drew a series of reports on an "Asian yuan". The idea of an Asian yuan, to be used throughout the region, was first proposed by former Malaysian Prime Minister Mahathir Mohamad in 1997 at the ASEAN summit. In 2003, the "Father of the Euro", Nobel Prize in Economics laureate, Robert Mondell, also proposed the establishment of a common currency in Asia, such as an "Asian yuan". In 2005, at the Bo'ao Asian Forum Annual Meeting in Hainan province, Hong Kong SAR's then acting chief, Donald Tsang, spoke of an "Asian yuan". However, dreams do not take the place of reality. An Asian yuan looks to remain a dream for the foreseeable future. According to Sun (2006), there are a few stumbling blocks for the concept to be a reality as outlined below.

First, there are big differences in the level of economic development between Asian countries. Asia is different from Europe in that Asia's development is imbalanced. This difference is the major hindrance to an Asian yuan. In Asia, there are both economic powers and small countries whose economies are still based on traditional agriculture. There is a huge gap in economic development and income, not only between countries but also between regions within countries. In terms of economic structure, China and ASEAN countries are similar as they all have labour-intensive industries and big export markets, and their economies mainly rely on investment and exports. So in many ways, their relationship is somewhat competitive. Balanced economic development would be the foundation of an "Asian yuan", and to date, there is no such foundation in Asia.

Second, many Asian countries lack the political drive and incentive to instigate this kind of monetary reform. Due to historic, cultural and political differences, Asian countries lack cohesion. Unlike European countries, Asian countries are not politically coordinated or aligned. Asian countries are very different; there are still disputes over land, sea and sovereignty among them, which occasionally threaten to boil over into a war. Political and economic systems are very different; there are also great differences in religious beliefs. An Asian yuan would mean conceding some sovereignty. If Asia chose to adopt a unified currency, political restructuring would have to take place at a high level. Without common and equal political will, such restructuring would not be easy.

Third, there is no anchoring currency. Asia would encounter the issue of an "N" currency if they want to unify the currency. The initial objective of the unification of Asian currencies would be to gain the maximum benefit from trade with a minimum of rights releases. Consequently, choosing an anchoring currency would be an issue. Neither the Japanese yen nor the Chinese yuan is currently reliable enough to be a candidate. Japan's economic strength is comparable to that of Germany, but the Japanese yen is not the German mark. Japanese scholars propose using the yen to establish a foreign exchange rate linking mechanism, similar to that of the mark with the euro. However, the yen is not like Mark, which is a strong international currency. The Japanese yen only accounts for 13.5% of currency in the world foreign exchange market, 6.2% of official foreign exchange reserves, 0.2% in international banking loans, 8.6% in international security issuances and 5% in international settlement of trade. The yuan, the currency of the second economic power in Asia, has become a strong currency in Southeast Asia in recent years, but reforms of the yuan's exchange rate formulation mechanism have started and its future is unpredictable. Due to China's strict capital controls, weak financial sector and inflexible exchange timetable, the yuan cannot be the anchoring currency any time soon either.

All these obstacles would be difficult to be eliminated in a short period of time. Asian countries need to face this reality and begin work on the preliminary stage of economic integration and on strengthening regional economic cooperation. In the meantime, countries should avoid taking financial risks, establish a financial crisis prevention mechanism and aim for common and steady development in Asian countries.

The Malaysian government, under the leadership of the then fifth Prime Minister of Malaysia, Tun Abdullah Badawi, decided that slightly less than seven years was long enough for Malaysia to recover from the Asian financial crises and help put Malaysia back on the radar of international investors by announcing the de-pegging of the ringgit on 1 April 2005. The global economic crises in 2008 that started from the subprime mortgage crisis in the USA has since created a lot of uncertainty in the market place and it is interesting to watch the reaction from the government under the new leadership of the Prime Minister Datuk Sri Najib Tun Rajak. It is a real testing time for Datuk Sri Najib as there are also pressures from the opposition coalition party led by opposition leader Datuk Seri Anwar Ibrahim, who was sentenced to five years of jail term in February 2015. The central bank has also not internationalised Malaysian ringgit to date due to risks of offshore trading.

Whitt (1996) observed that the Mexican Crawling peg lasted up to December 1994. Less than 12 months after NAFTA, Mexico faced economic disaster in December 1994 when it devalued the peso. The main reason was Mexico's current account deficit which went up from USD6 billion in 1989 to USD20 billion in 1992–1993. Mexico had a crawling peg system with the US dollar. However, in real terms, the peso was appreciating, contributing to the growing current account deficit. Mexico's inflation rate was higher than the US inflation rate and the Mexican peso depreciated. This exchange rate depreciation contributed to a growing current account deficit and capital flight and loss of reserves. Eventually, it resulted in devaluation and the situation was made worse by an ongoing political crisis. Other research that has been conducted on the Mexican peso includes the study by Calvo *et al.* (1996), while Williamson (1993) focused on Chile, Colombia and Israel and the Asian financial crisis was investigated by Goldstein (1998) and Liu *et al.* (1998).

Spiegel (2002) concluded from the experience of Argentina's Fixed Exchange Rate Currency Board (from April 1991 to January 2002) that the exchange rate, regardless of its nature, is not a cure for improper macroeconomic policies. The unsustainability of Argentina's budget deficit led to the collapse of its currency board system. Eichengreen and Hausmann (1999) put forward a bipolar view of currency regimes in developing economies. Goldstein *et al.* (2000) conducted a series of empirical tests aimed at identifying the best leading indicators of currency and banking crises in developing economies.

Since exchange rate risk can affect cash flows and stock prices of firms, exposure to this risk is a key concern for investors, analysts and managers. As a result, there have been tremendous efforts over the past 20 years to quantify the impact of fluctuating exchange rates. Mun (2007) applied exponential GARCH (EGARCH) by Nelson (1991) to both the dynamic movements of the stock market and exchange rate volatility. He found that exchange rate movements have a significant influence on equity market volatility but have no measurable influence on the US/local market correlation in most cases.

Tai (2004) examined four Asian foreign exchange markets, namely, Japan, Hong Kong, Singapore and Taiwan, during the 1997 Asian crisis and found that the time-varying risk premium is a very strong candidate in explaining the predictable excess return puzzle (proposed by Lewis (1994)), as the risk premiums are both statistically and economically significant. Hurley and Santos (2001) found that for the ASEAN currencies prior to the financial crisis in 1997, the Indonesian rupiah was the most volatile, followed by the Philippine peso, while the Singapore dollar was the least volatile. They also found that the switch to *de facto* pegging against the US dollar in the mid-1980s stabilised the variability in the currencies of all ASEAN nations, with the exception of the Malaysian ringgit.

Now that the summaries of the development of the foreign exchange markets in Malaysia have been presented, the discussion on a more in-depth analysis of foreign exchange market in Malaysia is presented in the next section.

Data analysis of Malaysia's exchange rate

The monthly and daily nominal foreign exchange rates are downloaded from Bank Negara Malaysia's website. The nominal exchange rates are all quoted in direct terms, which are the prices of foreign currencies in terms of Malaysian ringgit. The daily rates used are the middle rates recorded at the 12.00 p.m. sessions. The ending record of the exchange rates is used for monthly data. Figure 3.1 plots the trend of the seven major currencies plus the Special Drawing Rights (which are denoted by standard abbreviations: GBP for British pound; DM for Deutsche Mark; HKD for Hong Kong dollar; JPY for Japanese yen, USD for US dollar, SGD for Singapore dollar and CHF for Swiss franc; and SDR for Special Drawing Rights) over the sample period from January 1983 to May 2005, resulting in 269 observations. The Asian financial crisis started on 2 July 1997 and ended on 14 August 1998.

The monthly exchange rate data are the first to be analysed in order to understand the big picture of what happened to the exchange market in Malaysia over a longer period. The focus that follows is the analysis of the daily data and the change of the period starting from 1 January 1997, as more recent data are more relevant for the understanding of the fluctuations in the exchange rate. Finally, the trimmed down of the currency pairs to the top five major currency pairs with respect to the Malaysian ringgit is to facilitate for a more in-depth analysis.

To commence with the analysis, the monthly data are split into three periods: the full sample which spans from January 1983 to May 2005; the pre-crisis sample which starts from January 1983 to June 1997; the post-crisis sample which runs from September 1998 until May 2005. A plot of the raw monthly nominal exchange rates in Figure 3.1 shows that volatility is greatest during the Asian financial crisis period from July 1997 until August 1998, after which the Malaysian government pegged the Malaysian ringgit to the US dollar.

Table 3.1 shows the descriptive statistics for the daily nominal exchange rates and they are split into three panels. Panel A consists of the full sample period, Panel B consists of pre-crisis statistics and Panel C consists of post-crisis statistics. They provided an overview of the relationships between Malaysian ringgit and the five currencies. US dollar seems to be the least volatile, if one uses standard deviation to measure volatility, in all periods. Euro was the most volatile currency with respect to Malaysia Ringgit before Malaysia imposed capital control; as the euro was relatively new and was in the price discovery process, there were relative volatile movements. The pound was the most volatile after Malaysia relaxed the capital control, and due to various issues UK was facing as a country. The important observations from Table 3.1 are that volatility of the exchange rates is different for periods before and after the capital control imposed by Malaysia, and

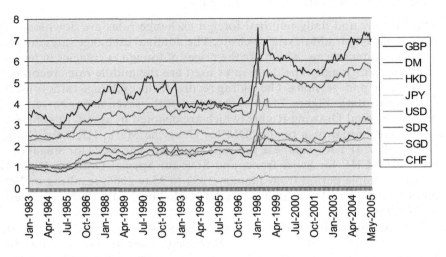

Data source: Bank Negara Malaysia

Figure 3.1   Time series of monthly data of major currencies with respect to Malaysian ringgit. Period: January 1993 to May 2005.

the skewness and kurtosis of the five series suggest that they do not exhibit normal distributions. These initial findings post important motivations for one to model volatility of these exchange rates in the next chapter by incorporating breaks and non-normal distributions.

Unit root testing is then carried out for all the level of nominal exchange rates, using the Augmented Dickey Fuller (ADF) tests by Dickey and Fuller (1981). The findings reveal that the hypothesis of unit root cannot be rejected as both the trend and intercept are significant for all the level series. These findings do not enable this study to proceed with building the autoregressive moving average (ARMA) and the conditional volatility models (see Chapters 4 and 5) as they are all stationary time series models. Hence, the first difference of the nominal exchange rates and the natural logarithm (now known as log) of the values to ensure stationarity of the transformed data are taken.

A closer look at the daily exchange rates in Figures 3.2–3.6 reveals much volatility of the five major exchange rates against the Malaysian ringgit, especially in early 1997, due to the Asian financial crisis. There were some major developments during this period. The USD was subsequently pegged at MYR3.8 to one USD by the Malaysian government and capital control was imposed subsequently. The Malaysian government later allowed the exchange rate of MYR/USD to float on 25 July 2005. The EUR was only launched on 4 January 1999, and hence there were no records prior to that date.

Table 3.1 Descriptive statistics of five daily major currencies against Malaysian ringgit

Panel A: 2 January 1997 to 28 February 2014

	USD	GBP	EUR	JPY	CHF
Mean	3.517911	5.84063	3.780817	3.31188	2.857369
Standard error	0.005458	0.012504	0.022214	0.006211	0.00686
Median	3.6735	5.9067	4.2121	3.2692	2.929
Mode	3.8	5.9464	0	3.2458	3.1051
Standard deviation	0.355622	0.814659	1.447291	0.404673	0.446946
Sample variance	0.126467	0.663669	2.094653	0.16376	0.199761
Kurtosis	0.302957	−0.97352	2.491904	1.003771	−0.18114
Skewness	−0.82089	−0.1183	−1.93086	−0.64481	−0.51043
Range	2.2533	3.7251	5.1859	2.2153	2.4885
Minimum	2.4717	3.9353	0	1.9737	1.6641
Maximum	4.725	7.6604	5.1859	4.189	4.1526

Panel B: 2 January 1997 to 30 December 2005

	USD	GBP	EUR	JPY	CHF
Mean	3.704916	6.034142	3.153888	3.182503	2.565412
Standard error	0.007412	0.016083	0.036859	0.008223	0.008172
Median	3.8	6.1018	3.7322	3.21495	2.55595
Mode	3.8	5.9464	0	3.1663	2.731
Standard deviation	0.350329	0.760174	1.74213	0.388639	0.386249
Sample variance	0.122731	0.577865	3.035018	0.15104	0.149188
Kurtosis	6.559586	0.605622	−0.44234	1.616772	−0.44884
Skewness	−2.63617	−0.73385	−1.08138	−1.29587	−0.26575
Range	2.2533	3.7251	5.1752	1.7808	1.6938
Minimum	2.4717	3.9353	0	1.9737	1.6641
Maximum	4.725	7.6604	5.1752	3.7545	3.3579
Count	2234	2234	2234	2234	2234

Panel C: 3 January 2006 to 28 February 2014

	USD	GBP	EUR	JPY	CHF
Mean	3.310169	5.625661	4.477267	3.455604	3.1817
Standard error	0.004918	0.018273	0.008005	0.008305	0.00528
Median	3.266	5.2874	4.5082	3.4903	3.186
Mode	3.1315	4.9519	3.9571	3.1635	3.1051
Standard deviation	0.220533	0.819432	0.358992	0.372428	0.236778
Sample variance	0.048635	0.671468	0.128875	0.138702	0.056064
Kurtosis	−1.15397	−1.36633	−1.17422	−1.34633	−0.21037
Skewness	0.318359	0.518596	0.019092	−0.01919	0.374142
Range	0.84	2.5725	1.3701	1.4119	1.397
Minimum	2.9385	4.5633	3.8158	2.7771	2.7556
Maximum	3.7785	7.1358	5.1859	4.189	4.1526
Count	2011	2011	2011	2011	2011

Data source: Bank Negara Malaysia.

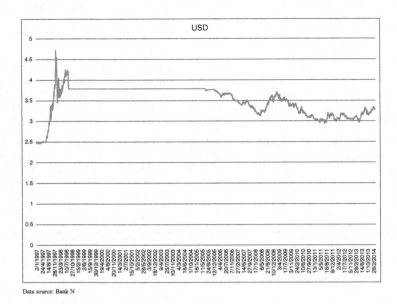

Data source: Bank N

Figure 3.2 Daily exchange rates of MYR/USD. Period: 2 January 1997 to 28 February
2014.

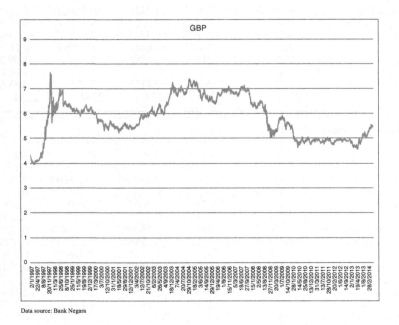

Data source: Bank Negara

Figure 3.3 Daily exchange rates of MYR/GBP. Period: 2 January 1997 to 28 February
2014.

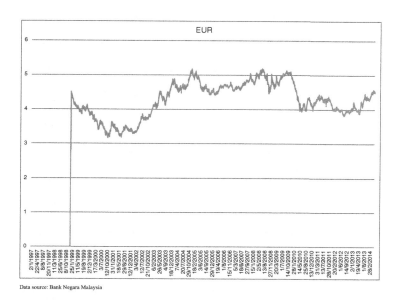

Data source: Bank Negara Malaysia

Figure 3.4 Daily exchange rates of MYR/EUR. Period: 2 January 1997 to 28 February 2014.

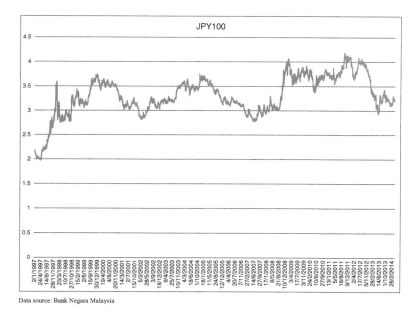

Data source: Bank Negara Malaysia

Figure 3.5 Daily exchange rates of MYR/JPY. Period: 2 January 1997 to 28 February 2014.

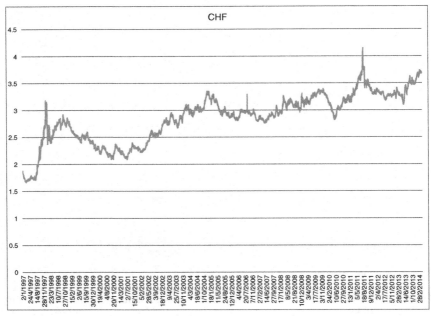

Data source: Bank Negara Malaysia

Figure 3.6 Daily exchange rates of MYR/CHF. Period: 2 January 1997 to 28 February 2014.

Figure 3.7 summarises the trend of the five major currencies with respect to the Malaysian ringgit. The period is now divided into two parts to capture the floatation of MYR/USD: 2 January 1997 to 30 December 2005 and 3 January 2006 to 28 February 2014. The starting date of the second part, 3 January 2006, allows the MYR/USD to settle down due to equilibrium path finding by various investors and speculators in the exchange rate market.

As there are three major developments in the first period of 4 January 1997 to 30 December 2005, i.e. the Asian financial crisis in July of 1997, floatation of EUR on 4 January 1999 and the liberalisation of MYR/USD on 25 July 2005, it can be expected that the volatility of the major exchange rates could be higher in the first period compared to the second period. The descriptive statistics of the exchange rate data summarised in Table 3.1 confirmed the increased volatility for the first period. Panel A of Table 3.1 shows the full period with more than 4,000 daily observations. Panel B of Table 3.1 shows higher volatility in terms of standard deviation and sample variance but it is quite similar to the full period. The Japanese yen is the only currency that had negative skewness, whereas all the major currencies had negative skewness in the first period. All currencies in all periods demonstrated non-normal density functions. This deviation from normal distribution is discussed further in the next two chapters.

Table 3.2 shows that the correlations of the different currency pairs varied over time. For panel A, only USD/CHF and GBP/JPY demonstrated negative correlations, while the other currency pairs exhibited positive correlations. For the period of January 1997 to December 2005, all currency pairs exhibited positive correlations as demonstrated in Panel B of Table 3.2. With respect to the post-liberalisation of the MYR/USD, less than half of the currency pairs demonstrated positive correlations, i.e. USD/GBP, USD/EUR, GBP/EUR and JPY/CHF. Both Japanese yen and Swiss franc revealed negative correlations with the US dollar, British pound and euro in the era after BNM relaxed capital control. The instability of the correlations of the currency pairs is also being examined in depth in Chapter 5, with the extension of the univariate analysis of the currency pair with respect to the Malaysian ringgit to the multivariate analysis of the five major currency pairs.

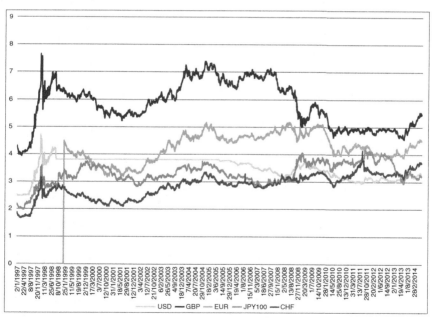

Data source: Bank Negara Malaysia

Figure 3.7 Daily exchange rates of MYR against the world top five currencies. Period: 2 January 1997 to 28 February 2014.

Table 3.2 Correlations of five major currencies against Malaysian ringgit

Panel A: 2 January 1997 to 28 February 2014

	USD	*GBP*	*EUR*	*JPY*	*CHF*
USD	1				
GBP	0.706082	1			
EUR	0.092628	0.257934	1		
JPY	0.101728	−0.04794	0.5663	1	
CHF	−0.19051	0.06274	0.581848	0.641334	1

Panel B: 2 January 1997 to 30 December 2005

	USD	*GBP*	*EUR*	*JPY*	*CHF*
USD	1				
GBP	0.741422	1			
EUR	0.480606	0.491491	1		
JPY	0.764203	0.752961	0.745143	1	
CHF	0.622526	0.950537	0.519471	0.656508	1

Panel C: 4 January 2006 to 28 February 2014

	USD	*GBP*	*EUR*	*JPY*	*CHF*
USD	1				
GBP	0.706427	1			
EUR	0.62971	0.69228	1		
JPY	−0.3399	−0.72665	−0.3775	1	
CHF	−0.56353	−0.66628	−0.27133	0.530913	1

Data source: Bank Negara Malaysia.

Implications

Post-liberalisation increases volatility of exchange rates, and therefore historical and static statistics like standard deviations and variances, as explained in section "Data analysis of Malaysia's exchange rate", are less reliable and effective as a measurement of risk in the case of exchange rate movements. These findings are similar to those of Thomas and Shah (1999) who observed that exchange rate volatilities are not well represented by historical standard deviations and variances, whereas GARCH models were found to better explain the exchange volatilities.

In the Markowitz (1952) portfolio theory, the variance is used as a risk measure. It might then seem natural, in a dynamic framework, to use the volatility as a risk measure. However, volatility does not take into account the signs of the differences from the conditional mean.

It can be seen in Figures 3.8–3.12 that all five major currency pairs demonstrated clustering of volatility over time. This time-varying heteroscedasticity

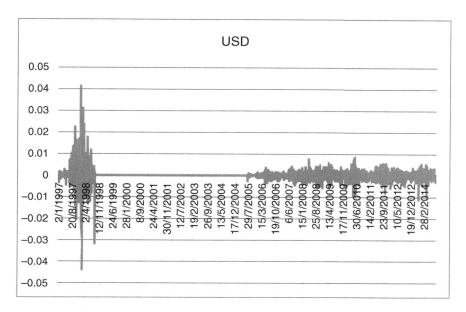

Figure 3.8 Log difference of daily exchange rates of MYR/USD. Period: 2 January 1997 to 28 February 2014.

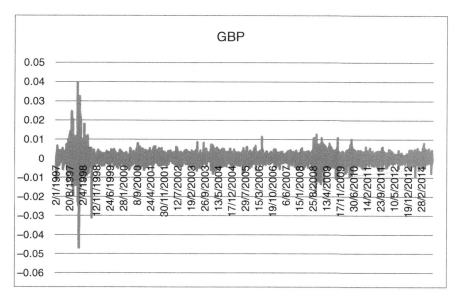

Figure 3.9 Log difference of daily exchange rates of MYR/GBP. Period: 2 January 1997 to 28 February 2014.

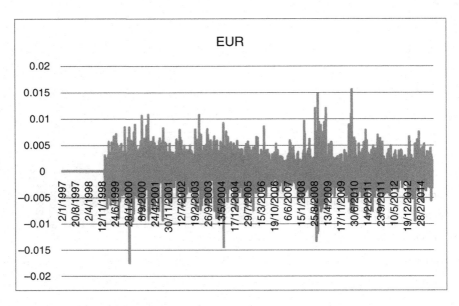

Figure 3.10 Log difference of daily exchange rates of MYR/EUR. Period: 2 January 1997 to 28 February 2014.

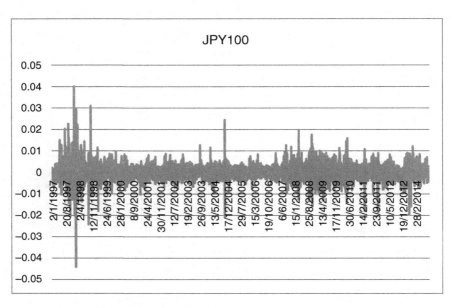

Figure 3.11 Log difference of daily exchange rates of MYR/JPY. Period: 2 January 1997 to 28 February 2014.

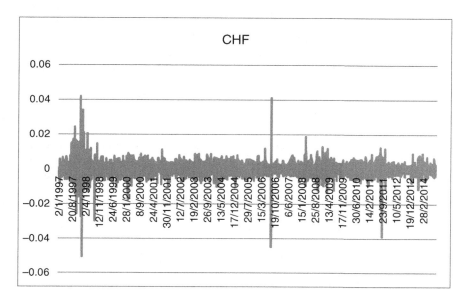

Figure 3.12 Log difference of daily exchange rates of MYR/CHF. Period: 2 January 1997 to 28 February 2014.

can be found in all five major currency pairs, and hence GARCH models are analysed in more detail as risk models for exchange rates in Chapters 4 and 5. Once the risk models are calibrated and chosen according to diagnostic tests, risk measures are compiled and compared to see whether there are significant differences in the different period of capital control in 1997 and exchange rate liberalisation post 2005.

Given the unstable correlations between five currency pairs across different periods, multivariate GARCH might be the better risk models to capture exchange rate volatility. These correlations between the different currency pairs are examined in more detail in Chapter 5 to analyse the dependence of different currency pairs.

Conclusion

This chapter has first provided a basic analysis of the exchange rates of the seven major currencies, using monthly data. It was then decided that more recent data should be used to analyse more closely the effect of liberalising the MYR/USD. Thus, due to the above reason, the change of the frequency to daily observations and the reduction of the financial time series to five major currency pairs of Malaysia were made. The reasons to use more recent and higher frequency data for analysis in later chapters are the concern of effectiveness and relevance. Since the measurement is in relation to the risk of exchange rates, the movement of exchange rates of recent periods is more relevant and the literature in this area has shown that higher frequency data have more tendency of volatility clustering. The reason to shorten the currency pairs from seven to five later is also the significance of the currency pairs where the major currency pairs are analysed.

In this chapter, the evidence provided indicates the need to extend the analysis of exchange rate volatility from standard measurement like static variance-covariance and standard deviations to stochastic volatility modelling in order to capture the time-varying volatility clustering, which was evident in the results found in section "Data analysis of Malaysia's exchange rate". This chapter has, therefore, presented us with a good platform, following Thomas and Shah (1999), to extend our analysis of exchange rate volatility from static historical standard deviation statistics to discrete stochastic volatility modelling for the next chapter.

4 Volatility modelling of exchange rates in a univariate framework

Introduction

The economic and financial crises, market instability and high volatility in developing stock markets became worldwide phenomena in the late 1990s. In 1997, macroeconomic conditions such as foreign exchange and interest rates saw adverse developments and severe fluctuations in most Asian countries. The crisis affected trade, investment and financial linkages, increasing risk premiums between many developing markets, especially in Asian countries and the rest of the world (see Mishkin, 1999 and Kettell, 2001). Following the Asian economic crisis, coupled with the devaluation of the Thai baht, most financial markets in the South East Asian region experienced a crash in capital markets and a dramatic decline in exchange rates of major currencies (Titman and Wei, 1999). The Thai currency, for example, lost half of its value against the US dollar within a few months after the announcement of its currency devaluation in 1997. As a result of the crisis, the Thai stock market became very volatile and stock prices suddenly fell by 70% by the end of 1997, which in turn generated a flow-on effect of similar consequences in the surrounding regional economies. Edmonds and So (2004) believed that the financial crises in developing markets had raised a debate about whether increased volatility may suppress international trade, investment and financial linkages and what could be done to discourage currency and stock speculation.

As the impacts of financial crises and volatility have been widespread in developing exchange rate markets, the question of how to simulate the real life behaviour of volatile exchange rate markets is crucial since such an appropriate simulation can help in understanding the factors and processes which are associated with the movements of exchange rates. However, there is no systematic study of the volatility aspect of these foreign exchange markets. Therefore, the objectives of this chapter are to undertake a comprehensive study of the volatility aspect of exchange rate for the Malaysian ringgit by adopting some recent popular econometric models and to analyse the implications of the model results and risk measurements.

There are many models that can be adopted to simulate the behaviour of exchange rate markets, especially the volatility aspect, which involve nonlinear and complex dynamic movements. Autoregressive Conditional

Heteroscedasticity (ARCH) models are widely used in finance for simulating nonlinear and complex market behaviour, especially for analysing and predicting volatility. However, ARCH models have not been systematically applied to simulate the behaviour of foreign exchanges. This chapter presents the theoretical models (various ARCH models) and the empirical results for the volatility of the exchange rate of the Malaysian ringgit. The data consist of monthly nominal exchange rates from 1983 to 2004. The modelling performance of several different conditional variance models, within the parametric Generalised ARCH (GARCH) class of models, is compared. Several GARCH-type models are analysed, including GARCH, EGARCH, GARCH-M and PGARCH.

In this book, ARCH- and GARCH-type models are adopted due to the accepted view in the literature about the appropriateness of these volatility models in providing empirical evidence of volatility in a market. The purpose of this study is not to test the models but to compare the results of five ARCH- and GARCH-type models, consisting of both linear and nonlinear models, used for identifying and predicting volatility of the ringgit exchange rate and seasonal anomalies in Malaysia.

This book focuses on the analysis of time-varying volatility of the Malaysian exchange markets, as the results presented in Chapter 3 confirmed the need to model these stochastic volatility models and to ascertain whether there have been changes in the behaviour of exchange rate volatility before and after the Asian financial crises. This chapter is structured as follows: section "Framework and estimation process" presents the methodology and data being used in this research; empirical evidence generated from this research is presented for volatility modelling in section "Empirical results". Section "Value-at-Risk" discusses the implications of the findings, and section "Implications" presents the conclusions for this chapter.

Framework and estimation process

Volatility modelling has been a very active area of research in recent years due to the importance of volatility in financial markets. Volatility estimates are often used as simple risk measures in many asset pricing models. There are various methods of measuring volatility in empirical work, including Autoregressive Conditional Heteroscedasticity (ARCH) models and Stochastic Volatility (SV) models among others. ARCH-type models have been reviewed by many authors including Bera and Higgins (1995), Bollerslev *et al.* (1992), Bollerslev *et al.* (1994) and Diebold and Lopez (1995). Ghysels *et al.* (1996) provided an excellent survey of SV models, while Aydemir (2002) suggested that one can consider both ARCH and SV models as well as other techniques for modelling volatility.

In this chapter, a time series approach, Generalised Autoregressive Conditional Heteroskedasticity (GARCH), is used to model discrete time-varying volatility rather than the time-varying moving average method used by Hurley and Santos (2001).

Conditional mean

Let one consider a univariate time series y_t. If Ω_{t-1} is the information set at time $t-1$, its functional form can be defined as

$$y_t = E(y_t | \Omega_{t-1}) + \varepsilon_t \tag{4.1}$$

where $E(\cdot|\cdot)$ denotes the conditional expectation operator and ε_t is the disturbance term (or unpredictable part), with $E(\varepsilon_t) = 0$ and $E(\varepsilon_t \varepsilon_s) = 0$, $\forall\, t \neq s$.

Equation (4.1) is the conditional mean equation which has been studied and modelled in many ways. Two of the most famous specifications are the Autoregressive (AR) and Moving Average (MA) models. Combining these two processes and introducing n_1 explanatory variables in the equation, the ARMAX (n, s) process is obtained:

$$\psi(L)(y_t - \mu_t) = \Theta(L)\varepsilon_t$$
$$\mu_t = \mu + \sum_{i=1}^{n-1} \delta_i x_{i,t} \tag{4.2}$$

where L is the lag operator, $\psi(L) = 1 - \sum_{i=1}^{n} \psi_i L^i$ and $\Theta(L) = 1 + \sum_{j=1}^{s} \theta_j L^j$.

Several studies have shown that the dependent variables (interest rate returns, exchange rate returns, etc.) may exhibit significant autocorrelation between observations widely separated in time. In such a case, y_t is said to display long memory (or long-term dependence) and is best modelled by a fractionally integrated ARMA (ARFIMA) process. This ARFIMA process was initially developed by Granger (1980) and Granger and Joyeux (1980) among others. The ARFIMA(n, ζ, s) is given by

$$\psi(L)(1-L)^{\zeta}(y_t - \mu_t) = \Theta(L)\varepsilon_t \tag{4.3}$$

where the operator $(1 - L)^{\zeta}$ accounts for the long memory of the process and is defined as

$$1 - (L)^{\zeta} = \sum_{k=0}^{\infty} \frac{\Gamma(\zeta+1)}{\Gamma(k+1)\Gamma(\zeta-k+1)} L^k$$
$$= 1 - \zeta L - \frac{1}{2}\zeta(1-\zeta)L^2 - \frac{1}{6}\zeta(1-\zeta)(2-\zeta)L^3 - \ldots \tag{4.4}$$
$$= 1 - \sum_{k=1}^{\infty} c_k(\zeta)L^k$$

with $0 < \zeta < 1, c_1(\zeta) = \zeta, c_2(\zeta) = \frac{1}{2}\zeta(1 - \zeta), \dots$ and $\Gamma(.)$ denoting the Gamma function (see Baillie, 1996, for a survey on this topic). The truncation order of the infinite summation is set to $t - 1$.

Autoregressive conditional heteroscedastic models

The ε_t term in equations (4.1)–(4.3) is the innovation of the process. More than two decades ago, Engle (1982) defined an Autoregressive Conditional Heteroscedastic (ARCH) process, all ε_t of the form

$$\varepsilon_t = z_t \sigma_t \qquad (4.5)$$

where z_t is an independently and identically distributed (*i.i.d.*) process with $E(z_t) = 0$ and $Var(z_t) = 1$. By assumption, ε_t is serially uncorrelated with a mean equal to zero but its conditional variance equals σ_t^2. Therefore, it may change over time, contrary to what is assumed in the standard regression model.

Various forms of ARCH models differ on the functional form of σ_t^2 but the basic principles are the same. Besides the traditional ARCH and GARCH models, there are two categories of models: the asymmetric models and the fractionally integrated models. The former models are defined to account for the so-called "leverage effect" observed in many stock returns, while the latter allow for long memory in the variance. Early evidence of the "leverage effect" can be found in Black (1976), while persistence in volatility is a common finding of many empirical studies (see for instance the excellent surveys on ARCH models proposed by Bollerslev *et al.* (1992) and Bera and Higgins (1995)).

The ARCH (q) model can be expressed as

$$\begin{aligned}
\varepsilon_t &= z_t \sigma_t \\
z_t &\sim i.i.d. \ D(0,1) \\
\sigma_t^2 &= \omega + \sum_{i=1}^{q} \alpha_i \varepsilon_{t-i}^2
\end{aligned} \qquad (4.6)$$

where $D(.)$ is a probability density function with mean 0 and unit variance.

The ARCH model can describe volatility clustering. The conditional variance of ε_t is indeed an increasing function of the square of the shock that occurred in $t - 1$. Consequently, if ε_{t-1} was large in absolute value, σ_t^2 and thus ε_t are expected to be large (in absolute value) as well. Notice that even if the conditional variance of an ARCH model is time-varying, i.e. $\sigma_t^2 = E(\varepsilon_t^2 | \psi_{t-1})$, the unconditional variance of ε_t is constant and, provided that $\omega > 0$ and $\sum_{i=1}^{q} \alpha_i$, one would have

$$\sigma^2 \equiv E\left[E\left(\varepsilon_t^2 | \psi_{t-1} \right) \right] = \frac{\omega}{1 - \sum\limits_{i=1}^{q} \alpha_i} \tag{4.7}$$

If z_t is normally distributed, $E(z_t^3) = 0$ and $E(z_t^4) = 3$. Consequently, $E(\varepsilon_t^3) = 0$ and the skewness of y is zero. The kurtosis coefficient for the ARCH(1) is $3\dfrac{1-\alpha_1^2}{1-3\alpha_1^2}$ if $\alpha_1 < \sqrt{\frac{1}{3}} \approx 0.577$. In this case, the unconditional distribution of the returns features fat tails whenever $\alpha_1 > 0$.

In most applications, the excess kurtosis implied by the ARCH model (coupled with a normal density) is not enough to mimic what one observes in real data. Other density functions are possible. For example, one could assume that z_t follows a Student distribution with unit variance and υ degrees of freedom, i.e. z_t is $ST(0,1,\upsilon)$. In that case, the unconditional kurtosis of the ARCH(1) is $\lambda\dfrac{1-\alpha_1^2}{1-\lambda\alpha_1^2}$ with $\lambda = 3(\upsilon - 2)/(\upsilon - 4)$. Because of the additional coefficient υ, the ARCH(1) model based on the Student distribution does feature fatter tails than the corresponding model based on the Normal distribution (see sections "Student *t*-distribution", "Generalised error distribution" and "Skewed Student distribution" for more details).

The computation of σ_t^2 in equation (4.6) depends on past (squared) residuals (ε_t^2), which are not observed for t = 0, −1,..., −q+1. To initialise the process, the unobserved squared residuals are set to their sample mean.

Generalised autoregressive conditional heteroscedastic models

The Generalised Autoregressive Conditional Heteroscedastic (GARCH) models introduced by Bollerslev (1986) extended the concept of ARCH proposed by Engle (1982). An ordinary ARCH model is a special case of a GARCH specification in which there are no lagged forecast variances in the conditional variance equation.

The GARCH model is based on an infinite ARCH specification and it allows the reduction of the number of estimated parameters by imposing nonlinear restrictions on them. The GARCH (p, q) model can be expressed as

$$\sigma_t^2 = \omega + \sum_{i=1}^{q} \alpha_i \varepsilon_{t-i}^2 + \sum_{j=1}^{p} \beta_j \sigma_{t-j}^2 \tag{4.8}$$

Using the lag (or backshift) operator L, the GARCH (p, q) model becomes

$$\sigma_t^2 = \omega + \alpha(L)\varepsilon_t^2 + \beta(L)\sigma_t^2$$

with $\alpha(L) = \alpha_1 L + \alpha_2 L^2 + \cdots + \alpha_q L^q$ and $\beta(L) = \beta_1 L + \beta_2 L^2 + \cdots + \beta_p L^p$

If all the roots of the polynomial $|1 - \beta(L)| = 0$ lie outside the unit circle, one gets:

$$\sigma_t^2 = \omega[1 - \beta(L)]^{-1} + \alpha(L)[1 - \beta(L)]^{-1}\varepsilon_t^2 \tag{4.9}$$

which may be seen as an ARCH(∞) process since the conditional variance linearly depends on all previous squared residuals. In this case, the conditional variance of y_t can become larger than the unconditional variance given by

$$\sigma^2 \equiv E\left[\varepsilon_t^2\right] = \frac{\omega}{1 - \sum_{i=1}^q \alpha_i - \sum_{j=1}^p \beta_j}$$

if past realisations of ε_t^2 are larger than σ^2 (Palm, 1996).

Applying variance targeting to the GARCH model implies replacing ω by $\sigma^2 (1 - \sum_{i=1}^q \alpha_i - \sum_{j=1}^p \beta_j)$, where σ^2 is the unconditional variance of ε_t, which can be consistently estimated by its sample counterpart.

Bollerslev (1986) has shown that for a GARCH(1,1) with normal innovations, the kurtosis of y is $3[1 - (\alpha_1 + \beta_1)2]/1 - (\alpha_1 + \beta_1)^2 - 2\alpha_1^2 > 3$. The autocorrelations of ε_t^2 have been derived by Bollerslev (1986). For a stationary GARCH(1,1), $\rho_1 = \alpha_1 + \left[\alpha_1^2\beta_1/(1 - 2\alpha_1\beta_1 - \beta_1^2)\right]$, and $\rho_k = (\alpha_1 + \beta_1)^{k-1}\rho_1$, $\forall k = 2,3,\ldots.$ In other words, the autocorrelations decline exponentially with a decay factor of $\alpha_1 + \beta_1$. As in the ARCH case, some restrictions are needed to ensure σ_t^2 is positive for all t. Bollerslev (1986) shows that imposing $\omega > 0$, $\alpha_i \geq 0$ (for $i = 1,\ldots, q$) and $\beta_j \geq 0$ (for $j = 1,\ldots, p$) is sufficient for the conditional variance to be positive. In practice, the GARCH parameters are often estimated without the positivity constraints. Nelson and Cao (1992) argued that imposing all coefficients to be nonnegative is too restrictive and that some of these coefficients are found to be negative in practice, while the conditional variance remains positive (by checking on a case-by-case basis). Consequently, they relaxed this constraint and gave sufficient conditions for the GARCH(1,q) and GARCH(2,q) cases based on the infinite representation given in equation (4.9). Indeed, the conditional variance is strictly positive provided $\omega[1 - \beta(L)]^{-1}$ is positive and all the coefficients of the infinite polynomial $\alpha(L)^{-1}$ in equation (4.9) are nonnegative.

Density functions of GARCH's innovation process

Estimation of GARCH-type models is commonly done by maximum likelihood so that one has to make an additional assumption about the innovation process z_t, i.e. choosing a density function $D(0,1)$ with a mean 0 and a unit variance. The logic of Maximum Likelihood (ML) is to interpret the density as a function of the parameter set, conditional on a set of sample outcomes. This function is called the *likelihood function*. The ML estimation is not perfectly exact as recursive evaluation of this function is conditional on unobserved values. To solve the problem of unobserved values, these quantities to their unconditional expected values have been set. For this reason, one talks about approximate (or conditional) ML and not exact ML.

Weiss (1986) and Bollerslev and Wooldridge (1992) showed that under the normality assumption, the Quasi-Maximum Likelihood (QML) estimator is consistent if the conditional mean and the conditional variance are correctly specified. This estimator is, however, inefficient with the degree of inefficiency increasing with the degree of departure from normality (Engle and González-Rivera, 1991).

As reported by Palm (1996), Pagan (1996) and Bollerslev *et al.* (1992), the use of fat-tailed density functions is widespread in the literature. In particular, Bollerslev (1987), Hsieh (1989), Baillie and Bollerslev (1989) and Palm and Vlaar (1997) among others showed that these density functions perform better in order to capture the higher observed kurtosis.

Normal distribution

If one expresses the mean equation as in equation (4.1) and $\varepsilon_t = z_t \sigma_t$, the log-likelihood function of the standard normal distribution is given by

$$L_{\text{norm}} = -\frac{1}{2} \sum_{t=1}^{T} \left[\log(2\pi) + \log\left(\sigma_t^2\right) + z_t^2 \right] \tag{4.10}$$

where T is the number of observations.

Student -distribution

For a Student t-distribution, the log-likelihood is

$$L_{\text{Stud}} = T \left\{ \log\Gamma\left(\frac{\upsilon+1}{2}\right) - \log\Gamma\left(\frac{\upsilon}{2}\right) - \frac{1}{2}\log\left[\pi(\upsilon-2)\right] \right\} - \frac{1}{2} \sum_{t=1}^{T} \left[\log\left(\sigma_t^2\right) + (1+\upsilon)\log\left(1 + \frac{z_t^2}{\upsilon-2}\right) \right] \tag{4.11}$$

where υ is the degrees of freedom, $2 < \upsilon \leq \infty$ and $\Gamma(.)$ is the gamma function.

Generalised error distribution

The generalised error distribution (GED) log-likelihood function of a normalised random variable is given by:

$$L_{\text{GED}} = \sum_{t=1}^{T}\left[\log\left(\frac{\upsilon}{\lambda_{\upsilon}}\right) - 0.5\left|\frac{z_t}{\lambda_{\upsilon}}\right|^{\upsilon} - \left(1+\upsilon^{-1}\right)\log(2) - \log\Gamma\left(\frac{1}{\upsilon}\right) - 0.5\log\left(\sigma_t^2\right)\right]$$

(4.12)

where $0 < \upsilon < \infty$ and

$$\lambda_{\upsilon} \equiv \sqrt{\frac{\Gamma\left(\frac{1}{\upsilon}\right)2^{\left(-\frac{2}{\upsilon}\right)}}{\Gamma\left(\frac{3}{\upsilon}\right)}}.$$

The main drawback of the last two densities is that even if they may account for fat tails, they are symmetric. Skewness and kurtosis are important in financial applications in many respects (in asset pricing models, portfolio selection, option pricing theory or Value at Risk among others).

Skewed Student distribution

Lambert and Laurent (2000) applied and extended the skewed Student density proposed by Fernández and Steel (1998) to the GARCH framework.

The log-likelihood of a standardised (zero mean and unit variance) skewed Student is

$$L_{\text{SkSt}} = \left\{\log\Gamma\left(\frac{\upsilon+1}{2}\right) - \log\Gamma\left(\frac{\upsilon}{2}\right) - \frac{1}{2}\log\left[\pi(\upsilon-2)\right] + \log\left(\frac{2}{\xi+\frac{1}{\xi}}\right) + \log(s)\right\}$$
$$-\frac{1}{2}\sum_{t=1}^{T}\left[\log\left(\sigma_t^2\right) + (1+\upsilon)\log\left[\left(1+\frac{(sz_t+m)^2}{\upsilon-2}\xi^{-2I_t}\right)\right]\right]$$

(4.13)

where

$$I_t = \begin{cases} 1 & \text{if } z_t \geq -\dfrac{m}{8} \\[2mm] 1 & \text{if } z_t < -\dfrac{m}{8} \end{cases}$$

ζ is the asymmetry parameter, v is the degree of freedom of the distribution,

$$m = \frac{\Gamma\left(\frac{v+1}{2}\right)\sqrt{v-2}}{\sqrt{\pi}\,\Gamma\left(\frac{v}{2}\right)}\left(\xi - \frac{1}{\xi}\right)$$

and

$$s = \sqrt{\left(\xi^2 + \frac{1}{\xi^2} - 1\right) - m^2}.$$

Exponential GARCH

The Exponential GARCH (EGARCH) model, originally introduced by Nelson (1991), is re-expressed in Bollerslev and Mikkelsen (1996) as follows:

$$\log\sigma_t^2 = \omega + \left[1 - \beta(L)\right]^{-1}\left[1 + \alpha(L)\right]g(z_{t-1}) \tag{4.14}$$

The value of $g(z_t)$ depends on several elements. Nelson (1991) notes that "to accommodate the asymmetric relation between stock returns and volatility changes (…) the value of $g(z_t)$ must be a function of both the magnitude and the sign of z_t". That is why he suggests expressing the function $g(\cdot)$ as

$$g(z_t) \equiv \underbrace{\gamma_1 z_t}_{\text{sign effect}} + \underbrace{\gamma_2\left[|z_t| - E|z_t|\right]}_{\text{magnitude effect}} \tag{4.15}$$

where $E|z_t|$ depends on the assumption made on the unconditional density of z_t. Indeed, for the normal distribution,

$$E|z_t| = \sqrt{2/\pi} \tag{4.16}$$

For the skewed Student distribution,

$$E|z_t| = \frac{4\xi^2}{\xi + 1/\xi}\,\frac{\Gamma\left(\frac{1+v}{2}\right)\sqrt{v-2}}{\sqrt{\pi}\,\Gamma(v/2)} \tag{4.17}$$

where $\xi = 1$ for the symmetric Student.
For the GED, one has

$$E|z_t| = 2^{(1/v)}\lambda_v\,\frac{\Gamma(2/v)}{\Gamma(1/v)} \tag{4.18}$$

where ξ, v and λ_v concern the shape of the non-normal densities.

Note that the use of a log transformation of the conditional variance ensures that σ_t^2 is always positive.

Applying variance targeting to the EGARCH model implies replacing ω by $\log(\sigma^2)$, where σ^2 is the unconditional variance of ε_t, which can be consistently estimated by its sample counterpart.

Misspecification tests

Various misspecification tests are performed on the GARCH modelling to access the goodness of fit of the volatility models.

Information criteria (divided by the number of observations)

$$Akaike = -2\frac{LogL}{n} + 2\frac{k}{n};$$

$$Hannan - Quinn = -2\frac{LogL}{n} + 2\frac{kLog[\log(n)]}{n};$$

$$Schwartz = -2\frac{LogL}{n} + 2\frac{Log(k)}{n};$$

$$Shibata = -2\frac{LogL}{n} + Log\left(\frac{n+2k}{n}\right).$$

Skewness and kurtosis

The value of the skewness and the kurtosis of the standardised residuals of the estimated model ($\hat{z}_t$), their t-tests and p-values are calculated. Moreover, the Jarque-Bera normality test (Jarque and Bera, 1987) is also reported.

Box-Pierce statistics

The Box-Pierce statistics at lag l^* for both standardised, i.e. $BP^{(l^*)}$, and squared standardised, i.e. $BP^{2(l^*)}$, residuals are also calculated. Under the null hypothesis of no autocorrelation, the statistics $BP^{(l^*)}$ and $BP^{2(l^*)}$ should be evaluated against $\chi^{2(l^*-m-l)}$ and $\chi^{2(l^*-p-q)}$, respectively (see McLeod and Li, 1983).

Lagrange Multiplier ARCH test

Engle's Lagrange Multiplier (LM) ARCH test (Engle, 1982) is also performed to test the presence of ARCH effects in a series. For each specified order, the squared residual series is regressed on p of its own lags. The test statistic is distributed $\chi^2(p)$ under the null hypothesis of no ARCH effects.

Leverage effect test

The diagnostic test of Engle and Ng (1993) that investigates possible mis-specification of the conditional variance equation is also conducted. Let S_t^- denote a dummy variable which takes the value 1 when $\hat{\varepsilon}_{t-1} < 0$, and 0 other-wise (and $S_t^+ \equiv 1 - S_t^-$). The Sign Bias Test (SBT) examines whether $\hat{\varepsilon}_t^2$ can be predicted by S_{t-1}^-, $S_{t-1}^- \hat{\varepsilon}_{t-1}$ and/or $S_{t-1}^+ \hat{\varepsilon}_{t-1}$. To test the presence of leverage effects, Engle and Ng (1993) proposed to run the following regressions:

$$\hat{\varepsilon}_t^2 = a_0 + a_1 S_{t-1}^- + u_t \: : \text{SBT}$$
$$\hat{\varepsilon}_t^2 = b_0 + b_1 S_{t-1}^- \hat{\varepsilon}_{t-1} + u_t : \text{NSBT}$$
$$\hat{\varepsilon}_t^2 = c_0 + c_1 S_{t-1}^+ \hat{\varepsilon}_{t-1} + u_t : \text{PSBT}$$

and test the significance of a_1, b_1 and c_1 through a t-test. The tests are re-spectively called Sign Bias Test (SBT), Negative Sign Bias Test (NSBT) and Positive Sign Bias Test (PSBT). The NSBT and PSBT also test whether the effect of negative and positive shocks on the conditional variance depends on their size.

Instead of running three different regressions, G@RCH follows Engle and Ng (1993) in estimating jointly the three effects, i.e.

$$\hat{\varepsilon}_t^2 = d_0 + d_1 S_{t-1}^- + d_2 S_{t-1}^- \hat{\varepsilon}_{t-1} + d_3 S_{t-1}^+ \hat{\varepsilon}_{t-1} + u_t \tag{4.19}$$

T-stats corresponding to $H_0: d_i = 0$ ($H_1: d_i \neq 0$), $\forall i = 1, 2$ and 3 are reported, as well as their p-value. Finally, a joint test for $H_0 : d_1 = d_2 = d_3 = 0$ is also provided.

Adjusted Pearson goodness-of-fit test

The adjusted Pearson goodness-of-fit test that compares the empirical distri-bution of the innovations with the theoretical one is also performed. In order to carry out this testing procedure, it is necessary to first classify the residuals in cells according to their magnitude. Let n be the number of observations, r the number of categories considered, p_i ($i = 1, ..., r$) the observed proportion of observations being in the ith category and p_i^t ($i = 1, ..., r$) the theoreti-cal probability for an observation to be in the ith category. The Pearson goodness-of-fit test has the null $H_0: p_1 = p_1^t, p_2 = p_2^t, ..., p_r = p_r^t$. The statistic is computed as

$$P(g) = \sum_{i=1}^{r} \frac{(n_i - En_i)^2}{En_i} \tag{4.20}$$

where n_i is the observed number in the sample that fall into the ith category and En_i is the number of observations expected to be in this ith category when H_0 is true. The Pearson statistic is therefore "small" when all of the observed counts (proportions) are close to the expected counts (proportions) and it is "large" when one or more observed counts (proportions) differ noticeably from what is expected when H_0 is true. For independent and identically distributed (i.i.d.) observations, Palm and Vlaar (1997) showed that under the null of a correct distribution the asymptotic distribution of $P(g)$ is bounded between $\chi^2(r - 1)$ and $\chi^2(r - k - 1)$, where k is the number of estimated parameters. As explained by Palm and Vlaar (1997), the choice of r is far from obvious. According to König and Gaab (1982), the number of cells must increase at a rate equal to T.

Residual-based diagnostic

The Residual-Based Diagnostic (RBD) for conditional heteroscedasticity is based on the study of Tse (2002). The Box-Pierce portmanteau statistic is perhaps the most widely used diagnostic for conditional heteroscedasticity models. Although it has been noted that the portmanteau statistics do not have an asymptotic χ^2 distribution, many researchers, nonetheless, apply the χ^2 distribution as an approximation (the problem lies in the fact that estimated residuals are used to calculate the portmanteau statistics). To overcome this problem, Tse (2002) proposed a Residual-Based Diagnostic for conditional heteroscedasticity. The diagnostic involves running artificial regressions and testing for the statistical significance of the regression parameters. The key problem is that since the regressors are estimated, the usual ordinary least squares (OLS) result does not apply.

The rationale for the test is as follows: after estimating the model, the standardised residuals $\hat{z}_t = \hat{\varepsilon}_t / \hat{\sigma}_t$ can be computed. It is obvious that $\hat{z}_t$ depends on the set of estimated parameters $E\left(\hat{z}_t^2\right) = 1$ by construction, so one can run a regression of $E(\hat{z}_t^2) - 1$ on some information variables and examine the statistical significance of the regression parameters. Tse (2002) proposed to run the following OLS regression to test the presence of remaining heteroscedasticity in the standardised residuals:

$$E\left(\hat{z}_t^2\right) - 1 = d_1 \hat{z}_{t-1}^2 + \cdots + d_M \hat{z}_{t-M}^2 + u_t.$$

Since the regressors are not observed (but estimated), standard inference procedures of OLS are invalid. Tse (2002) derived the asymptotic distribution of the estimated parameters and showed that a joint test of significance of the $d_1, \ldots, d_M$ is now $\chi^2(M)$ distributed.

Empirical results

The study discussed in this chapter used Oxmetrics software and the G@RCH module developed by Laurent (2006). Oxmetrics uses the Ox language and the syntax of Ox is modelled on C and C++ as well as on Java. The code written by Doornik and Ooms (1999) in the Ox programming language provides a dialogue-oriented interface with features that are not available in standard econometric software. More information on the Ox language can be found in the study by Doornik (2007b). The GARCH models are estimated using quasi-maximum likelihood (QML) approach by Bollerslev and Wooldridge (1992), where the estimator is generally consistent with a normal limiting distribution and provides asymptotic standard errors that are valid under non-normality. Basically, this method uses the quasi-Newton method of Broyden, Fletcher, Goldfarb and Shanno (BFGS) to maximise the QML and the inverse of the Hessian is used to calculate the covariance matrix of the estimates.

By applying the identification procedures introduced by Box and Jenkins (1970), it was found that all the log (first difference) exchange rate series are white noise by plotting the correlograms. Hence, the move to model the conditional second moment by applying the GARCH models. The GARCH(1,1) model is by far the most widely used by practitioners who wish to estimate the volatility of daily returns. In general, this model is chosen *a priori*, without implementing any statistical identification procedure. This practice is motivated by the common belief that the GARCH(1,1) (or its simplest asymmetric extensions) is sufficient to capture the properties of the financial series, and that higher-order models may be unnecessarily complicated. There are many empirical studies that have used GARCH(1,1) models, such as those by Thomas (1995) and Mohammed *et al.* (2014), even though Francq and Zakoïan (2010) showed that GARCH(1,1) is overrepresented in empirical studies. This book, however, follows Thomas and Shah (1999) in using GARCH(1,1) models as the benchmark for analysis as Hansen and Lunde (2005) proved that GARCH(1,1) is a better model than ARCH(1) for exchange rate data. Table 4.1 summarises the findings for the monthly data (more details of the analysis of monthly data can be found in Appendix 2). Proceeding from here is the analysis of the daily exchange rate data of the five major currency pairs.

Table 4.1 reveals poorly fitting models as some estimates are negative but statistically significant. A review of the adjusted R-square statistics of all the GARCH models above reconfirms such findings, as they are all negative.

As the previous analysis did not find any significant GARCH effects for the monthly exchange rate data, the study next carries out more in-depth analysis to cover more recent and higher frequency data, from monthly to daily, as well as some extensions of basic GARCH models to incorporate non-Gaussian density functions and asymmetric effects:

1   Daily exchange rates are used instead of monthly data. These were downloaded from Bank Negara Malaysia's website. The major trading currencies of USD, GBP, EUR, JPY and CHF are the subject of this sub-section.

2   Studies are conducted for the period when Bank Negara Malaysia decided to allow the Malaysian ringgit to float again instead of pegging

Table 4.1 GARCH(1,1) estimates for the logarithm of first difference of exchange rates (*p*-values are in parentheses)

Panel A: Full sample

$N = 268$	GBP	DM	HKD	JPY	USD	SDR	SGD	CHF
February 1983 to May 2005								
Intercept	0.0003 (0.0007)	0.0006 (0.0044)	0.000 (0.0000)	0.0000 (0.0215)	0.0000 (0.1073)	0.0000 (0.0000)	0.0000 (0.0066)	0.0002 (0.1444)
α1	0.2289 (0.0001)	0.2248 (0.0011)	0.7233 (0.0000)	0.1661 (0.0004)	0.4411 (0.0000)	0.2919 (0.0000)	0.3173 (0.0001)	0.1242 (0.0058)
β1	0.4969 (0.0000)	0.3101 (0.1474)	0.6687 (0.0000)	0.7642 (0.0000)	0.7414 (0.0000)	0.5180 (0.0000)	0.5936 (0.0000)	0.7301 (0.0000)

Panel B: Pre-Asian financial crisis

$N = 173$	GBP	DM	HKD	JPY	USD	SDR	SGD	CHF
February 1983 to June 1997								
Intercept	0.0010 (0.0359)	0.0001 (0.2965)	0.0000 (0.0045)	0.0000 (0.0295)	0.0000 (0.4945)	0.0003 (0.0339)	0.0000 (0.0366)	0.0000 (0.0000)
α1	0.1509 (0.0206)	0.0039 (0.9001)	−0.0007 (0.9491)	0.0057 (0.7919)	0.0201 (0.3704)	0.1378 (0.1620)	0.3190 (0.0050)	−0.0938 (0.0000)
β1	−0.1595 (0.7534)	0.8874 (0.0000)	0.9338 (0.0000)	0.9541 (0.0000)	0.8643 (0.0000)	−0.2881 (0.5622)	0.3505 (0.1158)	1.0339 (0.0000)

Panel C: Post-Asian financial crisis

$N = 79$	GBP	DM	HKD	JPY	USD	SDR	SGD	CHF
October 1998 to April 2005								
Intercept	0.0000 (0.0972)	0.0004 (0.0771)	−.0000 (0.0269)	0.0000 (0.0000)	N.A.	0.0000 (0.3359)	0.0000 (0.4977)	0.0004 (0.1575)
α1	−0.0713 (0.3889)	−0.1492 (0.0059)	−0.0112 (0.0617)	−0.1805 (0.0000)	N.A.	−0.0783 (0.4175)	−0.1176 (0.0189)	−0.1919 (0.0417)
β1	1.0504 (0.0000)	0.6560 (0.0167)	1.0891 (0.0000)	1.0459 (0.0000)	N.A.	0.7411 (0.0842)	1.0551 (0.0000)	0.7394 (0.0035)

Note: β1 stands for the ARCH (first term), while γ1 stands for the GARCH (first term). Bold fonts denote the significant estimates, while italic fonts highlight the violations of GARCH rules of non-negativity for all estimates. N.A. stands for not applicable.

to the USD, i.e. after August 2005. The use of more recent and higher frequency data provides more relevant analysis.

3   More advanced GARCH models are used to capture some of the effects that were not addressed in the previous sub-section. Some of the issues that this sub-section looks at include the following, if the basic GARCH models with normal density functions are not appropriate:
a   Asymmetric effects;
b   Non-Gaussian distributions;
c   Conditional mean effects;
d   Value at Risk models.

Figure 4.1 demonstrates the summary of the time series properties of the log difference of the daily exchange rate data in two different periods, whereas graphs 3.8–3.12 in Chapter 3 show the plot of the full series. All plots indicated that the log difference series fluctuates close to zero as the expected return in the long run should be close to zero. This is expected in the exchange rate market due to speculators and arbitragers ensuring that no arbitraged profits can be made in the long run.

Panel I of Figure 4.1 includes periods where the Central Bank of Malaysia or Bank Negara Malaysia (BNM) imposed capital control, whereas Panel II of Figure 4.1 includes periods after BNM relaxed the capital control and allowed the MYR/USD to float within a given band, i.e. managed float. For periods after the Asian financial crisis and when BNM imposed the capital control, the MYR/GBP and the MYR/CHF seemed to fluctuate more when the MYR/USD was fixed. After BNM relaxed capital control in Malaysia, the MYR/JPY seemed to be relatively more volatile. Nevertheless, all five currency pairs exhibited time-varying volatility and volatility clustering over time. Analysis of the stochastic volatility in a discrete time frame and application of the GARCH models to the daily exchange rate data is then carried out.

Tables 4.2 and 4.3 summarise the standard GARCH models with normal density functions as applied in most empirical studies documented in the literature, and are used as the benchmark for other extensions in the analysis for this chapter. Table 4.2 includes the period when BNM applied capital control, while Table 4.3 includes periods when BNM relaxed capital control in Malaysia. Both tables report the estimates of the GARCH parameters, tabulate the unconditional variance of the underlying data and provide diagnostic tests including normality tests, information criteria and leverage tests.

For the period when BNM imposed capital control, all currency pairs except the MYR/USD demonstrated GARCH effects in the log difference series as both the ARCH and GARCH parameters are statistically significant. For the period after BNM relaxed capital control in Malaysia, all currency pairs again demonstrated significant GARCH effects except for the MYR/USD where the ARCH parameter is not statistically significant.

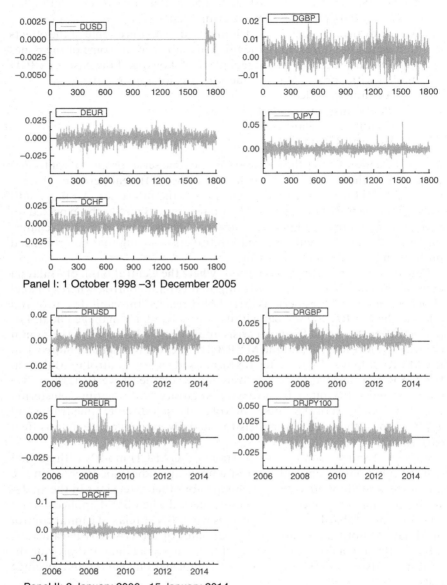

Figure 4.1 Plot of first difference of natural log of five different daily exchange rates (DRUSD: log difference of USD; DRGBP: log difference of GBP; DREUR: log difference of EUR; DRJPY: log difference of JPY; DRCHF: log difference of CHF).

Table 4.2 Estimation results and diagnostic tests of the five different daily exchange rates using GARCH models with normal density functions (Period: 1 October 1998 to 31 December 2005)

1 October 1998 to 31 December 2005	USD	GBP	EUR	JPY	CHF
Intercept (Var)	N.A.	0.0053	0.007664	0.024767	0.012693
		(0.0457)	(0.0669)	(0.2045)	(0.0075)
ARCH	N.A.	0.0347	0.029290	0.053415	0.019885
		(0.0007)	(0.0029)	(0.0125)	(0.0017)
GARCH	N.A.	0.9453	0.954407	0.885166	0.9547
		(0.0000)	(0.0000)	(0.0000)	(0.0000)
Unconditional variance	N.A.	2.659E−05	4.701E−05	4.032E−05	4.994E−05
Log-likelihood	N.A.	662.2310	6131.4750	6267.7800	6053.2530
Skewness	N.A.	−0.0353	−0.1323	0.1228	−0.0507
Kurtosis	N.A.	3.5868	4.2269	9.8259	3.7927
Diagnostic tests Normality test (*p*-values)					
Skewness	N.A.	0.7328	0.0264	0.0000	0.4147
Excess kurtosis	N.A.	0.0138	0.0000	0.0000	0.0000
Jarque-Bera	N.A.	0.0460	0.0000	0.0000	0.0000
Akaike information criteria	N.A.	−7.7351	−7.1594	−7.3187	−7.0681
Schwartz information criteria	N.A.	−7.7316	−7.1499	−7.3091	−7.0585
EGARCH vs GARCH (*p*-values)					
Sign bias *t*-test	N.A.	0.9900	0.1014	0.2999	0.0442
Negative size bias *t*-test	N.A.	0.5326	0.1793	0.7720	0.1398
Positive size bias *t*-test	N.A.	0.5727	0.1474	0.0970	0.0858
Joint test for three effects	N.A.	0.6329	0.2676	0.4160	0.1507

Note: N.A. stands for not applicable.

However, it can be inferred from Tables 4.2 and 4.3 that the normality tests of the error terms failed badly and there seem to be some leverage/asymmetric effects in the MYR/EUR, MYR/JPY and MYR/CHF series. In order to test for asymmetric effects and the non-normal distribution of the error terms, the non-Gaussian distribution of skewed Student distribution is now being incorporated (see section "Skewed Student distribution" for more details). Lambert and Laurent (2000) applied and extended the skewed Student density proposed by Fernández and Steel (1998) to the GARCH framework. Tables 4.4 and 4.5 summarise the GARCH model estimation

Table 4.3 Estimation results and diagnostic tests of the five different daily exchange rates using GARCH models with normal density functions (Period: 2 January 2006 to 15 January 2014)

2 January 2006 to 15 January 2014	USD	GBP	EUR	JPY	CHF
Intercept (Var)	0.0105	0.0030	0.0042	0.0110	0.0486
	(0.0003)	(0.0002)	(0.0306)	(0.0227)	(0.2670)
ARCH	0.1099	0.0600	0.0512	0.1009	0.1049
	(0.1111)	(0.0000)	(0.0001)	(0.0000)	(0.0019)
GARCH	0.8351	0.9312	0.9347	0.8867	0.8087
	(0.0000)	(0.0000)	(0.0000)	(0.0000)	(0.0000)
Unconditional variance	1.901E−05	3.409E−05	2.984E−05	8.921E−05	5.624E−05
Log-likelihood	8598.6910	7928.2250	7947.4560	7215.6500	7369.8280
Skewness	−0.1977	−0.3424	0.2711	0.0425	−0.9978
Kurtosis	5.9237	7.3905	6.7391	6.0981	42.1644
Diagnostic tests					
Normality test (*p*-values)					
Skewness	0.0011	0.1358	0.0001	0.2590	0.0000
Excess kurtosis	0.0000	0.0000	0.0000	0.0000	0.0000
Jarque-Bera	0.0000	0.0000	0.0000	0.0000	0.0000
Akaike information criteria	−8.3130	−7.6646	−7.6832	−6.9755	−7.1246
Schwartz information criteria	−8.3049	−7.6565	−7.6751	−6.9673	−7.1164
EGARCH vs GARCH (*p*-values)					
Sign bias *t*-test	0.8203	0.7426	0.2760	0.0032	0.3907
Negative size bias *t*-test	0.7416	0.6617	0.9597	0.4353	0.9601
Positive size bias *t*-test	0.7014	0.1656	0.0094	0.6580	0.5929
Joint test for three effects	0.9524	0.4057	0.0753	0.0007	0.4592

using skewed Student distribution for the error terms for the period during which BNM imposed and relaxed capital control in Malaysia, respectively.

The main difference of relaxing the normal distribution and symmetric effects for the log difference or movements of the exchange rate data resulted in higher log-likelihood statistics as well as better information criteria. One of the key findings from Tables 4.4 and 4.5 is that not only are all the ARCH and GARCH parameters statistically significant, but all the tail parameters under the skewed Student distribution are also statistically significant, implying that important information is captured in the tail parameter of the skewed Student distribution. The leverage effects test failed for most exchange rate data, implying that Exponential GARCH (EGARCH) models are not appropriate compared to GARCH models. The asymmetric parameters of the skewed distribution provided mixed results for the different currency pairs. Diagnostic

Table 4.4 Estimation results and diagnostic tests of the five different daily exchange rates using GARCH models with skewed Student density function (Period: 1 October 1998 to 31 December 2005)

1 October 1998 to 31 December 2005	USD	GBP	EUR	JPY	CHF
Intercept (Var)	N.A.	0.0047	0.0068	0.0111	0.0101
		(0.0682)	(0.0041)	(0.1010)	(0.0132)
Asymmetry	N.A.	−0.0096	0.0276	−0.0081	0.0241
		(0.7547)	(0.0005)	(0.8293)	(0.4714)
Tail	N.A.	20.9513	11.9530	6.8599	12.9842
		(0.0136)	(0.0003)	(0.0000)	(0.0011)
ARCH	N.A.	0.0309	0.0276	0.0382	0.2021
		(0.0018)	(0.0005)	(0.0012)	(0.0006)
GARCH	N.A.	0.9509	0.9577	0.9319	0.9595
		(0.0000)	(0.0000)	(0.0000)	(0.0000)
Unconditional variance	N.A.	2.609E−05	4.657E−05	3.700E−05	4.988E−05
Log-likelihood	N.A.	6878.6570	6144.3170	6339.9040	6063.0690
Skewness	N.A.	−0.0305	−0.1323	0.1228	−0.0507
Kurtosis	N.A.	3.5614	4.2269	9.8259	3.7927
Diagnostic tests Normality test (*p*-values)					
Skewness	N.A.	0.8163	0.0274	0.0000	0.4214
Excess kurtosis	N.A.	0.0170	0.0000	0.0000	0.0000
Jarque-Bera	N.A.	0.0569	0.0000	0.0000	0.0000
Akaike information criteria	N.A.	−7.7395	−7.1709	−7.3994	−7.0760
Schwartz information criteria	N.A.	−7.7210	−7.1518	−7.3803	−7.0569
EGARCH vs GARCH (*p*-values)					
Sign bias *t*-test	N.A.	0.99015	0.09377	0.23077	0.02962
Negative size bias *t*-test	N.A.	0.54151	0.16239	0.86217	0.13362
Positive size bias *t*-test	N.A.	0.67934	0.14692	0.03904	0.06256
Joint test for three effects	N.A.	0.71573	0.25074	0.23045	0.11209

Note: N.A. stands for not applicable.

tests of these skewed Student distributions, however, did not improve on the normality tests as reported in Tables 4.2 and 4.3 earlier.

The next required test is to determine whether the conditional standard deviation derived from the GARCH models can help predict or explain the movements of the exchange rate data using GARCH in mean or GARCH-M models. GARCH-M models do have similar concepts to the Capital Asset Pricing Model (CAPM) or more precisely the conditional CAPM model. If the conditional standard deviation is statistically significant, then it can be inferred that conditional standard deviation drives the conditional mean of the daily exchange rate data; and hence one can derive an appropriate conditional CAPM for the particular exchange rate movements or returns.

Table 4.5 Estimation results and diagnostic tests of the five different daily
exchange rates using GARCH models with skewed Student density
functions (Period: 2 January 2006 to 15 January 2014)

2 January 2006 to 15 January 2014	USD	GBP	EUR	JPY	CHF
Intercept (Var)	0.0092	0.0027	0.0034	0.0110	0.0267
	(0.0000)	(0.0031)	(0.0258)	(0.0132)	(0.0050)
Asymmetry	0.0158	−0.0108	0.0486	0.0860	0.0686
	(0.5747)	(0.7352)	(0.1166)	(0.0115)	(0.0159)
Tail	4.5283	7.9622	7.7772	6.6916	5.1515
	(0.0000)	(0.0000)	(0.0000)	(0.0000)	(0.0000)
ARCH	0.1325	0.0469	0.0430	0.0971	0.1129
	(0.0000)	(0.0018)	(0.0000)	(0.0000)	(0.0000)
GARCH	0.8478	0.9445	0.9454	0.8901	0.8313
	(0.0000)	(0.0000)	(0.0000)	(0.0000)	(0.0000)
Unconditional variance	4.684E−05	3.130E−05	2.893E−05	8.576E−05	4.779E−05
Log-likelihood	8642.5540	7860.7910	7983.9110	7266.4970	7600.2440
Skewness	−0.1977	−0.3424	0.2711	0.0425	−0.9978
Kurtosis	5.9237	7.3905	6.7391	6.0981	42.1644
Diagnostic tests					
Normality test (p-values)					
Skewness	0.0012	0.1196	0.0001	0.2774	0.0000
Excess kurtosis	0.0000	0.0000	0.0000	0.0000	0.0000
Jarque-Bera	0.0000	0.0000	0.0000	0.0000	0.0000
Akaike information criteria	−8.3535	−7.6934	−7.7156	−7.0218	−7.3445
Schwartz information criteria	−8.3399	−7.6798	−7.6992	−7.0054	−7.3282
EGARCH vs GARCH (p-values)					
Sign bias t-test	0.7999	0.7322	0.2588	0.0052	0.3139
Negative size bias t-test	0.9656	0.3663	0.8477	0.3862	0.8812
Positive size bias t-test	0.9219	0.2817	0.0034	0.5428	0.9882
Joint test for three effects	0.9894	0.4065	0.0326	0.0011	0.5617

As similar to Tables 4.4 and 4.5, this study continues to extend the basic
GARCH models with skewed density functions but add on an additional exogenous variable of conditional standard deviation in the estimation equations. The results are summarised in Tables 4.6 and 4.7 for these GARCH-M
models with skewed density functions for the period of imposed and relaxed
capital control in Malaysia respectively.

The findings reported in Tables 4.6 and 4.7 are very similar to those in
Tables 4.4 and 4.5 in that all ARCH and GARCH variables as well as the
tail variables are statistically significant. The results reported in Tables 4.6
and 4.7 do confirm, however, that the in-mean variables are statistically

Table 4.6 Estimation results and diagnostic tests of the five different daily exchange rates using GARCH-M models with skewed Student distribution (Period: 1 October 1998 to 31 December 2005)

1 October 1998 to 31 December 2005	USD	GBP	EUR	JPY	CHF
Intercept (Var)	N.A.	0.0048	0.0065	0.0114	0.0900
		(0.0663)	(0.0491)	(0.0101)	(0.0223)
Asymmetry	N.A.	−0.0061	−0.0007	0.0039	0.0247
		(0.8421)	(0.9829)	(0.9156)	(0.4580)
Tail	N.A.	21.8164	12.1323	6.9051	12.8560
		(0.0141)	(0.0004)	(0.0000)	(0.0009)
ARCH	N.A.	0.0307	0.0274	0.0389	0.021015
		(0.0018)	(0.0005)	(0.0014)	(0.003)
GARCH	N.A.	0.9507	0.9584	0.9304	0.9607
		(0.0000)	(0.0000)	(0.0000)	(0.0000)
GARCH-M	N.A.	0.0018	0.0031	−0.0108	0.0030
		(0.9379)	(0.8949)	(0.6429)	(0.9012)
Unconditional variance	N.A.	2.581E−05	4.591E−05	3.699E−05	4.923E−05
Log-likelihood	N.A.	6998.2390	6258.9510	6455.1040	6179.0500
Skewness	N.A.	−0.0274	−0.1322	0.1295	−0.0516
Kurtosis	N.A.	3.5537	4.2308	9.7927	3.8079
Diagnostic tests Normality test (*p*-values)					
Skewness	N.A.	0.8611	0.0280	0.0000	0.4172
Excess kurtosis	N.A.	0.0198	0.0000	0.0000	0.0000
Jarque-Bera	N.A.	0.0657	0.0000	0.0000	0.0000
Akaike information criteria	N.A.	−7.7433	−7.1790	−7.4043	−7.0870
Schwartz information criteria	N.A.	−7.7251	−7.1602	−7.3854	−7.0685
EGARCH vs GARCH (*p*-values)					
Sign bias *t*-test	N.A.	0.9372	0.0959	0.2037	0.0294
Negative size bias *t*-test	N.A.	0.5620	0.1522	0.8506	0.1323
Positive size bias *t*-test	N.A.	0.7372	0.1409	0.0274	0.0578
Joint test for three effects	N.A.	0.7336	0.2364	0.1782	0.1065

Note: N.A. stands for not applicable.

insignificant and, hence, do not support the hypothesis of conditional CAPM for the five daily currency pairs. These results indicate that conditional standard deviations are not drivers of the conditional mean of the daily exchange rates. The findings do not necessarily mean that the conditional standard deviation is not important. If conditional standard deviation is not driving the conditional mean of the data generating process of the underlying exchange rate data, other factors like news or exogenous shocks will drive the conditional mean instead.

Table 4.7 Estimation results and diagnostic tests of the five different daily exchange rates using GARCH-M models with skewed Student density functions (Period: 2 January 2006 to 15 January 2014)

2 January 2006 to 15 January 2014	USD	GBP	EUR	JPY	CHF
Intercept (Var)	0.0090	0.0027	0.0034	0.0110	0.0267
	(0.0000)	(0.0000)	(00258)	(0.0132)	(0.0050)
Asymmetry	−0.0025	−0.0143	0.0486	0.0860	0.0686
	(0.9938)	(0.6588)	(0.1166)	(0.0115)	(0.0159)
Tail	4.5605	7.9608	7.7772	6.6916	5.1515
	(0.0000)	(0.0000)	(0.0000)	(0.0000)	(0.0000)
ARCH	0.1311	0.0468	0.0430	0.0971	0.1129
	(0.0000)	(0.0000)	(0.0000)	(0.0000)	(0.0000)
GARCH	0.8492	0.9447	0.9454	0.8901	0.8313
	(0.0000)	(0.0000)	(0.0000)	(0.0000)	(0.0000)
GARCH-M	−0.0230	−0.0088	−0.0016	−0.0191	0.0083
	(0.1141)	(0.6815)	(0.9409)	(0.3673)	(0.6993)
Unconditional variance	4.572E−05	3.139E−05	2.893E−05	8.576E−05	4.779E−05
Log-likelihood	8643.1020	7960.0840	7983.9110	7266.4970	7600.2440
Skewness	−0.1977	−0.3424	0.2711	0.0425	−0.9978
Kurtosis	5.9237	7.3905	6.7391	6.0981	42.1644
Diagnostic tests					
Normality test (*p*-values)					
Skewness	0.0010	0.1178	0.0001	0.2774	0.0000
Excess kurtosis	0.0000	0.0000	0.0000	0.0000	0.0000
Jarque-Bera	0.0000	0.0000	0.0000	0.0000	0.0000
Akaike information criteria	−8.3531	−7.6925	−7.7156	−7.0218	−7.3445
Schwartz information criteria	−8.3368	−7.6762	−7.6992	−7.0054	−7.3282
EGARCH vs GARCH (*p*-values)					
Sign bias *t*-test	0.8816	0.7193	0.2588	0.0052	0.3139
Negative size bias *t*-test	0.7771	0.3623	0.8477	0.3862	0.8817
Positive size bias *t*-test	0.8925	0.2760	0.0034	0.5428	0.9882
Joint test for three effects	0.9909	0.4030	0.0326	0.0011	0.5617

Moving on from modelling the conditional variance of the exchange rate to the risk measurement of the exchange rate, the objective is to investigate whether volatilities of the daily exchange rate do increase or decrease after BNM relaxed capital control in Malaysia.

Following Tan and Chong (2008), the conditional variance that was estimated in Tables 4.2–4.7 is used to investigate whether the volatilities of the exchange rate increased after BNM relaxed capital control in Malaysia. The null hypothesis states that the sample variances of the currency pairs have no significant differences across the two alternative exchange rate regimes. The sample variances are distributed as *F*-test statistic with two-tailed testing as $F = S^2_A/S^2_B$, with A and B being the two different exchange rate regimes. The null hypothesis can be rejected if the *F*-statistic is significantly greater than the critical value in the upper tail or smaller than the critical value in the lower tail. Tan and Chong (2008) found that using GARCH models, the volatilities of most macroeconomic variables reduced significantly except for export in the case of Malaysia after BNM relaxed capital control.

Table 4.8 summarises the tests for any significant change in volatilities in different exchange regimes using the standard GARCH models with Gaussian or normal density functions. The results show that all currency pairs exhibited change in volatilities under different exchange rate regimes. The US dollar, British pound and Japanese yen all exhibited greater volatilities, while the euro and Swiss franc demonstrated reduction in volatilities.

The above results do not change significantly when one relaxes the normal distribution for the error terms (Table 4.9) or by incorporating the conditional CAPM framework or GARCH-M models with skewed Student density functions. Hence, the choice of conditional models does not change the

Table 4.8 Test of volatility persistence using GARCH models with normal density functions

Unconditional variance	USD	GBP	EUR	JPY	CHF
Period I	N.A.	2.6591E−05	4.7010E−05	4.0324E−05	4.9940E−05
Period II	1.9006E−05	3.4093E−05	2.9837E−05	8.9212E−05	5.6239E−05
Change	1.9006E−05	7.5022E−06	−1.7173E−05	4.8888E−05	6.2994E−06
F-test	N.A.	1.2821	1.5756	2.2124	1.1261

Note:
1 Period I: 1 October 1998–31 December 2005.
2 Period II: 2 January 2006–15 January 2014.
3 N.A. stands for not applicable.

Table 4.9 Test of volatility persistence using GARCH models with skewed Student density functions

Unconditional variance	USD	GBP	EUR	JPY	CHF
Period I	N.A.	2.6086E−05	4.6569E−05	3.7004E−05	4.9879E−05
Period II	4.6840E−05	3.1296E−05	2.8931E−05	8.5760E−05	4.7794E−05
Change	4.6840E+01	5.2097E−06	−1.7639E−05	4.8756E−05	−2.0847E−06
F-test	N.A.	1.1997	1.6097	2.3176	1.0436

Note:
1 Period I: 1 October 1998–31 December 2005.
2 Period II: 2 January 2006–15 January 2014.
3 N.A. stands for not applicable.

Table 4.10 Test of volatility persistence using GARCH-M models with skewed
Student density functions

Unconditional variance	*USD*	*GBP*	*EUR*	*JPY*	*CHF*
Period I	N.A.	2.5814E−05	4.5910E−05	3.6994E−05	4.9227E−05
Period II	4.5720E−05	3.1390E−05	2.8930E−05	8.5760E−05	4.7790E−05
Change	4.5720E−05	5.5760E−06	−1.6980E−05	4.8766E−05	−1.4370E−06
F-test	N.A.	1.2160	1.5869	2.3182	1.0301

Note:
1 Period 1: 1 October 1998–31 December 2005.
2 Period 2: 2 January 2006–15 January 2014.
3 N.A. stands for not applicable.

implications that while MYR/USD, MYR/GBP and MYR/JPY all exhibited increase in volatility after BNM relaxed capital control, MYR/EUR and MYR/CHF demonstrated reduced volatility after exchange rate liberalisation in Malaysia (Table 4.10).

The next challenge is to investigate the sensitivity of the volatility models to one popular form of risk measurement among risk managers, Value at Risk, as discussed in the next section.

Value at Risk

Value at Risk (VaR) has become a popular technique in recent times as it provides a simple answer to risk managers; with a given probability of α, one will know the quantification of the risk or potential financial loss over a given time horizon. It turns out that the VaR has a simple statistical definition: the VaR at level α for a sample of returns is defined as the corresponding empirical quantile at α%. Because of the definition of the quantile, with probability of $1-\alpha$, the returns will be larger than the VaR. In other words, with probability $1-\alpha$, the losses will be smaller than the dollar amount given by the VaR. From an empirical point of view, the computation of the VaR for a collection of returns thus requires the computation of the empirical quantile at level α of the distribution of the returns of the portfolio.

There are many empirical studies that used GARCH models to calculate VaR. Cera *et al.* (2013) applied the concept to the Albanian Lek exchange rate, Madhavi and Malleswaramma (2013) applied VaR to the Indian banking sector and Žiković (2008) used it for the financial markets of the European Union. Cera *et al.* (2013) found that it was appropriate to use the GARCH model to measure VaR for the Euro-Albanian Lek exchange rate.

There are also many studies that compute VaR. Van den Goorbergh and Vlaar (1999) and Jorion (2000) focused on computation of VaR for negative returns. Giot and Laurent (2003) showed that models that rely on a symmetric density distribution for the error term underperformed with respect to skewed density models when the left and right tails of the distribution of return were modelled. In the case of long position, the risk comes from a drop in the price of the asset (hence, focusing on the left-hand side of the distribution of return), while traders or speculators lose money when the price increases for short position (thereby focusing on the right-hand side of the distribution of return). Following Giot and Laurent (2003), the next sub-sections compare the popular RiskMetrics of J.P. Morgan (section "RiskMetrics") with APARCH models introduced by Ding, Granger and Engle (1993) (section "Asymmetric Power ARCH").

RiskMetrics

In its simplest form, it can be shown that the basic RiskMetrics model (please see Mina and Xiao, 2001) is equivalent to a normal Integrated GARCH (IGARCH) model of Engle and Bollerslev (1986), where the Auto-Regressive parameter is set at a pre-specified value λ and the coefficient of ε^2_{t-1} is equal to $1-\lambda$. In the RiskMetrics specification for daily data, λ is fixed to 0.94. In the previous section (section "Empirical results"), there are some signs of skewness in the exchange rate return and skewed Student density functions are used in replacement of normal density functions for all five major foreign exchange rates to determine the effects on the analysis.

Tables 4.11 and 4.12 summarise the parameter estimates and diagnostic tests of the RiskMetrics for the two exchange rate eras using a skewed

Table 4.11 Summary table of RiskMetrics models of the five different daily exchange rates (Period: 1 October 1998 to 31 December 2005)

1 October 1998 to 31 December 2005	USD	GBP	EUR	JPY	CHF
Asymmetry	N.A.	−0.0080	0.0042	−0.0057	0.0274
		(0.7799)	(0.8939)	(0.8661)	(0.3821)
Tail	N.A.	20.6720	11.3663	7.1854	11.2375
		(0.0059)	(0.0000)	(0.0000)	(0.0000)
Log-likelihood	N.A.	6866.7700	6131.1720	6324.3500	6046.1890
Skewness	N.A.	−0.0305	−0.1323	0.1228	−0.0507
Kurtosis	N.A.	3.5614	4.2269	9.8259	3.7927
Diagnostic tests					
Normality test (*p*-values)					
Skewness	N.A.	0.6637	0.1038	0.0000	0.5633
Excess kurtosis	N.A.	0.0118	0.0000	0.0000	0.0000
Jarque-Bera	N.A.	0.0386	0.0000	0.0000	0.0000
Akaike information criteria	N.A.	−7.7306	−7.1602	−7.3859	−7.0610
Schwartz information criteria	N.A.	−7.7244	−7.1539	−7.3796	−7.0546
EGARCH vs GARCH (*p*-values)					
Sign bias *t*-test	N.A.	0.6902	0.1480	0.2981	0.0453
Negative size bias *t*-test	N.A.	0.4331	0.7101	0.4617	0.8808
Positive size bias *t*-test	N.A.	0.1940	0.0070	0.3464	0.0022
Joint test for three effects	N.A.	0.3197	0.0581	0.6840	0.0203

Note: N.A. stands for not applicable.

Table 4.12 Summary table of RiskMetrics models of the five different daily exchange rates (Period: 2 January 2006 to 15 January 2014)

2 January 2006 to 15 January 2014	USD	GBP	EUR	JPY	CHF
Asymmetry	0.011438	−0.006926	0.052285	0.078330	0.060749
	(0.6628)	(0.8169)	(0.0642)	(0.0106)	(0.0140)
Tail	6.149390	8.740769	8.508145	7.153707	5.577868
	(0.0000)	(0.0000)	(0.0000)	(0.0000)	(0.0000)
Log-likelihood	8626.2100	7953.9020	7976.0850	7254.0060	7568.8640
Skewness	−0.1977	−0.3424	0.2711	0.0425	−0.9978
Kurtosis	5.9237	7.3905	6.7391	6.0981	42.1644
Diagnostic tests					
Normality test (p-values)					
Skewness	0.0000	0.1700	0.0001	0.4690	0.0000
Excess kurtosis	0.0000	0.0000	0.0000	0.0000	0.0000
Jarque-Bera	0.0000	0.0000	0.0000	0.0000	0.0000
Akaike information criteria	−8.3406	−7.6904	−7.7119	−7.0135	−7.3181
Schwartz information criteria	−8.3352	−7.6850	−7.7064	−7.0081	−7.3126
EGARCH vs GARCH (p-values)					
Sign bias t-test	0.9606	0.7525	0.2353	0.0048	0.3657
Negative size bias t-test	0.2946	0.9640	0.2971	0.2840	0.9276
Positive size bias t-test	0.4262	0.0720	0.1539	0.3044	0.9947
Joint test for three effects	0.6189	0.2588	0.3704	0.0003	0.6707

Student density function, as it was explained in section "Empirical results" that GARCH models with normal density function do not capture the asymmetric and tail effects. Asymmetric effects are not significant across all currency pairs when BNM imposed capital control, while MYR/EUR, MYR/JPY and MYR/CHF all exhibited asymmetric effects post exchange rate liberalisation when BNM removed capital control for Malaysia. Earlier, it was found in section "Empirical results" that only MYR/JPY and MYR/CHF exhibited asymmetric effects during periods after BNM relaxed capital control in Malaysia. Tail distributions continue to be significant for all currency pairs regardless of the exchange rate regime, which are very similar to the earlier findings in section "Empirical results". The conclusion is that RiskMetrics is not superior to using GARCH models with skewed Student density functions as discussed in section "Empirical results". Nevertheless, Giot and Laurent (2003) are followed, and RiskMetrics with skewed Student density function is used as the benchmark for the purpose of evaluating VaR performances.

Table 4.13 summarises the VaR performances and shows that RiskMetrics models performed well under a controlled exchange rate environment

Table 4.13 Dynamic quantile test – Engle and Manganelli (2004) for RiskMetrics models

Panel I: 1 October 1998 to 31 December 2005

Short positions: p-values	USD	GBP	EUR	JPY	CHF
0.9500	N.A.	0.4112	0.4084	0.2408	0.0915
0.9750	N.A.	0.4539	0.0520	0.8952	0.1292
0.9900	N.A.	0.3083	0.6143	0.1473	0.9619
0.9950	N.A.	0.9997	0.0097	0.9192	0.9783
0.9975	N.A.	1.0000	0.9909	0.7305	0.9998

Long positions: p-values	USD	GBP	EUR	JPY	CHF
0.0500	N.A.	0.2572	0.1442	0.0310	0.6798
0.0250	N.A.	0.5875	0.5118	0.4305	0.9384
0.0100	N.A.	0.1334	0.5746	0.5948	0.8579
0.0050	N.A.	0.0001	0.9192	0.9998	0.9783
0.0025	N.A.	1.0000	0.9999	0.9757	0.9222

Panel II: 2 January 2006 to 15 January 2014

Short positions: p-values	USD	GBP	EUR	JPY	CHF
0.9500	0.0199	0.3929	0.1497	0.0047	0.4398
0.9750	0.0101	0.6241	0.1616	0.0306	0.3619
0.9900	0.1216	0.7115	0.6962	0.0059	0.4007
0.9950	0.3434	0.0052	0.0334	0.0281	0.0281
0.9975	0.7609	0.9995	0.7841	0.9998	0.9998

Long positions: p-values	USD	GBP	EUR	JPY	CHF
0.0500	0.7428	0.2296	0.5059	0.8078	0.6916
0.0250	0.9051	0.0429	0.8480	0.1555	0.3046
0.0100	0.0083	0.0005	0.6287	0.9648	0.9827
0.0050	0.9785	0.9997	0.9758	0.9758	0.9224
0.0025	0.9883	0.7841	0.9919	0.5432	0.5432

Note: N.A. stands for not applicable.

but relatively badly with more rejections of the null hypothesis that the failure rate is equal to the chosen level of confidence level. This rejection is even more relevant for short positions than long positions of the exchange rates, after BNM abolished capital control.

Asymmetric power ARCH

The Asymmetric Power ARCH (APARCH) model was introduced by Ding, Granger and Engle (1993). The APARCH (p, q) model can be expressed as

$$\sigma_t^\delta = \omega + \sum_{i=1}^{q} \alpha_i \left(|\varepsilon_{t-i}| - \gamma_i \varepsilon_{t-i} \right)^\delta + \sum_{j=1}^{p} \beta_j \sigma_{t-j}^\delta \qquad (4.21)$$

where $\delta > 0$ and $-1 < \gamma_i < 1$ ($i = 1, ..., q$).

The parameter δ plays the role of a Box-Cox transformation of σ_t, while γ_i reflects the leverage effect. Properties of the APARCH model are studied in He and Teräsvirta (1999).

The APARCH nests seven ARCH models as special cases as shown by Laurent and Peters (2006):

i   The ARCH of Engle (1982) when $\delta = 2$, $\gamma i = 0$ ($i = 1, ..., p$) and $\beta j = 0$ ($j = 1, ..., p$).

ii   The GARCH of Bollerslev (1986) when $\delta = 2$, $\gamma_i = 0$ ($i = 1, ..., p$).

iii Taylor (1986)/Schwert (1990)'s GARCH when $\delta = 1$, $\gamma_i = 0$ ($i = 1, ..., p$).

iv   The GJR of Glosten *et al.* (1993) when $\delta = 2$.

v   The TGARCH of Zakoian (1994) when $\delta = 1$.

vi   The NARCH of Higgins and Bera (1992) when $\gamma_i = 0$ ($i = 1, ..., p$) and $\beta_j = 0$ ($j = 1, ..., p$).

vii The Log-ARCH of Geweke (1986) and Pentula (1986) when $\delta \rightarrow 0$.

Giot and Laurent (2003) found that APARCH models with skewed Student density functions perform similarly to RiskMetrics when applying to daily stock markets. The estimates and diagnostics tests generated are reported in Tables 4.14 and 4.15. Both the asymmetric effects and tail effects are similar to those as explained in section "RiskMetrics". The VaR performance summarised in Table 4.16 indicated that APARCH models performed relatively better than RiskMetrics (see Table 4.13). VaR performance under APARCH models improved for long positions even after BNM relaxed capital control and also relatively better than RiskMetrics for short positions for both different periods.

Implications

Risk modelling

GARCH models with Gaussian density functions were first estimated, and it was found that both ARCH and GARCH parameters are significant for both periods, implying that GARCH effects are prevalent in all five currency pairs. However, the normality tests of the error terms failed badly and there seem to be some leverage/asymmetric effects in the MYR/EUR, MYR/JPY and MYR/CHF series.

In order to test for asymmetric effects and the non-normal distribution of the error terms, the non-Gaussian distribution of skewed Student density function was incorporated. Not only are all the ARCH and GARCH parameters

Table 4.14 Summary table of APARCH models of the five different daily exchange rates (Period: 1 October 1998 to 31 December 2005)

1 October 1998–31 December 2005	USD	GBP	EUR	JPY	CHF
ARCH	N.A.	0.0277	0.0273	0.0398	0.0151
		(0.0091)	(0.0167)	(0.0154)	(0.0075)
GARCH	N.A.	0.9743	0.975567	0.9684	0.9813
		(0.0000)	(0.0000)	(0.0000)	(0.0000)
APARCH (gamma)	N.A.	−0.001879	−0.1192	0.0534	−0.1725
		(0.9836)	(0.2674)	(0.6207)	(0.1688)
APARCH (delta)	N.A.	1.8911	1.7344	1.3752	2.3916
		(0.0182)	(0.003)	(0.0000)	(0.0000)
Asymmetry	N.A.	−0.0110	−0.0011	−0.0110	0.0283
		(0.7269)	(0.9736)	(0.7634)	(0.3974)
Tail	N.A.	16.3414	11.2295	6.3250	11.4522
		(0.0024)	(0.0001)	(0.0000)	(0.0004)
Log-likelihood	N.A.	6622.5200	6140.8930	6333.2300	6060.0650
Skewness	N.A.	−0.0353	−0.1323	0.1228	−0.0507
Kurtosis	N.A.	3.5868	4.2269	9.8259	3.7927
Diagnostic tests					
Normality test (*p*-values)					
Skewness	N.A.	0.7163	0.0522	0.0000	0.4153
Excess kurtosis	N.A.	0.0019	0.0000	0.0000	0.0000
Jarque-Bera	N.A.	0.0078	0.0000	0.0000	0.0000
Akaike information criteria	N.A.	−7.7296	−7.1669	−7.3916	−7.0725
Schwartz information criteria	N.A.	−7.7105	−7.1478	−7.3725	−7.0534
EGARCH vs GARCH (*p*-values)					
Sign bias *t*-test	N.A.	0.8862	0.0741	0.0359	0.0355
Negative size bias *t*-test	N.A.	0.5558	0.1574	0.8283	0.1203
Positive size bias *t*-test	N.A.	0.5523	0.0710	0.0001	0.0571
Joint test for three effects	N.A.	0.5208	0.1530	0.0019	0.1047

Note: N.A. stands for not applicable

statistically significant, but all the tail parameters under the skewed Student distribution are also statistically significant, implying that important information is captured in the tail parameter of the skewed Student distribution.

The leverage effects test failed for most exchange rate data, suggesting that Exponential GARCH (EGARCH) models are not appropriate compared to GARCH models. The asymmetric parameters of the skewed distribution provided mixed results for the different currency pairs.

In conclusion, both the hypotheses of normality density functions and symmetric effects are rejected by the findings in section "Empirical results". Chong and Tan (2007) used EGARCH models to estimate the conditional standard deviation for Malaysia and it was found that the leverage tests failed for most currency pairs. GARCH models with skewed Student density

Table 4.15 Summary table of APARCH models of the five different daily exchange rates (Period: 2 January 2006 to 15 January 2014)

2 January 2006 to 15 January 2014	USD	GBP	EUR	JPY	CHF
ARCH	0.1524	0.0692	0.0405	0.1020	0.0689
	(0.0000)	(0.0000)	(0.0262)	(0.0000)	(0.0359)
GARCH	0.8876	0.9458	0.9593	0.9233	0.9497
	(0.0000)	(0.0000)	(0.0000)	(0.0000)	(0.0000)
APARCH (gamma)	0.0113	0.0330	0.0920	0.1255	−0.2739
	(0.0477)	(0.7012)	(0.4949)	(0.0622)	(0.0164)
APARCH (delta)	1.1806	1.3220	2.1039	1.2836	0.7869
	(0.0000)	(0.0000)	(0.0000)	(0.0000)	(0.0000)
Asymmetry	0.0097	−0.0057	0.0527	0.0865	0.0641
	(0.7266)	(0.8545)	(0.0759)	(0.0076)	(0.0205)
Tail	5.0100	7.9529	7.7343	6.5533	4.9633
	(0.0000)	(0.0000)	(0.0000)	(0.0000)	(0.000)
Log likelihood	8638.7450	7956.9140	7979.2560	7262.3880	7609.0000
Skewness	−0.1977	−0.3424	0.2711	0.0425	−0.9978
Kurtosis	5.9237	7.3905	6.7391	6.0981	42.1644
Diagnostic tests					
Normality test (*p*-values)					
Skewness	0.0000	0.1988	0.0001	0.6598	0.0000
Excess kurtosis	0.0000	0.0000	0.0000	0.0000	0.0000
Jarque-Bera	0.0000	0.0000	0.0000	0.0000	0.0000
Akaike information criteria	−8.3489	−7.6895	−7.7111	−7.0178	−7.3530
Schwartz information criteria	−8.3325	−7.6731	−7.6947	−7.0014	−7.3367
EGARCH vs GARCH (*p*-values)					
Sign bias *t*-test	0.9532	0.8122	0.2035	0.0025	0.1722
Negative size bias *t*-test	0.7215	0.9549	0.5660	0.4922	0.9155
Positive size bias *t*-test	0.6609	0.0904	0.0173	0.6956	0.0000
Joint test for three effects	0.9518	0.2784	0.1059	0.0037	0.0001

function were then utilised to address these two issues and they perform relatively better than the standard GARCH models with normal density function and symmetric effects. The tail parameters under the skewed Student distribution are statistically significant, implying that important information is captured in the tail parameter of the skewed Student distribution. The asymmetric parameters of the skewed distribution however provided mixed results for the different currency pairs.

Risk measurement

Following Tan and Chong (2008), conditional variances were first used to investigate whether the volatilities of the exchange rate increased after BNM

Table 4.16 Dynamic quantile test – Engle and Manganelli (2002) for APARCH models

Dynamic quantile test – Engle and Manganelli (2002)

Short positions: p-values	USD	GBP	EUR	JPY	CHF
0.9500	N.A.	0.9407	0.5738	0.4253	0.8496
0.9750	N.A.	0.7670	0.2398	0.8908	0.6206
0.9900	N.A.	0.2033	0.3587	0.1552	0.9828
0.9950	N.A.	0.9998	0.9998	0.9812	0.9908
0.9975	N.A.	0.9998	0.9988	1.0000	0.9980

Long positions: p-values	USD	GBP	EUR	JPY	CHF
0.0500	N.A.	0.2122	0.3027	0.1677	0.8767
0.0250	N.A.	0.1339	0.8043	0.4389	0.6420
0.0100	N.A.	0.0839	0.6204	0.4348	0.9811
0.0050	N.A.	0.0000	0.9998	0.8725	0.9964
0.0025	N.A.	0.9757	1.0000	0.9988	0.9988

Dynamic quantile test – Engle and Manganelli (2002)

Short positions: p-values	USD	GBP	EUR	JPY	CHF
0.9500	0.0604	0.5573	0.6854	0.1939	0.8901
0.9750	0.0945	0.9273	0.8388	0.8506	0.8013
0.9900	0.0182	0.6259	0.6159	0.1805	0.0303
0.9950	0.2050	0.0001	0.9991	0.9992	0.0018
0.9975	0.7609	1.0000	0.9917	0.9883	1.0000

Long positions: p-values	USD	GBP	EUR	JPY	CHF
0.0500	0.6933	0.4684	0.9222	0.4502	0.5138
0.0250	0.6977	0.1488	0.6479	0.3191	0.5174
0.0100	0.0723	0.3417	0.6159	0.6962	0.9734
0.0050	0.5130	0.9997	0.9992	0.9991	0.9948
0.0025	0.7609	0.7841	0.9917	0.5432	0.9998

Note: N.A. stands for not applicable.

relaxed the capital control in Malaysia. Tan and Chong (2008) found that using GARCH models, the volatilities of most macroeconomic variables reduced significantly except for export in the case of Malaysia after BNM relaxed capital control. The GARCH models were determined based on the Schwartz criterion, while regime-shift GARCH were employed to capture the effect of regime shifts within the estimation period.

The results from this book showed that all currency pairs exhibited change in volatilities under different exchange rate regimes. It is therefore reasonable to use regime-shifting models or one can estimate the volatilities separately. The US dollar, British pound and Japanese yen all exhibited greater volatilities, while the euro and Swiss franc demonstrated reduction in volatilities. The choice of conditional models does not change the implications that while MYR/ USD, MYR/GBP and MYR/JPY all exhibited increase in volatility after BNM relaxed capital control, MYR/EUR and MYR/CHF demonstrated reduced volatility post exchange rate liberalisation in Malaysia.

The euro and Swiss franc demonstrated reduced volatility suggests that these two exchange rates are safe haven currencies, with respect to Malaysian ringgit regardless of exchange rate era. An asset can be considered as a safe haven if it gives hedging benefits in times of stress according to Ranaldo and Söderlind (2010). An asset that offers hedging benefits on average is uncorrelated or negatively correlated with its reference asset. For instance, Campbell *et al.* (2009) considered the currency allocation that minimises portfolio risks for global equity and bond investors and found that Swiss franc and euro are negatively related to equity returns.

The next analysis undertaken is on the popular risk measurement of Value at Risk which is discussed in depth by Jorion (2000). GARCH models with normal density function do not capture the asymmetric and tail effects. Asymmetric effects are not significant across all currency pairs when BNM imposed capital control, while MYR/EUR, MYR/JPY and MYR/CHF all exhibited asymmetric effects post exchange rate liberalisation when BNM removed capital control for Malaysia. Tail distributions continue to be significant for all currency pairs regardless of the exchange rate regime. Nevertheless, Giot and Laurent (2003) were followed, and RiskMetrics with skewed Student density function was used as the benchmark for the purpose of evaluating VaR performances.

RiskMetrics models performed well under controlled exchange rate environment but relatively badly with more rejections of the null hypothesis that the failure rate is equal to the chosen level of confidence level, which is even more relevant for short positions than long positions, when BNM abolished capital control.

Giot and Laurent (2003) found that APARCH models with skewed Student density functions perform similarly to RiskMetrics when applying to daily stock market. The analysis for the exchange rate volatility for Malaysia data exhibited asymmetric effects and tail effects. VaR performance under APARCH models improved for long positions even after BNM relaxed capital control and was also relatively better than RiskMetrics for short positions for both different periods. With this improved performance, APARCH models are better suited compared to RiskMetrics when applied to exchange rate markets in Malaysia, while Giot and Laurent (2003) found that the two models are similar when applied to daily stock market.

There were no significant leverage effects across all five exchange rates and asymmetry effects were not significant except for Japanese yen and Swiss franc during the free-float period. The asymmetry effects for these two currencies are similar to those under RiskMetrics earlier. Finally, as the delta estimates for APARCH are all significantly different from zero, the use of conditional variance or GARCH models is more appropriate compared to conditional standard deviation models. This result is in contrast with those of Taylor (1986), Schwert (1990) and Ding *et al.* (1993) who indicate that there were substantially more correlations between absolute returns than squared returns, a stylised fact of high frequency financial returns (often called "long memory").

Conclusion

Initially this study did not manage to find the appropriate GARCH models fitting the monthly exchange rate data in Malaysia even though there is strong evidence of significant GARCH effects in most cases before May 2005. It is, therefore, very critical that one checks the underlying data before applying the popular GARCH models in empirical work. Most empirical work confirmed that higher frequency financial data exhibit GARCH effects compared to lower frequency financial data.

The hypotheses of normal density functions and symmetric effects are rejected. When applied to daily exchange rates, the leverage tests also failed for most currency pairs. GARCH models with skewed Student density function were then utilised to address these issues. The tail parameters under the skewed Student distribution are statistically significant, suggesting that important information is captured in the tail parameter of the skewed Student distribution. The asymmetric parameters of the skewed distribution provided mixed results for the different currency pairs. However, it was found that skewed Student density functions do not address the non-Gaussian issues in terms of statistical significance.

All currency pairs exhibited change in volatilities under different exchange rate regimes. The US dollar, British pound and Japanese yen all exhibited greater volatilities, while the euro and Swiss franc demonstrated reduction in volatilities. The results do not change significantly when one relaxed the normal distribution for the error terms. MYR/USD, MYR/GBP and MYR/JPY all exhibited an increase in volatility after BNM relaxed capital control, while only MYR/EUR and MYR/CHF demonstrated reduced volatility post exchange rate liberalisation in Malaysia. There were no significant relationships between the conditional mean and the risk of the exchange rate markets in either era.

Analysis was also conducted on the popular risk measurement of Value at Risk which is discussed in depth by Jorion (2000). Asymmetric effects are found to be not significant across all currency pairs when BNM imposed capital control, while MYR/EUR, MYR/JPY and MYR/CHF all exhibited asymmetric effects post exchange rate liberalisation when BNM removed capital control for Malaysia. Earlier, under section "Empirical results" it was found that only MYR/JPY and MYR/CHF exhibited asymmetric effects during periods after BNM relaxed capital control in Malaysia. Tail distributions continue to be significant for all currency pairs regardless of the exchange rate regime, which are also very similar to earlier findings.

The conclusion is that RiskMetrics is not superior to using GARCH models with skewed Student density functions as discussed in section "Empirical results". It is found that RiskMetrics models performed well under controlled exchange rate environment but they performed relatively badly for short positions than long positions, especially after BNM abolished capital control.

Giot and Laurent (2003) found that APARCH models with skewed Student density functions perform similarly to RiskMetrics when applied to daily stock market. The results of this study indicated that APARCH models perform relatively better than RiskMetrics. VaR performance under APARCH models improved for long positions even after BNM relaxed capital control and also relatively better than RiskMetrics for short positions for both different periods.

There were no significant leverage or conditional asymmetry effects for all the five exchange rates in different periods, while only yen and Swiss franc exhibited significant unconditional asymmetry effects. Finally, no long-memory effects are found for all the five exchange rates.

The next chapter proceeds to extend the discussion of univariate stochastic volatility modelling framework to a multivariate modelling framework (as was found in Chapter 3 that the correlations of the different currency pairs do change significantly over time), to study the inter-relationships of exchange rate volatility of five different trading countries with Malaysia.

5 Volatility modelling of exchange rates in a multivariate framework

Introduction

It is often the case in finance that the covariance between two series is of interest, just as the variances of the individual series themselves. While univariate descriptions of GARCH models are useful and important, the problems of risk assessment, asset allocation, hedging in futures markets and options pricing, portfolio Value at Risk (VaR) and Capital Asset Pricing Model (CAPM) beta estimates require a multivariate framework. This is because all aforementioned problems require correlations or covariances as inputs. Multivariate GARCH (MGARCH) models specify equations for how the variances and covariances move over time. Since it was found in Chapter 3 that the correlations of the five major currency pairs do vary over time, the previous univariate analysis of the currency pairs to a multivariate analysis is extended to investigate whether there are any significant changes in the results of risk modelling and risk measurement that have different implications on risk management.

MGARCH models were first considered by Engle *et al.* (1984), in the guise of the diagonal model. This model was extended and studied by Bollerslev *et al.* (1988). Recent MGARCH models were partly discussed by Franses and van Dijk (2000) and Gouriéroux (1997), while Bauwens *et al.* (2006) compiled a comprehensive and up-to-date survey of MGARCH models. There are also many recent references on MGARCH models including Silvennoinen and Teräsvirta (2008) and a book by Engle (2009). Francq and Zakoïan (2010) provided a summary of MGARCH models including their statistical properties.

The most obvious application of MGARCH models is the study of the relationships between the volatilities and co-volatilities of several markets. Is the volatility of one market leading to the volatility of other markets? Is the volatility of an asset transmitted to another asset directly (through its conditional variance) or indirectly (through its conditional covariances)? Does a shock on one market increase the volatility on another market, and, if so, by how much? Is the impact the same for negative and positive shocks of the same amplitude? A related issue is whether the correlations between asset returns change over time. Are they higher during periods of higher volatility (sometimes associated with financial crises)? Are they increasing in the long run, perhaps because of the globalisation of financial markets? Such issues can be studied directly by using a multivariate model and raise the question of the specification of the dynamics of covariances or correlations.

From a slightly different perspective, a few researchers have used MGARCH models to assess the impact of volatility in financial markets on real variables such as exports and output growth rates, and the volatility of these growth rates. Another application of MGARCH models is the computation of time-varying hedge ratios. Traditionally, constant hedge ratios are estimated by OLS as the slope of a regression of the spot return on the futures return, because this is equivalent to estimating the ratio of the covariance between spot and futures over the variance of the futures. Since a bivariate MGARCH model for the spot and futures returns directly specifies their conditional variance-covariance matrix, the hedge ratio can be computed as a byproduct of estimation and updated by using new observations as they become available (see Lien and Tse (2002) for a survey on hedging and additional references).

Asset pricing models relate returns to "factors", such as the market return in the capital asset pricing model. A specific asset excess return (in excess of the risk-free return) may be expressed as a linear function of the market return. Assuming its constancy, the slope or beta coefficient may be estimated by OLS. As in the hedging case, since beta is the ratio of a covariance to a variance, an MGARCH model can be used to estimate time-varying beta coefficients (see Bollerslev *et al.* (1988), De Santis and Gerard (1998) and Hafner and Herwartz (1998) for examples). Given an estimated univariate GARCH model on a return series, one knows the return conditional distribution and can forecast the value-at-risk (VaR) of a long or short position. When considering a portfolio of assets, the portfolio return can be computed directly from the asset shares and returns. A GARCH model can be fitted to the portfolio returns for given weights. If the weight vector changes, the model has to be estimated again. On the contrary, if a multivariate GARCH model is fitted, the multivariate distribution of the returns can be used directly to compute the implied distribution of any portfolio. There is no need to re-estimate the model for different weight vectors. At the present state of the art, it is probably simpler to use the univariate framework if there are many assets, but the conjecture is that using a multivariate specification may become a feasible alternative. Whether the univariate "repeated" approach is more adequate than the multivariate one is an open question. The multivariate approach is illustrated by Giot and Laurent (2003) using a trivariate example with a time-varying correlation model. MGARCH models were initially developed in the late 1980s and the first half of the 1990s and after a period of tranquility in the second half of the 1990s, this area seems to be experiencing a quick expansion phase again.

Framework and estimation process

The models discussed in this chapter are multivariate extensions of the univariate GARCH model which was discussed in Chapter 4. The number of parameters increases rapidly when the conditional mean of several time series is considered. The same issue of parameter estimation occurs for multivariate GARCH models as straightforward extensions of the univariate GARCH model. Furthermore, since H_t is a variance matrix, positive definiteness has to be ensured. To make the model tractable for applied purposes, an additional structure may be imposed, for example, in the form of factors or diagonal parameter matrices. This class of models lends itself to relatively easy theoretical derivations of stationarity and ergodicity conditions, and unconditional moments (see e.g. He and Teräsvirta, 2002). A stationary sequence is said to be ergodic if it satisfies the strong law of large numbers (see Billingsley, 1995 for more information).

RiskMetrics

Morgan (1996) employed the exponentially weighted moving average model (EWMA) to forecast variance and covariances. Practitioners who study volatility processes often observe that their model is very close to the unit root case. To take this into account, RiskMetrics defines the variances and covariances as Integrated GARCH (IGARCH)-type models (Engle and Bollerslev, 1986).

Definition 1: The RiskMetrics model is defined as

$$H_t = (1 - \lambda)\epsilon_t \epsilon'_{t-1} + \lambda H_{t-1} \tag{5.1}$$

or alternatively as:

$$H_t = \frac{(1-\lambda)}{(1-\lambda)^{t-1}} \sum_{t=1}^{t-1} \lambda^{i-1} \epsilon_t \epsilon'_{t-1} \tag{5.2}$$

The decay factor λ ($0 < \lambda < 1$) proposed by RiskMetrics is equal to 0.94 for daily data and 0.97 for monthly data. The decay factor is not estimated but suggested by RiskMetrics. In this respect, this model is easy to work with in practice. However, imposing the same dynamics on every component in a multivariate GARCH model, no matter which data are used, is difficult to justify.

BEKK model

Engle and Kroner (1995) proposed a parametrisation for H_t that easily imposes its positivity, i.e. the BEKK model (the acronym comes from synthesised work on multivariate models by Baba *et al.* (1991)).

Definition 2: The BEKK(p, q) model is defined as

$$H_t = C'C + \sum_{i=1}^{q} A_i' \epsilon_{t-i} \epsilon_{t-i}' A_i + \sum_{j=1}^{p} G_j' H_{t-j} G_j \tag{5.3}$$

where C, As and Gs matrices are of dimension $N \times N$ but C is upper triangular.

The original BEKK model is a bit more general since it involves a summation over K terms. The BEKK model is actually a special case of the VEC model of Bollerslev *et al.* (1988).

The number of ARCH and GARCH parameters in the BEKK(1,1) model is $N(5N + 1)/2$. To reduce this number, and consequently to reduce the generality, one can impose a diagonal BEKK model, i.e. A_i and G_j in equation (5.3) are diagonal matrices.

Another way to reduce the number of parameters is to use a scalar BEKK model, i.e. A_i and G_j are equal to a scalar times a matrix of ones. The Diagonal-BEKK (Diag-BEKK) and Scalar-BEKK (without explanatory variables) are covariance stationary if $\sum_{i=1}^{q} a_{nn,i}^2 + \sum_{j=1}^{p} g_{nn,j}^2 < 1, \forall n = 1, ..., N$, $\sum_{i=1}^{q} a_i^2 + \sum_{j=1}^{p} g_j^2 < 1$, respectively. These conditions are imposed during the estimation.

When it exists, the unconditional variance matrix $\Sigma \equiv E(H_t)$ of the BEKK model (again without explanatory variables) is given by

$$vec(\Sigma) = \left[I_{N^2} - \sum_{i=1}^{q} (A_i \otimes A_i)' - \sum_{j=1}^{p} (G_j \otimes G_j)' \right]^{-1} vec(C'C) \tag{5.4}$$

where *vec* denotes the operator that stacks the columns of a matrix as a vector. Similar expressions can be obtained for the Diag-BEKK and Scalar-BEKK models.

As for univariate models, explanatory variables can be included in the volatility equation. For RiskMetrics and BEKK models, equations (5.1) and (5.3) are extended by adding the following term:

$$+F \cdot diag(|Z_t|) \cdot F' \tag{5.5}$$

where F is an $N \times n_2$ matrix and $diag(|Z_t|)$ is an $n_2 \times n_2$ diagonal matrix with $|Z_t|$ on the diagonal. The positivity of $|Z_t|$ and the quadratic form ensure the positive definiteness of the conditional variance-covariance.

What renders most MGARCH models difficult for estimation is their high number of parameters. Variance targeted by Engle and Mezrich (1996) is a simple trick to ensure a reasonable value of the model-implied unconditional covariance matrix and also help to reduce the number of parameters in the maximisation of the likelihood function. The conditional variance matrix of the BEKK model (and all its particular cases) may be expressed in terms of the unconditional variance matrix and other parameters. In doing so, one can reparametrise the model using the unconditional variance matrix and replace it with a consistent estimator (before maximising the likelihood). Applying variance targeting to the BEKK models implies replacing CC' with unvec $\left[I_{N^2} - \sum_{i=1}^{q} (A_i \otimes A_i)' - \sum_{j=1}^{p} (G_j \otimes G_j)' \right] \bar{\Sigma}$, where $\bar{\Sigma}$ is the unconditional variance-covariance matrix of ϵ and unvec is the reverse of the operator.

Orthogonal GARCH

In the orthogonal GARCH (O-GARCH) model, the observed data are assumed to be generated by an orthogonal transformation of N (or a smaller number of) univariate GARCH processes. The matrix of the linear transformation is the orthogonal matrix (or a selection) of eigenvectors of the population unconditional covariance matrix of the standardised returns. In the generalised version, this matrix must only be invertible. The orthogonal models can also be considered as factor models, where the factors are univariate GARCH-type processes. Alexander (2002) and Ding and Engle (2001) provided many references on O-GARCH models.

In the orthogonal GARCH model of Kariya (1988) and Alexander and Chibumba (1997), the $N \times N$ time-varying variance matrix H_t is generated by $m \leq N$ univariate GARCH models.

Definition 3: The O-GARCH(1,1,m) model is defined as

$$y_t = \mu_t + \epsilon_t \tag{5.6}$$

$$\epsilon_t = V^{1/2} u_t \tag{5.7}$$

$$u_t = Z_m f_t \tag{5.8}$$

where $V = \text{diag}(v_1, v_2, \ldots, v_N)$, with v_i being the population variance of ϵ_{it}, and Z_m is a matrix of dimension $N \times m$ given by

$$Z_m = P_m L_m^{1/2} = P_m diag\left(l_1^{1/2} \cdots l_m^{1/2} \right) \tag{5.9}$$

with $l_1 \geq \ldots \geq l_m > 0$ being the m largest eigenvalues of the population correlation matrix of ϵ_t (or of the covariance matrix of u_t), and P_m the $N \times m$ matrix of associated (mutually orthogonal) eigenvectors. The vector $f_t = (f_{1t} \ldots f_{mt})'$ is a random process such that

$$E_{t-1}(f_t) = 0 \text{ and } Var_{t-1}(f_t) = \Sigma_t = diag\left(\sigma^2_{f_{1t}} \cdots \sigma^2_{f_{mt}}\right) \tag{5.10}$$

$$\sigma^2_{f_{1t}} = (1 - \alpha_i - \beta_i) + \alpha_i f^2_{i,t-1} + \beta_i \sigma^2_{f_i,t-1} \quad i = 1,\ldots,m \tag{5.11}$$

Consequently,

$$H_t = Var_{t-1}(\epsilon_t) = V^{1/2} V_t V'^{1/2} \text{ where } V_t = Var_{t-1}(u_t) = Z_m \Sigma_t Z'_m \tag{5.12}$$

The parameters of the model are V, L_m, and the parameters of the GARCH factors (α_is and β_is). The number of parameters is $N(N+5)/2$ (if $m = N$). In practice, V and L_m are replaced by their sample counterparts and m is chosen by principal component analysis applied to the standardised residuals $\hat{u}_t$. Alexander (2001) illustrated the use of the O-GARCH model. She emphasised that using a small number of principal components compared to the number of assets is the strength of the approach (in one example, she fixes m at 2 for 12 assets). However, when $m < N$, the conditional variance matrix reduces rank and is very likely to be singular (not invertible). In this case, diagnostic tests based on standardised residuals (which depend on the inverse of H_t) are not reported. Provided that H_t is invertible, standardised residuals are computed as follows: $\epsilon_t = H_t^{-1/2}(y_t - \mu_t)$.

Note also that equation (5.11) is a GARCH(1,1) model with unit unconditional variance. Interestingly, one can permit the choice of all the specifications presented in Chapter 4, rather than just restricting to the standard GARCH model. Furthermore, explanatory variables can be included in the conditional variance of the m factors. For instance, for a GARCH(1,1) with an explanatory variable x_t, equation (5.11) becomes

$$\sigma^2_{f_{1t}} = \sigma^*_i + \gamma x_t + \alpha_i f^2_{i,t-1} + \beta_i \sigma^2_{f_i,t-1} \quad i = 1,\cdots,m \tag{5.13}$$

where $\sigma^*_i = (1 - \alpha_i - \beta_i) - \gamma_i$.

Estimation of the O-GARCH model can be done in three steps as follows:

1   The conditional mean equation (μ_t) is obtained by estimating N models by QMLE with normal errors. If $\mu_t = \mu$, the sample average of y_t is used instead. Note that explanatory variables can be included in μ_t as well as an AR(FI)MA specification.

2   P_m and L_m are computed by means of a principal component analysis (a scree plot is provided to help the user to choose m if the relevant option is selected).

3   Finally, m GARCH-type models are estimated on f_{it}, $i = 1,\ldots, M$, by QMLE (note that standard errors are not corrected for the uncertainty of the first two steps).

Generalised O-GARCH

Van der Weide (2002) proposed a generalisation of the O-GARCH model. In the Generalised O-GARCH (GO-GARCH), the orthogonality condition assumed in the O-GARCH model is relaxed by assuming that the matrix Z in the relation $u_t = Zf_t$ is square and invertible, rather than orthogonal. The matrix Z has N^2 parameters and is not restricted to be triangular. Boswijk and Van der Weide (2006) provided updated references on these models.

Definition 4: The GO-GARCH(1,1) model is defined as in Definition 3, where $m = N$ and $Z_m = Z = PL^{1/2}U$ is a non-singular matrix of parameters and U is orthogonal. The implied conditional correlation matrix of ϵt can be expressed as

$$R_t = J_t^{-1}V_tJ_t^{-1} \quad \text{where} \quad J_t = (V_t \odot I_m)^{1/2} \quad \text{and} \quad V_t = Z\Sigma_t Z' \tag{5.14}$$

P and L are defined as above (from the eigenvectors and eigenvalues). The O-GARCH model (when $m = N$) corresponds to the particular choice $U = I_N$. More generally, Van der Weide (2002) expressed U as the product of $N(N-1)/2$ rotation matrices:

$$U = \prod_{i<j}G_{ij}(\delta_{ij}), \quad -\pi \leq \delta_{ij} \leq \pi, \quad i,j = 1,2,\cdots,n \tag{5.15}$$

where $G_{ij}(\delta_{ij})$ performs a rotation in the plane spanned by the ith and the jth vectors of the canonical basis of R^N over an angle δ_{ij}. For example, in the trivariate case,

$$G_{12} = \begin{pmatrix} \cos\delta_{12} & \sin\delta_{12} & 0 \\ -\sin\delta_{12} & \cos\delta_{12} & 0 \\ 0 & 0 & 1 \end{pmatrix}, \quad G_{13} = \begin{pmatrix} \cos\delta_{13} & 0 & -\sin\delta_{13} \\ 0 & 1 & 0 \\ -\sin\delta_{13} & 0 & \cos\delta_{13} \end{pmatrix} \tag{5.16}$$

and G_{23} has the block with $\cos\delta_{23}$ and $\sin\delta_{23}$ functions in the lower right corner. The $N(N-1)/2$ rotation angles are parameters to be estimated.

For estimation, Van der Weide (2002) replaced in a first step P and L by their sample counterparts and the remaining parameters (those of U) were estimated together with the parameters of the GARCH factors in a second step.

The orthogonal models are particular F-GARCH models and thus are nested in the BEKK model. As a consequence, their properties follow those of the BEKK model. In particular, it is obvious that the (G)O-GARCH model is covariance stationary if the m univariate GARCH processes are themselves stationary.

Estimation of the GO-GARCH model can be done in three steps as follows:

1   The conditional mean equation (μ_t) is obtained by estimating N models by QMLE with normal errors. If $\mu_t = \mu$ the sample average of y_t is used instead. Note that explanatory variables can be included in μ_t as well as an AR(FI)MA specification.

2   P_m and L_m are computed by means of a principal component analysis. Note that the GO-GARCH imposes $m = N$.

3   Finally, U' and the GARCH parameters are estimated by QMLE. Note also that $f_t = U'L^{-1/2}P'u_t$, where u_t and f_t are $m \times 1$ vectors and U is a function of δ.

Nonlinear least squares generalised O-GARCH (NLS GO-GARCH)

As pointed out recently by Boswijk and Van der Weide (2006), the practical power of the O-GARCH has been lost in the GO-GARCH of Van der Weide (2002), i.e. the fact that all GARCH parameters can be conveniently estimated by appealing to the univariate GARCH model for the principal components of the original series.

Boswijk and Van der Weide (2006) have proposed an alternative method for estimating the GO-GARCH model that makes it more attractive from a purely practical point of view. The price to pay is a loss of efficiency.

Recall from Definition 3 that $u_t = Zf_t$ (when $m = N$) and from the GO-GARCH model that $Z = PL^{1/2}U$. Thus, $u_t = PL^{1/2}Uf_t = PL^{1/2}s_t$, where $s_t = Uf_t$ is the standardised and orthogonalised version of u_t. It is straightforward to show that $s_t = L^{-1/2}P'u_t$.

The idea of Boswijk and Van der Weide (2006) is to identify U from the (cross)-autocorrelation structure of $s_t s'_t$.

Consider the linear projection of $f_t f'_t$ on $f_{t-1}f'_{t-1}$:

$$\begin{bmatrix} f_{1t}^2 & \cdots & f_{1t}f_{mt} \\ \vdots & \ddots & \vdots \\ f_{mt}f_{1t} & \cdots & f_{mt}^2 \end{bmatrix} = \begin{bmatrix} a_1 & \cdots & 0 \\ \vdots & \ddots & \vdots \\ 0 & \cdots & a_m \end{bmatrix} +$$

$$\begin{bmatrix} b_1^2 f_{1,t-1}^2 & \cdots & 0 \\ \vdots & \ddots & \vdots \\ 0 & \cdots & b_m^2 f_{m,t-1}^2 \end{bmatrix} + e_t$$

or in matrix form,

$$f_t f'_t = D_a + D_b \odot f_{t-1}f'_{t-1} \odot D_b + e_t, \tag{5.17}$$

where $\odot$ denotes the Hadamar product, D_a and D_b are diagonal and e_t is uncorrelated with $f_{t-1}f'_{t-1}$.

Now suppose that one estimates the following model:

$$f_t f'_t = A + B f_{t-1} f'_{t-1} B + v_t \tag{5.18}$$

by means of NLS, i.e. by minimising $\sum_{t=1}^{T} tr\left(v_t^2\right)$ over symmetric matrices A and B. Then the pseudo-true values of A and B will be diagonal (under some conditions on fourth-order moments; see Boswijk and Van der Weide, 2006), although not equal to D_a and D_b.

Therefore, using $s_t = Uf_t$, if one estimates

$$s_t s'_t = C + Q s_{t-1} s'_{t-1} Q + w_t \tag{5.19}$$

over symmetric matrices C and Q, then the pseudo-true values will satisfy $C = UAU'$ and $Q = UBU'$ for diagonal matrices A and B. This implies that one may estimate U as eigenvectors from $\hat{Q}$ (or $\hat{C}$). The resulting estimator $\hat{U}$ may be used to construct $\hat{Z} = \hat{P}\hat{L}^{1/2}\hat{U}$, and hence $\hat{f}_t = \hat{Z}^{-1}u_t$.

The diagonal variance matrix V_t may be estimated from $\hat{f}_t$ using univariate GARCH models. In principle, different models for different components are possible. Some empirical applications and simulations suggest that the new procedure is worth considering. A formal (asymptotic) theory of inference is not yet available.

Having introduced the four linear multivariate GARCH models above, four different nonlinear correlation models will now be introduced in the next four sub-sections before proceeding to discuss about the estimation process for all these multivariate GARCH models in section "Estimation processes".

Constant conditional correlation

This sub-section collects models that may be viewed as nonlinear combinations of univariate GARCH models. This allows for models where one can specify separately, on the one hand, the individual conditional variances, and, on the other hand, the conditional correlation matrix. For models of this category, theoretical results on stationarity, ergodicity and moments may not be so straightforward to obtain as for models presented in the preceding sections. Nevertheless, they are less demanding in terms of parameters than the models of the first category, and therefore they are more easily estimable.

The conditional variance matrix for this class of models is specified in a hierarchical manner. First, one chooses a GARCH-type model for each conditional variance. Second, based on the conditional variances, one models the conditional correlation matrix (imposing its positive definiteness $\forall t$).

Bollerslev (1990) proposed a class of MGARCH models in which the conditional correlations are constant, and thus the conditional covariances are proportional to the product of the corresponding conditional standard deviations. This restriction significantly reduces the number of unknown parameters and thus simplifies estimation.

Definition 5: The Constant Conditional Correlation (CCC) model is defined as

$$H_t = D_t R D_t = \left(\rho_{ij} \sqrt{h_{iit} h_{jjt}} \right) \tag{5.20}$$

where

$$D_t = diag \left(h_{11t}^{1/2} \cdots h_{NNt}^{1/2} \right) \tag{5.21}$$

Here, h_{iit} can be defined as any univariate GARCH model, and

$$R = \left(\rho_{ij} \right) \tag{5.22}$$

is a symmetric positive definite matrix with $\rho_{ii} = 1, \forall\, i$.

R is the matrix containing the constant conditional correlations ρ_{ij}. The original CCC model has a GARCH(1,1) specification for each conditional variance in D_t:

$$h_{iit} = w_i + \alpha_i \epsilon_{i,t-1}^2 + \beta_i h_{ii,t-1} \quad i = 1, \cdots, N \tag{5.23}$$

This CCC model contains $N(N + 5)/2$ parameters. H_t is positive definite if and only if all the N conditional variances are positive and R is positive definite. The unconditional variances are easily obtained, as in the univariate case, but the unconditional covariances are difficult to calculate because of the nonlinearity in equation (5.20).

Dynamic conditional correlation

The assumption that the conditional correlations are constant may seem unrealistic in many empirical applications. Engle (2002) and Tse and Tsui (2002) put forward a generalisation of the CCC model by making the conditional correlation matrix time dependent. The model is then called a dynamic conditional correlation (DCC) model. An additional difficulty is that the time-dependent conditional correlation matrix has to be positive definite $\forall t$. The DCC models guarantee this requirement under simple conditions on the parameters.

Definition 6: The DCC model of Tse and Tsui (2002) is defined as

$$H_t = D_t R_t D_t \tag{5.24}$$

where D_t is defined in (5.21), h_{iit} can be defined as any univariate GARCH model and

$$R_t = (1 - \theta_1 - \theta_2) R + \theta_1 \psi_{t-1} + \theta_2 R_{t-1} \tag{5.25}$$

In equation (5.25), θ_1 and θ_2 are non-negative parameters satisfying $\theta_1 + \theta_2 < 1$, R is a symmetric $N \times N$ positive-definite parameter matrix with $\rho_{ii} = 1$ and Ψ_{t-1} is the $N \times N$ correlation matrix of ϵ_τ for $\tau = t-M, t-M+1,\ldots,$ $t-1$. Its ijth element is given by

$$\psi_{ij,t-1} = \frac{\displaystyle\sum_{m=1}^{M} u_{i,t-m} u_{j,t-m}}{\sqrt{\left(\displaystyle\sum_{m=1}^{M} u_{i,t-m}^2\right)\left(\displaystyle\sum_{h=1}^{M} u_{j,t-m}^2\right)}} \tag{5.26}$$

where $u_{it} = \epsilon_{it}\sqrt{h_{ii,t}}$. The matrix Ψ_{t-1} can be expressed as

$$\psi_{t-1} = B_{t-1}^{-1} L_{t-1} L_{t-1}' B_{t-1}^{-1} \tag{5.27}$$

where B_{t-1} is an $N \times N$ diagonal matrix with ith diagonal element given by $\left(\displaystyle\sum_{h=1}^{M} u_{i,t-h}^2\right)^{1/2}$ and $L_{t-1} = (u_{t-1},\ldots, u_{t-M})$ is an $N \times M$ matrix, with $u_t = (u_{1t}\, u_{2t}\, \ldots\, u_{Nt})'$.

A necessary condition to ensure the positivity of Ψ_{t-1}, and therefore also of R_t, is that $M \geq N$. Then R_t is itself a correlation matrix if R_{t-1} is also a correlation matrix (notice that $\rho_{iit} = 1 \forall i$). Alternatively, Engle (2002) proposed a different DCC model (see also Engle and Sheppard, 2001).

Definition 7: The DCC model of Engle (2002) is defined as in equation (5.24) with

$$R_t = diag\left(q_{11,t}^{-1/2} \cdots q_{NN,t}^{-1/2}\right) Q_t diag\left(q_{11,t}^{-1/2} \cdots q_{NN,t}^{-1/2}\right) \tag{5.28}$$

where the $N \times N$ symmetric positive-definite matrix $Q_t = (q_{ij,\,t})$ is given by

$$Q_t = (1 - \alpha - \beta)\bar{Q} + \alpha u_{t-1} u_{t-1}' + \beta Q_{t-1} \tag{5.29}$$

with u_t as in Definition 6. $\bar{Q}$ is the $N \times N$ unconditional variance matrix of u_t, and α and β are non-negative scalar parameters satisfying $\alpha + \beta < 1$.

To show more explicitly the difference between the two DCC models, one writes the expression of the correlation coefficient in the bivariate case: for the DCC of Tse and Tsui (2002),

$$\rho_{12,t} = \left(1 - \theta_1 - \theta_2\right)\rho_{12} + \theta_2\rho_{12,t-1} + \theta_1 \frac{\sum\limits_{m=1}^{M} u_{1,t-m}u_{2,t-m}}{\sqrt{\left(\sum\limits_{m=1}^{M} u_{1,t-m}^2\right)\left(\sum\limits_{h=1}^{M} u_{2,t-m}^2\right)}} \tag{5.30}$$

and for the DCC of Engle (2002),

$$\rho_{12,t} = \frac{\left(1 - \alpha - \beta\right)\bar{q}_{12} + \alpha u_{1,t-1}u_{2,t-1} + \beta q_{12,t-1}}{\sqrt{\left(\left(1 - \alpha - \beta\right)\bar{q}_{11} + \alpha u_{1,t-1}^2 + \beta q_{11,t-1}\right)\left(\left(1 - \alpha - \beta\right)\bar{q}_{22} + \alpha u_{2,t-1}^2 + \beta q_{22,t-1}\right)}} \tag{5.31}$$

Unlike Tse and Tsui (2002), Engle (2002) formulated the conditional correlation as a weighted sum of past correlations. Indeed, the matrix Q_t is written like a GARCH equation and then transformed to a correlation matrix. However, for both DCC models, one can test $\theta_1 = \theta_2 = 0$ or $\alpha = \beta = 0$ respectively to check whether imposing constant conditional correlations is empirically relevant.

A drawback of the DCC models is that θ_1, θ_2 and α, β are scalars, so that all the conditional correlations obey the same dynamics. This is necessary to ensure that R_t is positive definite $\forall t$ through sufficient conditions on the parameters. If the conditional variances are specified as GARCH(1,1) models then the *DCC* models contain $(N + 1)(N + 4)/2$ parameters. Interestingly, CCC and DCC models can be estimated consistently in two steps which makes this approach feasible when N is high. Of course, when N is large, the restriction of common dynamics gets tighter, but for large N the problem of maintaining tractability also gets harder.

To conclude, DCC models open the door for using flexible GARCH specifications in the variance part. Indeed, as the conditional variances (together with the conditional means) can be estimated using N univariate models, one can easily extend the DCC-GARCH models to more complex GARCH-type structures. One can also extend the bivariate CCC Fractional Integrated GARCH (FIGARCH) model of Brunetti and Gilbert (2000) to a model of the DCC family.

Dynamic equicorrelation

Definition 8: The dynamic equicorrelation (DECO) model of Engle and Kelly (2012) is defined as in equation (5.24) with

$$R_t = \left(1 - \rho_t\right)I_N + \rho_t J_{N \times N} \tag{5.32}$$

$$\rho_t = \frac{1}{N(N-1)} \sum_{i \neq j} \frac{q_{ij,t}}{\sqrt{q_{ii,t}q_{jj,t}}} \tag{5.33}$$

where ρ_t is the equicorrelation, $q_{ij,\,t}$ is the i, jth element of Q_t in equation (5.29), I_N denotes the N-dimensional identity matrix and $J_{N \times N}$ is an $N \times N$ matrix of ones.

According to Engle and Kelly (2012), R_t^{-1} exists if and only if $\rho_t \neq 1$ and $\rho_t \neq -1/(N-1)$, and R_t is positive definite if and only if $-1/(N-1) < \rho_t < 1$.

As already mentioned, a useful feature of the DCC models is that the parameters governing the variance and correlation dynamics can be estimated separately. For the correlation estimation, one typically first estimates Q as the empirical correlation matrix of u_t. Then the parameters α and β in the DCC are usually estimated by Gaussian quasi maximum likelihood.

Corrected DCC

Aielli (2009) showed that the estimation of Q as the empirical correlation matrix of u_t is inconsistent because

$$[u_t u_t] = E[E[u'_t u_t | \Omega_{t-1}] = E[R_t] \neq E[Q_t]$$

Definition 9: Let $P_t = \mathrm{diag}\ (q_{11,t}^{1/2} \dots q_{NN,\,t}^{1/2})$ and $u_t^* = P_t u_t$. The corrected DCC (cDCC) model of Aielli (2009) is defined as in the DCC model of Engle (2002) but the $N \times N$ symmetric positive-definite matrix $Q_t = (q_{ij,\,t})$ is now given by

$$Q_t = (1 - \alpha - \beta)\bar{Q} + \alpha u_{t-1}^* u_{t-1}^{*\prime} + \beta Q_{t-1} \tag{5.34}$$

where $\bar{Q}$ is the $N \times N$ unconditional variance matrix of u_t^* (since $E[u_t^* u_{t-1}^{*\prime} | \Omega_{t-1}] = Q_t$), and α and β are non-negative scalar parameters satisfying $\alpha + \beta < 1$.

For the cDCC model, the estimation of the matrix $\bar{Q}$ and the parameters α and β are intertwined, since $\bar{Q}$ is estimated sequentially as the correlation matrix of u_t^*. To obtain u_t^* one needs, however, a first-step estimator of the diagonal elements of Q_t. By virtue of the fact that the diagonal elements of Q_t do not depend on $\bar{Q}$ (because $Q_{ii} = 1$ for $i = 1, \dots, N$), Aielli (2009) proposed to obtain these values $q_{11,t}, \dots, q_{NN,\,t}$ as follows:

$$q_{ii,t} = (1 - \alpha - \beta) + \alpha u_{i,t-1}^2 + \beta q_{ii,t-1} \tag{5.35}$$

for $i = 1, \dots, N$. In short, given α and β, one can compute $q_{11,t}, \dots, q_{NN,\,t}$ and thus u_t^* and then one can estimate $\bar{Q}$ as the empirical covariance of u_t^*.

Estimation processes

Suppose the vector stochastic process $\{y_t\}$ (for $t = 1, \dots, T$) is a realisation of a DGP whose conditional mean, conditional variance matrix and conditional distribution are respectively $\mu_t(\theta_0)$, $H_t(\theta_0)$ and $p(y_t | \zeta_0, \Omega_{t-1})$, where

$\zeta_0 = (\theta_0 \; \eta_0)$ is a r-dimensional parameter vector and η_0 is the vector that contains the parameters of the distribution of the innovations z_t (there may be no such parameter). More importantly, to justify the choice of the estimation procedure, one assumes that the model to be estimated encompasses the true formulations of $\mu_t(\theta_0)$ and $H_t(\theta_0)$.

The procedure most often used in estimating θ_0 involves the maximisation of a likelihood function constructed under the auxiliary assumption of an *i.i.d.* distribution for the standardised innovations z_t. The *i.i.d.* assumption may be replaced by the weaker assumption that z_t is a martingale difference sequence with respect to Ω_{t-1}, but this type of assumption does not translate into the likelihood function. The likelihood function for the *i.i.d.* case can then be viewed as a quasi-likelihood function.

Consequently, one has to make an additional assumption on the innovation process by choosing a density function, denoted $g(z_t(\theta)|\eta)$, where η is a vector of nuisance parameters. The problem to solve is thus to maximise the sample log-likelihood function $L_T(\theta, \eta)$ for the T observations (conditional on some starting values for μ_0 and H_0), with respect to the vector of parameters $\zeta = (\theta, \eta)$, where

$$L_T(\zeta) = \sum_{t=1}^{T} \log f(y_t \mid \zeta, \Omega_{t-1}) \qquad (5.36)$$

with

$$f(y_t|\Omega_{t-1}) = |H_t|^{-1/2} \, g\left(H_t^{-1/2}(y_t - \mu_t)|\eta\right) \qquad (5.37)$$

and the dependence with respect to θ occurs through μ_t and H_t. The term $|H_t|^{-1/2}$ is the Jacobian that arises in the transformation from the innovations to the observables.

The most commonly employed distribution in the literature is the multivariate normal, uniquely determined by its first two moments (so that $\zeta = \theta$ since η is empty). In this case, the sample log-likelihood is

$$L_T(\theta) = -\frac{1}{2} \sum_{t=1}^{T} \left[N\log(2\pi) + \log|H_t| + (y_t - \mu_t)' \, H_t^{-1} (y_t - \mu_t) \right] \qquad (5.38)$$

It is well known that the normality of the innovations is rejected in most applications dealing with daily or weekly data. In particular, the kurtosis of most financial asset returns is larger than 3, which means that they have too many extreme values to be normally distributed. Moreover, their unconditional distribution often has fatter tails than what is implied by a conditional normal distribution: the increase of the kurtosis coefficient brought about by the dynamics of the conditional variance is not usually sufficient to adequately match the unconditional kurtosis of the data.

However, as shown by Bollerslev and Wooldridge (1992), a consistent estimator of θ_0 may be obtained by maximising equation (5.38) with respect to θ even if the DGP is not conditionally Gaussian. This estimator, called (Gaussian) quasi-maximum likelihood (QML) or pseudo-maximum likelihood (PML) estimator, is consistent, provided the conditional mean and the conditional variance are specified correctly. Jeantheau (1998) proved the strong consistency of the Gaussian QML estimator of multivariate GARCH models. He also provided sufficient identification conditions for the CCC model (see Gouriéroux (1997) for a detailed description of the QML method in an MGARCH context and its asymptotic properties). For these reasons and as far as the purpose of the analysis is to estimate consistently the first two conditional moments, estimating MGARCH models by QML is justified.

Nevertheless, in certain situations it is desirable to search for a better distribution for the innovation process. For instance, when one is interested in obtaining density forecasts (see Diebold *et al.*1998, in the univariate case and Diebold *et al.* 1999, in the multivariate case), it is natural to relax the normality assumption, keeping in mind the risk of inconsistency of the estimator (see Newey and Steigerwald, 1997).

A natural alternative to the multivariate Gaussian density is the Student density (see Harvey *et al.* (1994) and Fiorentini *et al.* (2003)). The latter has an extra scalar parameter, the degrees of freedom parameter, denoted by v hereafter. When this parameter tends to infinity, the Student density tends to the normal density. When it tends to zero, the tails of the density become increasingly thicker. The parameter value indicates the order of existence of the moments, e.g. if $v = 2$, the second-order moments do not exist, but the first-order moments exist. For this reason, it is convenient (although not necessary) to assume that $v > 2$, so that H_t is always interpretable as a conditional covariance matrix. Under this assumption, the Student density can be defined as

$$g(z_t|\theta,v) = \frac{\Gamma\left(\dfrac{v+N}{2}\right)}{\Gamma\left(\dfrac{v}{2}\right)[\pi(v-2)]^{\frac{N}{2}}}\left[1+\frac{z_t'z_t}{v-2}\right]^{-\frac{N+v}{2}} \tag{5.39}$$

where $\Gamma(.)$ is the Gamma function. Note that in this case $\eta = v$. The density function of y_t is easily obtained by applying equation (5.37).

The asymptotic properties of ML and QML estimators in multivariate GARCH models are not yet firmly established, and are difficult to derive from low-level assumptions. As mentioned previously, consistency has been shown by Jeantheau (1998). Asymptotic normality of the QMLE is not established generally. Gouriéroux (1997) proves it for a general formulation using high-level assumptions. Comte and Lieberman (2003) prove it for the BEKK formulation. Since (G)O-GARCH models are special cases of the BEKK model, this result also holds for these models (see Van der Weide, 2002). Researchers who use MGARCH models have generally proceeded as if asymptotic normality holds in all cases. Asymptotic normality of the MLE and QMLE has been proven in the univariate case under low-level assumptions, one of which being the existence of moments of order four or higher of the innovations (see Lee and Hansen, 1994, Lumsdaine, 1996, and Ling and McAleer, 2003).

Finally, it is worth mentioning that the conditional mean parameters may be consistently estimated in a first stage, prior to the estimation of the con-ditional variance parameters, for example for a Vector ARMA (VARMA) model, but not for a GARCH-in-mean model. Estimating the parameters simultaneously with the conditional variance parameters would increase the efficiency at least in large samples (unless the asymptotic covariance matrix is block diagonal between the mean and variance parameters), but this is computationally more difficult. For this reason, one either usually takes a very simple model for the conditional mean or considers $y_t - \hat{\mu}_t$ as the data for fitting the MGARCH model.

A useful feature of the CCC and DCC models presented in sections "Nonlinear least squares generalised O-GARCH (NLS GO-GARCH)" and "Constant conditional correlation", respectively, is that they can be esti-mated consistently using a two-step approach. Engle and Sheppard (2001) showed that in the case of a *DCC* model, the log-likelihood can be written as the sum of a mean and volatility part (depending on a set of unknown parameters θ_1^*) and a correlation part (depending on θ_2^*).

Indeed, recalling that the conditional variance matrix of a DCC model can be expressed as $H_t = D_t R_t D_t$, an inefficient but consistent estimator of the parameter θ_1^* can be found by replacing R_t with the identity matrix in equation (5.38). In this case, the quasi-log-likelihood function corresponds to the sum of log-likelihood functions of N univariate models:

$$QL1_T\left(\theta_1^*\right) = -\frac{1}{2}\sum_{t=1}^{T}\sum_{i=1}^{N}\left[\log(2\pi) + \log\left(h_{iit}\right) + \frac{\left(y_{it} - \mu_{it}\right)^2}{h_{iit}}\right] \qquad (5.40)$$

Given θ_1^* and under appropriate regularity conditions, a consistent, but inef-ficient, estimator of θ_2^* can be obtained by maximising

$$QL2_T\left(\theta_2^*|\theta_1^*\right) = -\frac{1}{2}\sum_{t=1}^{T}\left(\log|R_t| + u_t' R_t^{-1} u_t\right) \qquad (5.41)$$

where $u_t = D_t^{-1}\left(y_t - \mu_t\right)$.

Note that for the DECO model of Engle and Kelly (2012) (see Definition 8), equation (5.41) can be simplified as follows:

$$QL2_T\left(\theta_2^*|\theta_1^*\right) = -\frac{1}{2}\sum_{t=1}^{T}\left\{\begin{array}{l}\log[(1-\rho_t)^{N-1}(1+(N-1)\rho_t)]\\[2mm]+\dfrac{1}{1-\rho_t}\left[\sum_i u_{it}^2 - \dfrac{\rho_t}{1+(N-1)\rho_t}\left(\sum_i u_{it}\right)^2\right]\end{array}\right\} \quad (5.42)$$

Engle and Kelly (2012) argued as follows:

> The payoff from making the equicorrelation assumption can now be appreciated. In DCC, the conditional correlation matrices must be recorded and inverted for all t and their determinants calculated; further, these T inversions and determinant calculations are repeated for each of the many iterations required in a numeric optimization program. This is costly for small cross sections and potentially infeasible for very large ones.
>
> With DECO, only the scalar equicorrelation parameter for each t is recorded, and the compact analytical forms for the determinant and inverse of a covariance matrix under the assumption of equicorrelation makes the computational demands for solving the likelihood optimization problem manageable for large cross sections.

The sum of the likelihood functions in equations (5.40) and (5.41) or (5.42), plus half of the total sum of squared standardised residuals ($\sum_t u_t'u_t/2$, which is almost equal to $NT/2$), is equal to the log-likelihood in equation (5.38). It is thus possible to compare the log-likelihood of the two-step approach with that of the one-step approach and of other models.

Engle and Sheppard (2001) explained that the estimators $\hat{\theta}_1^*$ and $\hat{\theta}_2^*$, obtained by maximising equations (5.40) and (5.41) separately, are not fully efficient (even if z_t is normally distributed) since they are limited information estimators.

Diagnostic testing

Since estimating MGARCH models is time consuming, in terms of both computations and their programming (if needed), it is desirable to check *ex ante* whether the data present are evident of multivariate ARCH effects. *Ex post*, it is also of crucial importance to check the adequacy of the MGARCH specification. However, compared to the huge body of diagnostic tests devoted to univariate models, only few tests are specific to multivariate models.

In the current literature on MGARCH models, one can distinguish two categories of specification tests, namely univariate tests applied independently to each series and multivariate tests applied to the vector series as a whole. The first category of tests is deliberately left out, and for the univariate tests, interested readers may refer to Chapter 4. As emphasised by Kroner and Ng (1998), the existing literature on multivariate diagnostics is sparse compared to the univariate case. However, although univariate tests can provide some guidance, contemporaneous correlation of disturbances entails that statistics from individual equations are not independent. As a result, combining test decisions over all equations raises size control problems, so the need for joint testing naturally arises (Dufour *et al.*, 2003).

Portmanteau statistics

The most widely used diagnostics to detect ARCH effects are probably the Box-Pierce/Ljung-Box portmanteau tests. Following Hosking (1980), a multivariate version of the Ljung-Box test statistic is given by

$$HM(m) = T^2 \sum_{j=1}^{m} (T-j)^{-1} tr\left\{ C_{y_t}^{-1}(0) C_{y_t}(j) C_{y_t}^{-1}(0) C_{y_t}'(j) \right\} \qquad (5.43)$$

where y_t is the vector of observed returns and $C_{y_t}(j)$ is the sample autocovariance matrix of order j. Under the null hypothesis of no serial correlation in y_t, $HM(m)$ is distributed asymptotically as $\chi^2(N^2 m)$.

To detect misspecification in the conditional mean, y_t is replaced by $\hat{z}_t = H_t^{-1/2} \hat{\varepsilon}_t$ and to detect misspecification in the conditional variance, y_t is replaced by $\hat{z}_t^2$. The asymptotic distribution of the portmanteau statistics is, however, unknown in this case since $\hat{z}_t$ has been estimated. *Ad hoc* adjustments of degrees of freedom for the ARMA and GARCH orders are applied. In such a case, portmanteau tests should be interpreted with care even if simulation results reported by Tse and Tsui (1999) suggest that they provide a useful diagnostic in many situations.

Li and McLeod (1981) put forward an alternative portmanteau statistic to detect misspecification in the conditional mean of an ARMA model (i.e. it is applied on $\hat{z}_t$). Following their notation, the modified version of their statistic $Q_m^* = Q_m + \dfrac{k^2 m(m+1)}{2n}$ is asymptotically χ^2 distributed with $k^2(m-s)$ degrees of freedom, where m is the lag order, $k = N$ and s is the ARMA order (AR+MA orders). For more updated discussions, one can refer to Tse (2002) and Duchesne and Lalancette (2003).

CCC tests

To reduce the number of parameters in the estimation of MGARCH models, it is usual to introduce restrictions. For instance, the CCC model of

Bollerslev (1990) assumed that the conditional correlation matrix is constant over time. It is then desirable to test this assumption afterwards. Tse (2000) proposed a test for constant correlations. The null is $h_{ij,t} = \rho_{ij}\sqrt{h_{ii,t}h_{jj,t}}$ where the conditional variances are GARCH-type models, while the alternative is $h_{ij,t} = \rho_{ij,t}\sqrt{h_{ii,t}h_{jj,t}}$. The test statistic is an LM statistic, which under the null is asymptotically $\chi^2\left(N(N-1)/2\right)$.

Engle and Sheppard (2001) suggested another test of the constant correlation hypothesis, in the spirit of the DCC models. The null H_0: $R_t = R\ \forall t$ is tested against the alternative H_1: $vech\ (R_t) = vech\ (R) + \beta_1^*vech\ \left(R_{t-1}\right) + \cdots + \beta_p^*vech\ \left(R_{t-p}\right)$. The test is easy to implement since H_0 implies that coefficients in the regression $X_t = \beta_0^* + \beta_1^*X_{t-1} + \cdots + \beta_p^*X_{t-p} + u_t^*$ are equal to zero, where $X_t = vech^u\left(\hat{z}_t\hat{z}_t' - I_N\right)$, $vech^u$ is like the *vech* operator but it only selects the elements under the main diagonal, $\hat{z}_t = \widehat{R}^{-1/2}\hat{D}_t^{-1}\hat{\epsilon}_t$ is the $N \times 1$ vector of standardized residuals (under the null), and $D_t = diag(h_{11t}^{1/2}\ldots h_{NNt}^{1/2})$.

Empirical results

The multivariate analysis was conducted for the period of 2 January 2006 to 15 January 2014 as BNM imposed capital control and pegged MYR/USD before this period. Hence, multivariate analysis for the period of pegged exchange rate is not appropriate. There is less flexibility and more restrictions for multivariate in terms of asymmetric effects and non-Gaussian density functions for risk modelling, and there are no meaningful risk measurement statistics like volatility persistency, risk premium and VaR measurements available with G@RCH version 5. There is a lot of applied work that can be extended by MGARCH in the future with better theoretical frameworks and analytical tools available for applied research work.

The focus is only on the sensitivity of density functions over the performance of the different MGARCH models explained in this chapter and on trying to compare with the results of the univariate analysis in Chapter 4. The only alternative density function other than Gaussian function for MGARCH at this moment is Student's distribution, whereas skewed Student density function was justified and used in Chapter 4 for univariate analysis.

Tables 5.1 and 5.2 summarise the diagnostic statistics for nine different MGARCH models over the period of 2 January 2006 to 15 January 2014. The usage of more recent data is to avoid distortion of the analysis using MGARCH models and the fact that BNM imposed capital control and pegged exchange rate before this period. As can be seen in Chapter 3, the correlations of the exchange rate do change over the two different exchange rate regimes, and hence there is the necessity to investigate as to which MGARCH models perform better in terms of performance and whether MGARCH can overcome the issues of non-normality of the squared residuals as found in Chapter 4.

Table 5.1 Diagnostic tests for multivariate GARCH models with normal density functions for the period of 2 January 2006 to 15 January 2014

Normal distribution	Scalar BEKK	Diag-BEKK	RiskMetrics	CCC	DCC (Tse and Tsui)	DCC (Engle)	O-GARCH	GO-GARCH	NLS GO-GARCH
Log-likelihood	41,005.23	41,061.18	N.A.	40,370.73	40,663.69	40,751.62	40,661.81	40,970.30	40,970.30
Akaike	−39.64	−39.69	N.A.	−39.02	−39.30	−39.39	−39.31	−39.60	−39.60
Schwarz	−39.59	−39.62	N.A.	−38.97	−39.25	−39.33	−39.27	−39.53	−39.53
Shibata	−39.64	−39.69	N.A.	−39.02	−39.31	−39.39	−39.31	−39.60	−39.60
Hannan-Quinn	−39.62	−39.66	N.A.	−39.00	−39.28	−39.37	−39.30	−39.57	−39.57
Vector normality test	0.00	0.00	N.A.	0.00	0.00	0.00	0.00		0.00
Lags	Hosking's Multivariate Portmanteau statistics on standardised residuals								
5	0.17	0.14	N.A.	0.12	0.07	0.16	0.53	0.08	0.08
10	0.11	0.08	N.A.	0.04	0.07	0.10	0.41	0.08	0.08
20	0.52	0.53	N.A.	0.31	0.39	0.41	0.94	0.59	0.59
50	0.16	0.13	N.A.	0.16	0.23	0.29	0.53	0.26	0.26
Lags	Li and McLeod's Multivariate Portmanteau statistics on squared standardised residuals								
5	0.12	0.14	N.A.	0.82	0.78	0.78	0.00	0.00	0.00
10	0.04	0.03	N.A.	0.92	0.90	0.84	0.00	0.00	0.00
20	0.47	0.22	N.A.	0.72	0.99	0.99	0.00	0.00	0.00
50	1.00	0.97	N.A.	0.99	1.00	1.00	0.00	0.13	0.13

Note: All the above statistics are *p*-values except for log-likelihood and the four information criteria.

Table 5.2 Diagnostic tests for multivariate GARCH models with Student's distribution function for the period of 2 January 2006 to 15 January 2014

Student's distribution	Scalar BEKK	Diag-BEKK	RiskMetrics	CCC	DCC (Tse and Tsui)	DCC (Engle)	O-GARCH	GO-GARCH	NLS GO-GARCH
Log-likelihood	42,234.54	42,271.79	42,048.21	41,514.61	42,035.98	42,041.64	40,661.81	40,970.30	40,770.70
Akaike	−40.83	−40.86	−40.66	−40.12	−40.63	−40.63	−39.31	−39.60	−39.41
Schwarz	−40.78	−40.79	−40.66	−40.05	−40.55	−40.56	−39.27	−39.53	−39.34
Shibata	−40.83	−40.86	−40.67	−40.13	−40.63	−40.63	−39.31	−39.60	−39.41
Hannan-Quinn	−40.81	−40.83	−40.63	−40.10	−40.60	−40.60	−39.30	−39.57	−39.38
Vector normality test	0.00	0.00	0.00	0.00	0.00	0.00	0.00	0.00	0.00
Hosking's Multivariate Portmanteau statistics on standardised residuals									
Lags									
5	0.36	0.32	0.40	0.16	0.18	0.29	0.53	0.08	0.42
10	0.31	0.30	0.16	0.05	0.30	0.28	0.41	0.08	0.16
20	0.76	0.82	0.41	0.38	0.79	0.74	0.94	0.59	0.81
50	0.71	0.75	0.58	0.08	0.54	0.43	0.53	0.26	0.65
Li and McLeod's Multivariate Portmanteau statistics on squared standardised residuals									
Lags									
5	0.91	0.77	1.00	0.03	0.18	0.74	0.00	0.00	0.01
10	0.99	0.84	1.00	0.12	0.45	0.89	0.00	0.00	0.00
20	1.00	1.00	1.00	0.01	0.94	0.99	0.00	0.00	0.00
50	1.00	1.00	1.00	0.43	1.00	1.00	0.00	0.13	0.01

Note: All the above statistics are *p*-values except for log-likelihood and the four information criteria.

When the normal density functions for all the MGARCH models were utilised, it was found that only the conditional correlation models such as the Constant Conditional Correlations (CCC) by Bollerslev (1990) and Dynamic Conditional Correlations (DCC) by Tse and Tsui (2002) and Engle (2002) are acceptable compared to other MGARCH models. These three MGARCH models survived the Multivariate Portmanteau tests on the squared residuals proposed by Li and McLeod (1981). It was not possible to estimate RiskMetrics models under MGARCH with normal distribution as there were no parameters which need to be calculated.

The results in Table 5.2 demonstrate the sensitivity of MGARCH models with the underlying density functions. The Student distribution of the MGARCH now enables most of the MGARCH models to pass the Multivariate Portmanteau tests on the squared residuals, with the exception of the three orthogonal MGARCH models. Only DCC models of Tse and Tsui (2002) and Engle (2002) are able to withstand the sensitivity of density functions in both cases. Both the scalar and diagonal BEKK MGARCH models also seem to be mildly sensitive to the change in density functions. The forecasting conditional correlations of these four MGARCH models are presented in Figures 5.1–5.4. Details of MGARCH model estimation and corresponding univariate/multivariate diagnostic tests are reported in Appendix 5.

Implications

Survey articles by Bollerslev *et al.* (1994) and Bauwens *et al.* (2006) are useful sources of information and references for the multivariate GARCH models. The CCC-GARCH model was suggested by Bollerslev (1990), who used it to model European exchange rate data before and after the introduction of the European Monetary System (EMS) and came to the expected conclusion that conditional correlations after the introduction of the EMS were higher. The idea of the DCC model is explored by Engle (2002), Engle and Sheppard (2001) and Tse and Tsui (2002). Fitting in stages is promoted in the formation of Engle and Sheppard (2001) and asymptotic statistical theory for this procedure is given. Hafner and Franses (2003) suggested that the dynamics of CCC are too simple for collections of many asset returns and provide a generalisation.

The more general vector GARCH model is discussed in Engle and Kroner (1995) alongside BEKK model, named after these two authors as well as Baba and Kraft, in Baba *et al.* (1987), who co-authored an earlier unpublished manuscript. There is limited work on statistical properties of QMLEs in multivariate models: Jeantheau (1998) showed consistency for a general formulation and Comte and Liberman (2003) found asymptotic normality for the BEKK formulation.

The multivariate analysis was conducted for the period of 2 January 2006 to 15 January 2014 as BNM imposed capital control and pegged MYR/USD

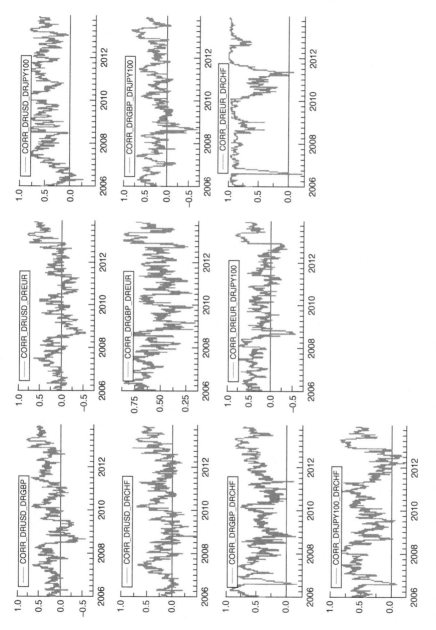

Figure 5.1 Forecasting conditional correlations using scalar BEKK models.

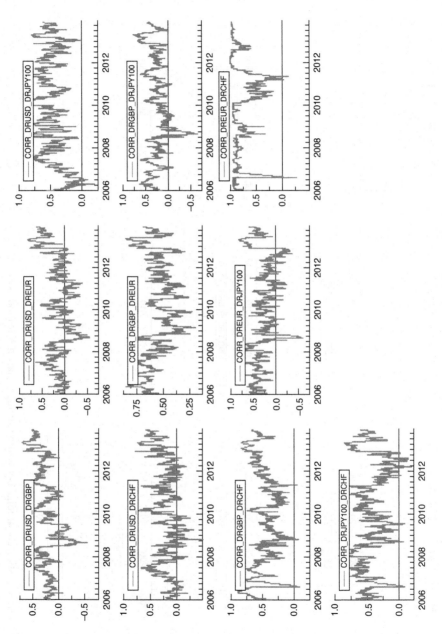

Figure 5.2 Forecasting conditional correlations using diagonal **BEKK** models.

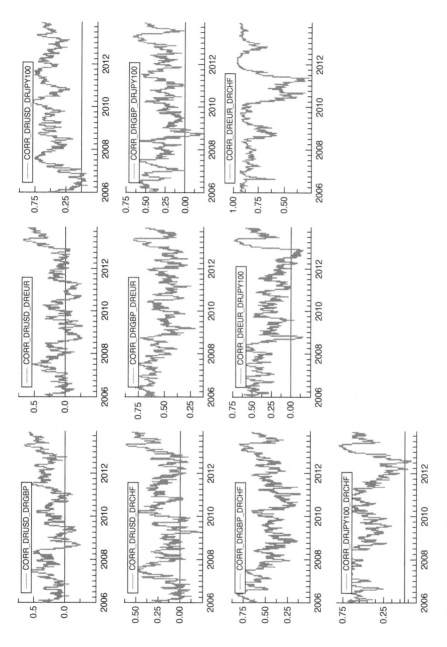

Figure 5.3 Forecasting conditional correlations using DCC (Tse and Tsui) models.

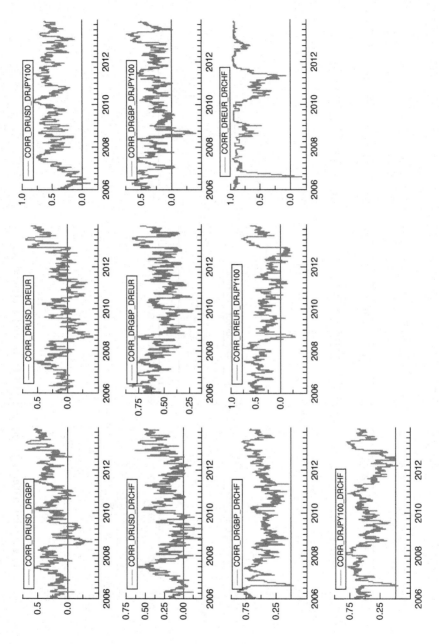

Figure 5.4 Forecasting conditional correlations using DCC (Engle) models.

before that period. Hence, the multivariate analysis for the period of pegged exchange rate is not appropriate. The focus was only on the sensitivity of density functions over the performance of the different MGARCH models as explained in this chapter and on trying to compare with the results of the univariate analysis from Chapter 4. The only alternative density function other than Gaussian function for MGARCH at this moment is Student distribution, whereas skewed Student density function was justified and used in Chapter 4 for univariate analysis.

Tables 5.1 and 5.2 summarise the diagnostic statistics for nine different MGARCH models over the period of 2 January 2006 to 15 January 2014. When the normal density functions for all the MGARCH models were utilised, it was found that only the Conditional Correlation models, like Constant Conditional Correlations (CCC) by Bollerslev (1990) and Dynamic Conditional Correlations (DCC) by Tse and Tsui (2002) and Engle (2002), are acceptable compared to other MGARCH models. These three MGARCH models survived the Multivariate Portmanteau tests on the squared residuals proposed by Li and McLeod (1981). It was not possible to estimate RiskMetrics models under MGARCH with normal distribution as there were no parameters which need to be calculated.

The results in Table 5.2 demonstrated the sensitivity of MGARCH models with the underlying density functions. The Student distribution of the MGARCH now enables most of the MGARCH models to pass the Multivariate Portmanteau tests on the squared residuals, with the exception of the three orthogonal MGARCH models. Only DCC models of Tse and Tsui (2002) and Engle (2002) are able to withstand the sensitivity of density functions in both cases. Both the scalar and diagonal BEKK MGARCH models also seem to be mildly sensitive to the change in density functions.

The conclusion on the discussion of multivariate GARCH models in Chapter 5 is presented in section "Conclusion", which is followed by some concluding remarks of this book in Chapter 6.

Conclusion

Unlike the univariate analysis in Chapter 4, this research is restricted by the current software constraints. There is less flexibility and more restrictions for multivariate in terms of asymmetric effects and non-Gaussian density functions for risk modelling, and there are no meaningful risk measurement statistics like volatility persistency, risk premium and VaR measurements available with the G@RCH module version 5. There are many applied studies that can be extended by MGARCH in the future with better theoretical frameworks and analytical tools available for applied research work.

Evidence deduced from the findings revealed that the sensitivity of MGARCH models is affected by the underlying density functions. The Student distribution of the MGARCH models enables most of the MGARCH models to pass the Multivariate Portmanteau tests on the squared residuals, with the exception of the three orthogonal MGARCH models. It was not possible to estimate RiskMetrics models under MGARCH with normal distribution as there were no parameters which need to be calculated. Only DCC models of Tse and Tsui (2002) and Engle (2002) are able to withstand the sensitivity of density functions in both cases. Both the scalar and diagonal BEKK MGARCH models also seem to be mildly sensitive to the change in density functions.

Applied researchers and investors who are doing research for developing markets may want to consider one or more of the four MGARCH models discussed above to simulate the conditional correlations for the purpose of portfolio analysis. The conclusion is that to model the conditional correlations of the currency pair of a small open economy such as Malaysia it is reasonable to use MGARCH models of DCC models and BEKK models. One however cannot use these MGARCH models for meaningful risk measurements and will need to fall back to univariate GARCH models.

6   Concluding remarks

Introduction

The analysis of exchange rate volatility in terms of risk modelling, followed by risk measurements, was discussed in Chapters 4 and 5 under the univariate and multivariate frameworks, respectively. The emphasis of this chapter will focus on issues and implications of exchange rate risk modelling, measurement and management relating to developing countries.

Some important issues in three different areas of exchange rate risk, as discussed earlier in Chapter 1, are listed below and they are based on the analysis and implications of Chapters 3–5 (see also Lum and Islam 2016a, 2016a, 2016c, and 2016d):

Risk modelling

Exchange rate volatility models

Analysis in Chapter 3 shows that traditional time series model like ARMA and static historical statistics like standard deviations or variance are not appropriate to model the time-varying movements of the daily exchange rates of the five major currency pairs with respect to the Malaysian ringgit. Chapters 4 and 5 provided some discrete stochastic volatility models and there is some evidence that exchange rate volatility can be modelled, but better refinements are required in the future, as normality density functions are not addressed in most cases.

Malaysian exchange rate volatility models

Standard GARCH models with normal density functions and symmetric effects are not suitable for Malaysia due to rejections of the hypotheses for these two areas. GARCH models with skewed Student density functions were utilised instead of EGARCH as leverage effect hypothesis were rejected. For risk measurement issues, these GARCH models with skewed Student density functions provide evidence of change in volatilities across different exchange rate era, no evidence of risk premiums for all five currency pairs, and APARCH models with skewed Student density functions perform better than the popular RiskMetrics models in terms of VaR performances.

Comparison of exchange rate volatility models
with other developing economies

The findings of this book are different from those of Thomas and Shah (1999), as Malaysia yields mixed findings in terms of change in exchange rate volatility during capital control, whereas Thomas and Shah (1999) found that India yielded greater exchange rate risk through a combination of months of fixed prices, followed by very large adjustments. Malaysia did not adjust the pegging of the MYR/USD during capital control, resulting in all currency pairs exhibiting changes in volatility under different exchange rate regimes. The US dollar, British pound and Japanese yen all exhibited greater volatilities, while the euro and Swiss franc demonstrated reduction in volatilities.

Effect of exchange rate liberalisation on models

For the period during which BNM imposed capital control, all currency pairs except the MYR/USD demonstrated GARCH effects in the log difference series, as both the ARCH and GARCH parameters are statistically significant. For the period after BNM relaxed capital control in Malaysia, all currency pairs again demonstrated significant GARCH effects except for the MYR/USD where the ARCH parameter is not statistically significant.

Multivariate vs univariate volatility models

Multivariate models are more restrictive and less flexible compared to univariate models but they do provide additional information on conditional correlations, which is important for portfolio investment analysis as demonstrated in Chapter 3 that the correlations of the different currency pairs changed over time.

Risk measurement

Persistency of exchange rate volatility

Table 4.8 in Chapter 4 summarises the tests for any significant changes in volatility in different exchange regimes using the standard GARCH models with Gaussian or normal density functions. The results showed that all currency pairs exhibited changes in volatility under different exchange rate regime.

Effect on exchange rate volatility post exchange rate liberalisation

The US dollar, British pound and Japanese yen all exhibited greater volatilities, while the euro and Swiss franc demonstrated reduction in volatilities. Only the euro and Japanese yen exhibit asymmetry effects.

Exchange rate risk premium

Analysis, using GARCH-M models, found no significant risk premium across all five currency pairs with respect to Malaysian ringgit. This book also did not find any risk premium across the two different exchange rate eras.

Multivariate vs univariate volatility models

Multivariate GARCH models only provided extra information of conditional correlations, of which the dynamic conditional correlation models are more appropriate compared to the other MGARCH models. These conditional correlations can be used for portfolio analysis.

Risk management

Section "Implications on risk measurement" will combine the analysis of next two sub-sections to link the implications to the following risk management perspectives:

a Government stabilisation policies;
b Individuals and institutions;
c Educational institutions and professional bodies;
d Efficient market hypothesis.

Volatility issues in the exchange rate market

General volatility issues

Some important volatility issues with univariate GARCH modelling, as discussed in Chapter 4, allow one to conduct many extensions such as asymmetric effects and non-Gaussian density functions. In addition to the extension of the popular GARCH models with normal density function and symmetric effects applied in most empirical studies, one can utilise those risk models to carry out meaningful risk measurements for analysis, which are discussed in section "Implications on risk measurement". Analyses in Chapters 4 and 5, however, do not provide any ideal discrete stochastic volatility models to capture the normality of the squared error terms, and hence more research is required in other aspects, such as the possible missing exogenous variables that might be driving the exchange rate volatilities.

GARCH models with Gaussian density functions were first modelled and it was found that both ARCH and GARCH parameters are significant for both periods, implying that GARCH effects are prevalent in all five currency pairs but the normality tests of the error terms failed badly and there seem to be some leverage/asymmetric effects in the MYR/EUR, MYR/JPY and MYR/CHF series.

In order to test for asymmetric effects and the non-normal distribution of the error terms, the non-Gaussian distribution of skewed Student density function was incorporated (see section "Skewed Student distribution" for more details). Lambert and Laurent (2000) applied and extended the skewed Student density function proposed by Fernández and Steel (1998) to the GARCH framework.

The main difference of relaxing the normal distribution and symmetric effects for the log difference or movements of the exchange rate data resulted in higher log-likelihood statistics as well as better information criteria. One of the key findings from Tables 4.4 and 4.5 is that not only are all the ARCH and GARCH parameters statistically significant, but all the tail parameters under the skewed Student distribution are also statistically significant, implying that important information is captured in the tail parameter of the skewed Student distribution. The leverage effect test failed for most exchange rate data, implying that Exponential GARCH (EGARCH) models are not appropriate compared to GARCH models. The asymmetric parameters of the skewed distribution provided mixed results for the different currency pairs. Diagnostic tests of these skewed Student distributions, however, did not significantly improve the normality tests as reported earlier in Tables 4.2 and 4.3.

In conclusion, both hypotheses of normality density functions and symmetric effects are rejected by the findings in section "Empirical results". Chong and Tan (2007) used EGARCH models to estimate the conditional standard deviation for Malaysia and it was found that the leverage tests failed for most currency pairs. GARCH models with skewed Student density function were utilised to address these two issues and they performed relatively better than the standardised GARCH models with normal density function and symmetric effects. It was also found that the tail parameters under the skewed Student distribution are statistically significant, suggesting that important information is captured in the tail parameter of the skewed Student distribution. The asymmetric parameters of the skewed distribution, however, provided mixed findings for the different currency pairs. Finally, diagnostic tests of these skewed Student distribution did not significantly improve the normality tests, implying that skewed Student density functions do not address the non-Gaussian issues.

Multivariate GARCH in the analysis of Chapter 5 is more restrictive in terms of flexibility and restrictions. The multivariate models were analysed for the period of 2 January 2006 to 15 January 2014 as BNM had imposed capital control and pegged MYR/USD before that period; hence, the multivariate analysis for the period of the pegged exchange rate would not be appropriate. This book focused only on the sensitivity of density functions over the performance of the different MGARCH models and on trying to compare with the results from the univariate analysis in Chapter 4. The only alternative density function other than Gaussian function for MGARCH at this moment is Student distribution, whereas skewed Student density function was justified and used in Chapter 4 for univariate analysis.

Tables 5.1 and 5.2 summarise the diagnostic statistics for nine different MGARCH models over the period of 2 January 2006 to 15 January 2014. When the normal density functions for all the MGARCH models were utilised, only the conditional correlation models, like Constant Conditional Correlations (CCC) by Bollerslev (1990) and Dynamic Conditional Correlations (DCC) by Tse and Tsui (2002) and Engle (2002), performed better than other MGARCH models. These three MGARCH models survived the Multivariate Portmanteau tests on the squared residuals proposed by Li and McLeod (1981).

The results in Table 5.2 demonstrated the sensitivity of MGARCH models with the underlying density functions. The Student distribution of the MGARCH now enables most of the MGARCH models to pass the Multivariate Portmanteau tests on the squared residuals, with the exception of the three orthogonal MGARCH models. Only DCC models of Tse and Tsui (2002) and Engle (2002) are able to withstand the sensitivity of density functions in both cases. Both the scalar and diagonal BEKK MGARCH models are also mildly sensitive to the change in density functions. In conclusion, MGARCH models are not able to provide risk measurements in terms of volatility persistency, risk premium and VaR except for the conditional correlations between the different currency pairs. The better MGARCH models can generate these conditional correlations, as discussions in Chapter 3 revealed that correlations between the different currency pairs changed over time. These conditional correlations will be important for investment portfolio in different currency pairs. More detailed analysis of exchange rate volatilities will have to be conducted using the methodologies discussed in Chapter 4.

Malaysia issues

Tan and Chong (2008) found that for Malaysia, the exchange rate volatilities were reduced when Malaysia switched from a managed float to a pegged system. They used various GARCH models with normal distributions to test for changes in volatility of the different macroeconomic variables. They then found that inappropriate exchange rate regime switch may worsen macroeconomic instability, especially in small open developing countries, even though there may be other contributing factors such as political and social unrest.

This book, however, focuses on exchange rate volatilities of Malaysia, and hence reference to the study of Chong and Tan (2007) is more appropriate. Chong and Tan (2007) applied the exponential GARCH (EGARCH) approach developed by Nelson (1991) to measure the exchange rate volatility instead of the level of exchange rate. The reason behind EGARCH is that it is able to account for asymmetric effect. Kim (1998) and Bond and Najand (2002) utilised the same method in computing exchange rate volatility. The empirical results in section "Empirical results", however, rejected EGARCH models when compared to GARCH models by running leverage tests.

The findings are different from those of Thomas and Shah (1999), as Malaysia yielded mixed findings in terms of change in exchange rate volatility during capital control, whereas Thomas and Shah (1999) found that India yielded greater exchange rate risk through a combination of months of fixed prices followed by very large adjustments. Malaysia did not adjust the pegging of the MYR/USD during the capital control, resulting in all currency pairs exhibiting change in volatilities under different exchange rate regimes. The US dollar, British pound and Japanese yen all exhibited greater volatilities, while the euro and Swiss franc demonstrated reduction in volatilities.

Chapter 4 provided evidence which revealed that skewed Student density functions perform better than Gaussian distribution as the former distribution captures asymmetric and tail parameters. Tail parameters are significant across all currency pairs across both exchange rate regimes, implying that important information is captured in the tail parameters, and hence it is fruitful for one to focus on the tail distribution such as extreme value theory.

The empirical findings of this book are also influenced by the characteristics of the developing Malaysian market, which can be classified under three major headings: (1) characteristics specific to the Malaysian ringgit such as the relatively low trading volume and restrictive trading by central banks in international foreign exchange market, (2) general market-related characteristics and (3) underdeveloped financial systems.

Implications on risk measurement

Thomas and Shah (1999) used GARCH models to calculate a risk measurement of Value-at-Risk and found that the volatility of the Dollar-Indian Rupee exchange rate dropped when there was economic liberalisation in India. This reduction in volatility illustrated the idea that a regime with price flexibility provided more realistic signals about price volatility to economic agents, and could actually yield less risk when compared to a regime with the illusion of zero price changes, punctuated by sharp movements.

Chong and Tan (2007) concluded that exchange rate volatility and relative macroeconomic factors move together to achieve long-run equilibrium in Malaysia. Tan and Chong (2008) found that for Malaysia, switching from the managed float to the pegged system successfully reduced the volatilities, and hence they strongly support central banks of small open developing economies to adopt a more fixed, rather than a more flexible system. The empirical findings of this study on risk measurement will next be compared with the above findings.

Univariate stochastic volatility modelling

The empirical results showed that all currency pairs exhibited changes in volatility under different exchange rate regimes. The US dollar, British pound and Japanese yen all exhibited greater volatilities, while the euro and Swiss franc demonstrated reduction in volatilities. Tan and Chong (2008) found that using GARCH models, the volatilities of most macroeconomic variables reduced significantly, except for export in the case of Malaysia after BNM relaxed capital control. The choice of conditional models does not change the implications that while MYR/USD, MYR/GBP and MYR/JPY all exhibited increase in volatility after BNM relaxed capital control, MYR/EUR and MYR/CHF demonstrated reduced volatility after exchange rate liberalisation in Malaysia.

The popular risk measurement of Value-at-Risk, which is discussed in depth by Jorion (2000), was analysed. Asymmetric effects are not significant across all currency pairs when BNM imposed capital control, while MYR/EUR, MYR/JPY and MYR/CHF all exhibited asymmetric effects post exchange rate liberalisation when BNM removed capital control for Malaysia. It was found earlier under section "Empirical results" that only MYR/JPY and MYR/CHF exhibited asymmetric effects during periods after BNM relaxed capital control in Malaysia. Tail distributions continued to be significant for all currency pairs regardless of the exchange rate regime, which are very similar to findings in section "Empirical results" earlier.

RiskMetrics is found to be not superior to GARCH models with skewed Student density functions as discussed in section "Empirical results". Nevertheless, following Giot and Laurent (2003), RiskMetrics models with skewed Student density functions were used as the benchmark for the purpose of evaluating VaR performances. RiskMetrics models performed well under controlled exchange rate environment, but relatively badly with more rejections of the null hypothesis that the failure rate is equal to the chosen level of confidence level, which is even more relevant for short positions than long positions, when BNM abolished capital control.

This book followed Giot and Laurent (2003) and applied APARCH models with skewed Student density functions and found that APARCH models performed relatively better than RiskMetrics (see Table 4.13). VaR performance under APARCH models improved for long positions even after BNM relaxed capital control and was also relatively better than RiskMetrics for short positions for both different periods.

Multivariate stochastic volatility modelling

McNeil *et al.* (2010) found that vector GARCH is of purely theoretical interest due to parsimoniousness of the parametrisation issue while BEKK is of very low dimensional use and the rest of the MGARCH models are the most practically useful. MGARCH models can also be useful for portfolio analysis when more than one currency pairs are involved.

The sensitivity of MGARCH models was found to be affected by the underlying density functions. The Student distribution of the MGARCH models enabled most of the MGARCH models to pass the Multivariate Portmanteau tests on the squared residuals, with the exception of the three orthogonal MGARCH models.

It was not possible to estimate RiskMetrics models under MGARCH with normal distribution as there were no parameters which need to be calculated. Only DCC models of Tse and Tsui (2002) and Engle (2002) were able to withstand the sensitivity of density functions in both cases. Both the scalar and diagonal BEKK MGARCH models also seemed to be mildly sensitive to the change in density functions.

Applied researchers and investors who conducted research for developing markets may want to consider one or more of the four MGARCH models discussed above to simulate the conditional correlations for the purpose of portfolio analysis.

Implications on risk management

Many empirical studies documented in the literature found that risk management is especially important in today's globalised world, where all markets are interconnected with one another. Thomas and Shah (1999) found that market institutions in India, which offer insurance and derivatives, are highly undeveloped. Alongside this development, firms and individuals need to obtain the skills required in risk measurement and derivatives. When firms and individuals are equipped with these knowledge and tools, price volatility will generate a smaller outcry in the public media. This transition will generate welfare gains, and pave the way for volatility-enhancing economic reforms.

As mentioned before, Tan and Chong (2008) found that for Malaysia the exchange rate volatilities were reduced when it switched from a managed float to a pegged system. Their empirical evidence provided support for central banks of small open economies to adopt a more fixed system, such as the managed float system or pegged system, rather than a more flexible one, such as an independent system. They, however, also acknowledged that a pegged system would easily and most probably be undervalued or overvalued in the medium and long run, which may carry significant economic and social costs. Risk management issues, relating to the findings and implications of sections "Volatility issues in the exchange rate market" and "Implications on risk measurement", are discussed below under four different aspects and broken into controlled and liberalised exchange rate eras. This chapter concludes with the discussion on some limitations of this book and provides some areas for further research in the future.

Government stabilisation policy

The financial crisis in East Asia has become the focal point of reference for critics of the IMF. East Asia was held to be the model economies by the

IMF before the crises occurred and currency crises were driven by exchange rates that were fixed to the dollar. When the dollar appreciated significantly in the mid-1990s, these countries' currencies became overvalued relative to regional trading partners. The IMF imposed programmes of structural adjustment and austerity. Economic conditions of these countries actually deteriorated after the IMF became involved and exchange rates also became more volatile. The analysis and implications of this book suggested that volatilities can be modelled and studied with the proper adjustments to the normal GARCH models including tail distributions and skewed Student density functions especially for developing countries which imposed capital controls or any structural breaks such as Malaysia. Hence, the central banks or IMF can use some of these revised discrete stochastic volatility models to help simulate some scenarios for policy-making decisions and avoid creating time-dependent adverse exchange rate movements in the future. The rejections of risk premiums in the exchange rate market do not imply that pricing of risk is not relevant but there are other macroeconomic or other factors that the IMF has to take into consideration. There are also mixed outcomes for different currency pairs post exchange rate liberalisation, and hence the government central banks and IMF will have to be more selective in monitoring different currency movements in the future.

The lack of long memory for the Malaysian exchange rate markets is in contrast with those findings from the stock market of Taylor (1986), Schwert (1990) and Ding *et al.* (1993) who indicated that there were substantially more correlations between absolute returns than squared returns, a stylised fact of high-frequency financial returns. This shows that central banks or IMF will need to address/manage more actively on the external shocks in the exchange rate markets, especially for developing markets. The central banks and IMF should also put more effort to dwell into the tail distribution of the exchange rates as they are found to be always statistical significant and will provide important information for future risk management purpose.

Gencay and Selcuk (2004) applied extreme value theory to generate the value-at-risk estimates for daily stock return of nine developing markets. They found that certain moments of the return distributions did not exist in some countries. In addition, daily return distributions have different moment properties at their right and left tails. Therefore, risk and reward are not equally likely in these economies. Other studies that incorporate extreme value theory to estimate volatility and value-at-risk include Bali (2003) and Gilli (2006).

Individuals and institutions

Financial development helps borrowers and lenders hedge, pool and diversify risk. Risk is an integral part of financial transactions because of imperfect and asymmetric information. One of the fundamental functions of financial systems is to transfer risk from people who prefer more certainty to those who are willing to tolerate more risk if they are compensated for it.

Financial systems fulfil this function through hedging, pooling and diversifying risk. The more that risk can be transferred efficiently from those who want to avoid it to those who are willing to accept it, the more economic activities will take place. Studies that focus on strategies to manage the exchange rate risks include Allayannis *et al.* (2001) that split them into financial and operational strategies; Bartram *et al.* (2010) discussed various types of exchange rate exposures and found that financial hedges are more effective in reducing exposures than operational hedging.

This book does not follow the traditional view of managing exchange rate risks via hedging using financial derivatives or natural hedging techniques as there are many standard textbooks that will explain on those techniques and issues. Instead, this book provided a systematic process for individuals and private institutions to manage not only exchange rate risks by looking at the first moment but also other higher moments as conditional variance and other higher moments can be captured, modelled and used for investment portfolio or risk management purposes.

Risk measurements can be improved with the application of APARCH to skewed Student density functions compared to the popular RiskMetrics models. Post exchange rate liberalisation, some exchange rates are more volatile than others, and hence more active risk management tools using financial instruments such as derivatives or natural hedging by individuals and institutions will be important in the future.

Finally, more complex risk models like APARCH with skewed Student density functions will provide better VaR, and hence the need for education on risk management for individuals and managers of institutions will also be more important in the future. APARCH models enable one to differentiate currencies that are safe haven and can be very useful especially in a turbulent external macroeconomic environment.

Education institutions and professional bodies

As explained above, there is a need for individuals and managers of institutions to better equip themselves with more advanced and complex risk models in order to calculate more accurate risk measures and have more effective risk management strategies to overcome any adverse exchange rate movements in the future. There are now many graduate schools in the region that understand this trend and are designing more quantitative-based education focusing on quantitative risk management. Professional accounting bodies are also ensuring that risk management is part of their syllabi, so that all professional accountants are better equipped to deal with financial risk management in the future.

Non-profit organisations of professional financial risk management, such as the Global Association of Risk Professionals (GARP), are also pioneers and helping members of the financial risk management industry to have a solid platform to share their experiences. GARP provides many risk accreditations for risk professionals around the world like Financial Risk Manager (FRM) and Energy Risk Professional (ERP). It also works very closely with many universities around the world to collaborate with them on financial risk management content especially for postgraduate students. GARP also delivers critical risk intelligences to ensure that the risk professional community has the very latest intelligence to make informed decisions.

The drivers for more risk professionals in the future are: (1) there are still many things risk managers do not know; (2) the world is becoming more inter-connected and hence risks are becoming more complicated; (3) technology is a two-edged sword: it can provide users with more power to run more complicated models but the same is also true for the financial markets which are getting deals done in faster, bigger and more complicated manner.

Efficient market hypothesis

The term "efficient market hypothesis" (EMH) was first coined by Fama (1970) and has been applied in many empirical studies in different financial markets. For example, Islam *et al.* (2007) studied the EMH of the Thailand stock market. Jensen (1978) defines a market as efficient with respect to information set X_t if it is impossible to make economic profits by trading on the basis of information set X_t. A capital market is said to be efficient if it fully and correctly reflects all relevant information in determining security prices. Formally, the market is said to be efficient with respect to some information set, X_t, if security prices would be unaffected by revealing that information to all participants. Moreover, efficiency with respect to an information set, X_t, implies that it is impossible to make economic profits by trading on the basis of X_t.

Three forms of market efficiency are commonly entertained in the EMH literature based on the set of variables contained in the information set, X_t, as documented by Fama (1970). If X_t only comprises past and current asset prices (as well as possibly dividends and variables such as trading volume), the EMH in its weak form is being tested. Expanding X_t to include all publicly available information gives rise to the EMH in its semi-strong form. Finally, if all public and private information is included in X_t, market efficiency in the strong form is being tested.

The efficient market hypothesis gives rise to forecasting tests that mirror those adopted when testing the optimality of a forecast in the context of a given information set. However, there are also important differences arising from the fact that market efficiency tests rely on establishing profitable trading opportunities in "real time". Forecasters constantly search for predictable patterns and affect prices when they attempt to exploit trading opportunities. Stable forecasting patterns are therefore unlikely to persist for long periods of time and will self-destruct when discovered by a large number of investors. This gives rise to nonstationarities in the time series of financial returns and complicates both formal tests of market efficiency and the search for successful forecasting approaches.

Surveys of market efficiency such as Fama (1970, 1991) have focused on testing informational efficiency. Fama (1970) concludes that the empirical evidence is largely supportive of weak form and semi-strong form efficiency, while Fama (1991) reports stronger evidence of predictability in returns based on both lagged values of returns and publicly available information.

Timmermann and Granger (2004) highlighted that an important weakness of the earlier definitions of market efficiency is that they do not account for investors' uncertainty about the "best" model to use when forecasting future returns. In reality, investors face the difficult task of choosing a specific forecasting model or combining a subset of forecasting models from a huge, possibly infinite-dimensional, space of potential forecasting models. This fundamental uncertainty about the best or even moderately successful prediction model is also the reason why predictability can exist in local "pockets in time". Investors with heterogeneous beliefs and information simultaneously search for forecasting models that might work for some time.

Many researchers have attempted to reject the EMH by presenting evidence that a particular model could forecast financial returns over a given sample period. However, conditioning on a specific model, $m_{it}{}^* \in M_t$, and showing that it could have been used to forecast asset returns is insufficient to disprove the EMH. Individual forecasting models are likely to go through stages of success, declining value and disappearance. The difficulty of selecting a successful forecasting model is of course compounded by the extremely noisy nature of most financial return series.

There is now substantial evidence that volatility of asset returns varies over time in a way that can be partially predicted. For this reason, there has been considerable interest in improved volatility forecasting models in the context of option pricing; see e.g. Engle *et al.* (1993). Does this violate market efficiency? Clearly the answer is no unless a trading strategy could be designed that would use this information in the options markets to identify under- and over-valued options. If options markets are efficient, option prices should incorporate the best volatility forecasts at all points in time.

The identified implications of volatility modelling in this book are that the popular GARCH models with normal distributions are not appropriate and will need to be adjusted for asymmetric effects as well as to focus on tail distributions. The book however finds no significance in the leverage effects for all the five currency pairs.

The analysis of this book strongly supported the evidence of volatility clustering, using Malaysia as a case study and compared it with other developing countries. There is volatility persistency post liberalisation and some exchange rates exhibit an increase in volatility for the case of Malaysia. No significant risk pricing was found in this study. All the above findings, however, do not refute the EMH but re-emphasise the importance of EMH, as there are still no perfect models to explain some of the stylised facts such as fat tails of the exchange rate volatilities and asymmetric effects. Market imperfections are common issues, especially for small open economies and developing markets such as Malaysia; hence, there are opportunities to study these characteristics in more depth and one can have a more comprehensive understanding of the risk management of the exchange rate in the future. This opportunity to continuously research and discover new models and theories to better understand the dynamics of asset return is reflecting the importance of education and continuous professional development in risk management, as discussed in the previous sub-section.

Limitations and areas of further research

The limitations of this research can be classified into two main areas for future researchers to explore. The first limitation is data issues. This book has used five major currencies with respect to the Malaysian ringgit. However, one can include different countries such as other ASEAN countries and currencies such as the Chinese Yuan. The former is relevant due to the ASEAN Economic Community, while the latter is due to the recent rise of China's global influence as well as gradual internationalisation of the Chinese Renminbi in recent years. Daily exchange rates were used as monthly exchange rate data did not provide much evidence of GARCH effects. One can investigate the stochastic volatilities in higher frequencies or even branch out into continuous stochastic volatility instead of discrete stochastic volatility.

These data issues lead to the second area of possible extensions of this research's volatility modelling. Future researchers can focus on the many extensions of discrete stochastic volatility modelling applied in this book, for examples, to include copulas, copulas GARCH and continuous stochastic volatility modelling. One can also use Bayesian concepts and apply the learning process to estimate GARCH models. Significant tail distributions were found in all estimations, and hence more in-depth analysis for tail density functions will be crucial and extreme value theory can be applied to provide complementary information. Finally, one can also explore non-parametric estimation of exchange rate volatility to overcome the issues of parametric estimation. In conclusion, there are still many gaps to be filled for one to fully understand risk modelling, risk measurements and risk management. The limitations of this book, however, provide many opportunities for academics and professionals to explore in the future and to develop better understanding of risk management theories and framework.

Conclusion

This book provided an in-depth analysis and attempted to answer some important questions posed, in terms of risk modelling, risk measurement and risk management, focusing on the exchange rate markets of small open economies and developing markets, using Malaysia as a case study due to the many special and unique characteristics discussed earlier in this book.

For risk modelling, both hypotheses of normality density functions and symmetric effects are rejected by the findings in section "Empirical results". Chong and Tan (2007) used EGARCH models to estimate the conditional standard deviation for Malaysia and it was found that the leverage tests failed for most currency pairs. GARCH models with skewed Student density function were utilised to address these two issues and they performed relatively better than the standardised GARCH models with normal density function and symmetric effects. The tail parameters under the skewed Student distribution are found to be statistically significant, implying that important information is captured in the tail parameter of the skewed Student distribution. The asymmetric parameters of the skewed distribution, however, provided mixed results for the different currency pairs. Finally, diagnostic tests of these skewed Student distributions did not significantly improve the normality tests, implying that skewed Student density functions did not address non-Gaussian issues. Multivariate GARCH in the analysis in Chapter 5 was more restrictive in terms of flexibility and restrictions. Only DCC models of Tse and Tsui (2002) and Engle (2002) were able to withstand the sensitivity of density functions in both cases. Both the scalar and diagonal BEKK MGARCH models were also mildly sensitive to the change in density functions. In conclusion, MGARCH models are not able to provide risk measurements in terms of volatility persistency, risk premium and VaR except for the conditional correlations between the different currency pairs. The better MGARCH models can generate these conditional correlations, as the discussions in Chapter 3 revealed that correlations between the different currency pairs changed over time. These conditional correlations will be important for investment portfolio in different currency pairs.

The findings of this book are different from those of Thomas and Shah (1999), as Malaysia yielded mixed findings in terms of change in exchange rate volatility during capital control, whereas Thomas and Shah (1999) found that India yielded greater exchange rate risk through a combination of months of fixed prices, followed by very large adjustments. Malaysia did not adjust the pegging of the MYR/USD during capital control, resulting in all currency pairs exhibiting changes in volatility under different exchange rate regimes. The US dollar, British pound and Japanese yen all exhibited greater volatilities, while the euro and Swiss franc demonstrated reduction in volatilities with respect to the Malaysian ringgit.

Chapter 4 provided evidence that skewed Student density functions perform better than Gaussian distribution as the former distribution captures asymmetric and tail parameters. Tail parameters are significant across all currency pairs and across both exchange rate regimes, suggesting that important information is captured in the tail parameters, and hence it is fruitful for one to focus on the tail distribution such as extreme value theory.

RiskMetrics models are not superior to GARCH models with skewed Student density functions, as discussed in section "Empirical results". Nevertheless, following Giot and Laurent (2003), RiskMetrics models with skewed Student density function were used as the benchmark for the purpose of evaluating VaR performances. RiskMetrics models performed well under controlled exchange rate environments but relatively badly with more rejections of the null hypothesis and the failure rate is equal to the chosen level of confidence level, which is even more relevant for short positions than for long positions, when BNM abolished capital control. Following Giot and Laurent (2003), this book applied APARCH models with skewed Student density functions and found that APARCH models performed relatively better than RiskMetrics. VaR performance under APARCH models improved for long positions even after BNM relaxed capital control and was also relatively better than RiskMetrics for short positions in both periods.

The empirical findings of this book are influenced by the characteristics of the developing Malaysian exchange rate market, which can be classified under three major headings: (1) characteristics specific to the Malaysian ringgit, such as the relatively low trading volume and restrictive trading by central banks in international foreign exchange markets; (2) general market-related characteristics and (3) underdeveloped financial systems. These three characteristics, which are also common to many developing countries, help to explain some of the empirical findings of this book and also help build new theories in this area.

There are three new academic contributions and theories that can be derived from this book and can provide new insights into the study of exchange rate volatility, especially for developing countries. There are strong pieces of evidences to support that Asymmetric Power ARCH (APARCH) models, introduced by Ding *et al.* (1993), perform better than the popular RiskMetrics models, regardless of exchange rate eras. Giot and Laurent (2003) found that APARCH models with skewed Student density functions perform similar to RiskMetrics when applying to stock markets. Exchange rate volatility models with skewed Student density, rather than Gaussian density, are also more suitable for modelling exchange rate volatility models for developing countries. Finally, there are no significant relationships between conditional mean and conditional risk for the developing countries' exchange rate markets. This does not mean that risk is not important in the exchange rate markets. On the contrary, forecasting the risk for exchange rate is useful for portfolio decisions, risk management and option pricing.

This chapter can be concluded by relating the implications discussed above to exchange rate risk modelling, measurement and management. There are many market imperfections for developing countries, and hence a more balanced approach, using both quantitative and qualitative analyses, to risk management for exchange rate in the future is proposed. Systematic development of human capital in the exchange rate risk management area will help bridge the gaps between what one thinks one knows today and what one needs to know in the future.

Appendix 1

Foreign exchange changes in Malaysia on 1 April 2005

Key areas:

1   Forward foreign exchange contracts by residents and non-residents
2   Maintenance of foreign currency accounts by residents and conversion of Ringgit into foreign currency for credit into FCA
3   Domestic credit facilities to non-resident–controlled companies
4   Investment abroad by individuals, unit trust management companies and resident insurance companies
5   Foreign currency credit facilities
6   Activities by approved operational headquarters

Summary of some of the changes:

1   Unit trust companies will be allowed to invest up to 30% of the NAV overseas (current 10%).
2   Fund managers may invest up to 30% of funds of resident clients with domestic credit facilities (current 10%).
3   Individuals without domestic credit facilities are free to invest abroad in foreign currency from their own foreign currency or conversion of ringgit funds.
4   Individuals with domestic credit facilities may invest abroad any amount of their foreign currency funds or conversion of ringgit up to RM100,000 per annum.
5   Individuals are free to open foreign currency accounts (FCAs) onshore and offshore without prior permission from BNM.
6   No limit on the amount of foreign currency funds which individual is able to retain onshore or offshore.
7   For education or overseas employment purposes, individuals can convert up to USD150,000 (previously USD100,000) for credit into FCA onshore or offshore in Labuan and up to USD50,000 into an overseas FCA (need approval previously).

8 Aggregate limit for foreign currency borrowing by individuals is increased to RM10 million, while corporations may obtain foreign currency credit facilities up to RM50 million.
9 Foreign currency borrowing by individuals used to finance overseas investment is increased from RM5 million to RM10 million.
10 Transactions that need to be registered include remittance of funds from Malaysia that exceeds RM50,000 and the procurement of foreign currency credit facilities exceeding RM1 million.

Source: http://www.bnm.gov.my and http://www.sc.com.my

Appendix 2
Analysis of monthly exchange rate data

From Figure A2.1, we can see that all the log return series do not exhibit any trends and intercept and we now found that all of them are stationary as the null hypotheses of unit root are all rejected.

Table A2.2 provides the descriptive statistics for the natural logarithm of the first difference of the nominal exchange rates. One interesting note from the table is that there were negative correlations for some currency parings before the financial crisis but after the crisis all the correlations are positive. So there were some arbitrage opportunities available in the exchange market in Malaysia, and hence the crisis took place.

The above analysis has provided us with a big picture that correlations among the different currency pairs are not constant and from the diagrams there seems to be volatility clustering for all the currency pairs. It can be seen that the currencies are highly correlated within each geographical location from Panel A. This is, however, not true if they are broken into the two sub-periods of pre- and post-crisis, as reflected in Panels B and C. The

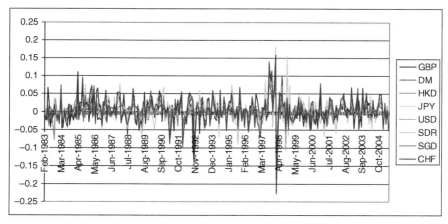

Data source: Bank Negara Malaysia

Figure A2.1 Natural logarithm of the first difference of the nominal exchange rates.

Table A2.1 Basic statistics of the raw nominal monthly foreign exchange rates

N = 269	**Panel A: Full sample**							
January 1983 to May 2005	*GBP*	*DM*	*HKD*	*JPY*	*USD*	*SDR*	*SGD*	*CHF*
Mean	4.7947	1.6397	0.3853	0.0236	2.9893	3.9784	1.7082	1.9956
Standard deviations	1.1403	0.4310	0.0770	0.0080	0.6069	0.9845	0.4239	0.5682
Correlations *GBP*	1							
DM	0.9016	1						
HKD	0.9115	0.7686	1					
JPY	0.8525	0.9050	0.8448	1				
USD	0.9146	0.7754	0.9965	0.8532	1			
SDR	0.9545	0.9423	0.9288	0.9586	0.9347	1		
SGD	0.8644	0.8936	0.8892	0.9485	0.8918	0.9582	1	
CHF	0.9222	0.9868	0.8240	0.9246	0.8302	0.9657	0.9141	1

N = 174	**Panel B: Pre-Asian financial crisis**							
January 1983 to June 1997	*GBP*	*DM*	*HKD*	*JPY*	*USD*	*SDR*	*SGD*	*CHF*
Mean	4.0671	1.4137	0.3302	0.0188	2.5555	3.3323	1.4361	1.6686
Standard deviations	0.5541	0.3159	0.0149	0.0054	0.1255	0.4858	0.2501	0.3648
Correlations *GBP*	1							
DM	0.7448	1						
HKD	0.6835	0.5634	1					
JPY	0.5243	0.9132	0.4474	1				
USD	0.7222	0.6225	0.8694	0.5222	1			
SDR	0.7536	0.9858	0.6247	0.9380	0.7023	1		
SGD	0.4185	0.8488	0.3795	0.8880	0.4146	0.8512	1	
CHF	0.7170	0.9874	0.5219	0.9150	0.5821	0.9703	0.8389	1

N = 81	**Panel C: Post-Asian financial crisis**							
September 1998 to May 2005	*GBP*	*DM*	*HKD*	*JPY*	*USD*	*SDR*	*SGD*	*CHF*
Mean	6.1338	2.0527	0.4880	0.0332	3.8000	5.1967	2.1987	2.6099
Standard deviations	0.5582	0.2790	0.0012	0.0023	0.0000	0.3086	0.0683	0.3377
Correlations *GBP*	1							
DM	0.9610	1						
HKD	0.2683	0.3361	1					
JPY	0.5934	0.4762	0.1067	1				
USD	0.0000	0.0000	0.0000	0.0000	1			
SDR	0.9798	0.9750	0.2615	0.6458	0.0000	1		
SGD	0.7875	0.7549	0.4930	0.7112	0.0000	0.7969	1	
CHF	0.9303	0.9752	0.1834	0.4047	0.0000	0.9462	0.6481	1

Data source: Bank Negara Malaysia.

Table A2.2 Basic statistics of the natural logarithm of the first difference of the nominal exchange rates

N = 268	**Panel A: Full sample**							
February 1983 to May 2005	*GBP*	*DM*	*HKD*	*JPY*	*USD*	*SDR*	*SGD*	*CHF*
Mean	0.0025	0.0035	0.0013	0.0049	0.0019	0.0031	0.0027	0.0037
Standard deviations	0.0360	0.0366	0.0247	0.0370	0.0237	0.0258	0.0185	0.0383
Correlations *GBP*	1							
DM	0.7784	1						
HKD	0.5291	0.5060	1					
JPY	0.5669	0.6559	0.4721	1				
USD	0.5363	0.5095	0.9569	0.4996	1			
SDR	0.8035	0.8912	0.7454	0.7898	0.7695	1		
SGD	0.6199	0.6491	0.7511	0.6825	0.7756	0.8023	1	
CHF	0.7712	0.9537	0.4781	0.6879	0.4860	0.8686	0.6326	1

N = 173	**Panel B: Pre-Asian financial crisis**							
February 1983 to June 1997	*GBP*	*DM*	*HKD*	*JPY*	*USD*	*SDR*	*SGD*	*CHF*
Mean	0.0011	0.0026	−0.0004	0.0048	0.0006	0.0020	0.0027	0.0024
Standard deviations	0.0324	0.0303	0.0146	0.0301	0.0119	0.0170	0.0119	0.0334
Correlations *GBP*	1							
DM	0.6954	1						
HKD	0.0197	−0.0044	1					
JPY	0.4345	0.5778	−0.0295	1				
USD	−0.0154	−0.0564	0.7957	0.0017	1			
SDR	0.7183	0.8684	0.2191	0.7354	0.2463	1		
SGD	0.3809	0.3836	0.4494	0.4356	0.5266	0.5672	1	
CHF	0.6960	0.9254	−0.0261	0.6322	−0.0598	0.8400	0.4012	1

N = 80	**Panel C: Post-Asian financial crisis**							
October 1998 to May 2005	*GBP*	*DM*	*HKD*	*JPY*	*USD*	*SDR*	*SGD*	*CHF*
Mean	0.0007	0.0003	−0.0013	0.0020	−0.0013	0.0002	−0.0005	0.0008
Standard deviations	0.0221	0.0292	0.0116	0.0333	0.0116	0.0154	0.0144	0.0295
Correlations *GBP*	1							
DM	0.6592	1						
HKD	0.2283	0.1477	1					
JPY	0.1762	0.3509	0.2196	1				
USD	N.A.	N.A.	N.A.	N.A.	1			
SDR	0.6326	0.8828	0.2363	0.6540	N.A.	1		
SGD	0.2931	0.5252	0.1633	0.6456	N.A.	0.6120	1	
CHF	0.6307	0.9557	0.3039	0.3960	N.A.	0.8603	0.5240	1

Data source: Bank Negara Malaysia.

Asian currencies, with respect to the Malaysian ringgit, are found to be less correlated with one another. They, however, exhibit the lowest deviations outside the crisis period. Finally, it can be seen in Panel C that the unconditional second moments have been reduced for all currencies except for the British pound and the correlations for most pairings of currencies have also reduced compared to the pre-crisis period.

Analysis of the exchange rates in more detail using daily series and more recent data from 2 January 1997 to 28 February 2014 is carried out in Chapter 4. The reason for using more recent data is that old data prior to 1997 are not relevant to today's development and we compensate the shortening of the data by using daily instead of monthly data. The Singapore dollar and the Special Drawing Rights were dropped in Chapter 4, to focus on the major currencies in terms of trading volumes, and have also replaced the Deutsche mark with the euro with the formation of Eurozone. The rest of the book focuses on using more recent data and daily data (see Chapters 4 and 5 for more details on the estimation and results).

Appendix 3

Forecasting diagrams of various GARCH models

MYR/USD

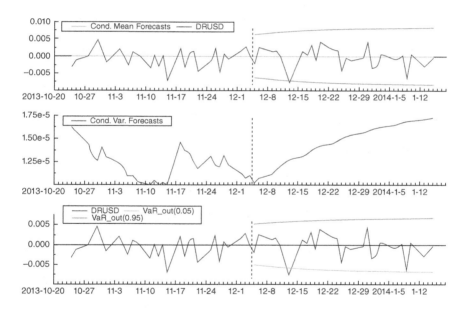

Figure A3.1 Forecasting GARCH(1,1) with normal distribution for MYR/USD.

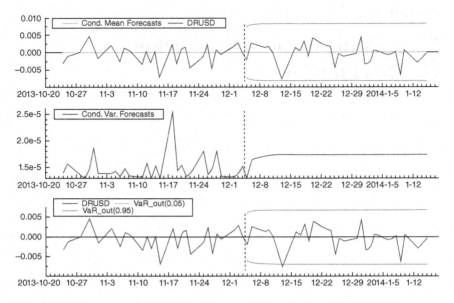

Figure A3.2 Forecasting ARCH(1) with normal distribution for MYR/USD.

MYR/GBP

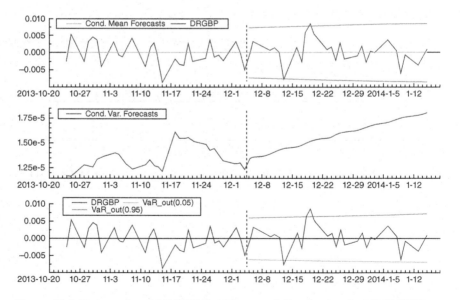

Figure A3.3 Forecasting GARCH(1,1) with normal distribution for MYR/GBP.

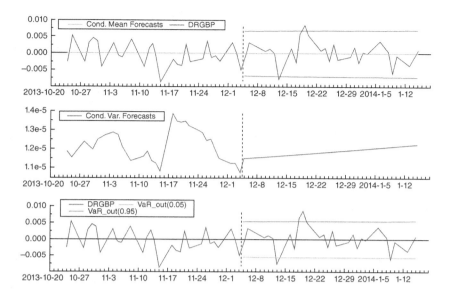

Figure A3.4 Forecasting GARCH(1,1) with skewed Student distribution for MYR/GBP.

MYR/EUR

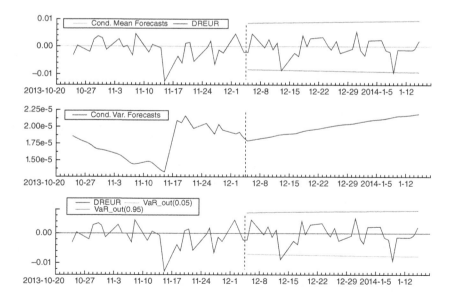

Figure A3.5 Forecasting GARCH(1,1) with normal distribution for MYR/EUR.

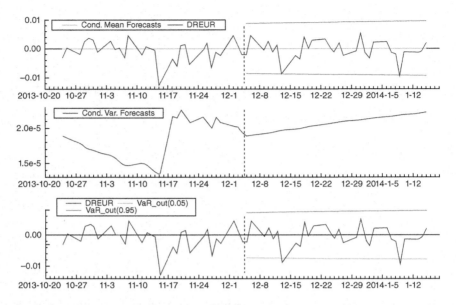

Figure A3.6 Forecasting GJR with normal distribution for MYR/EUR.

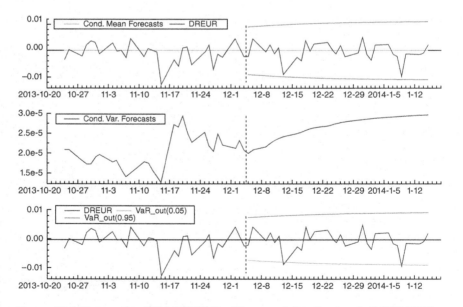

Figure A3.7 Forecasting EGARCH(1,1) with normal distribution for MYR/EUR.

MYR/JPY

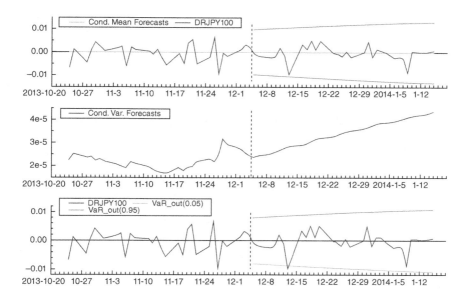

Figure A3.8 Forecasting GARCH(1,1) with normal distribution for MYR/JPY.

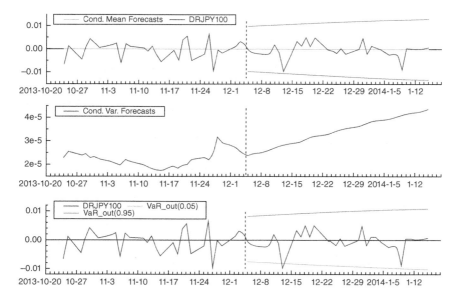

Figure A3.9 Forecasting GARCH(1,1) with skewed Student distribution for MYR/JPY.

MYR/CHF

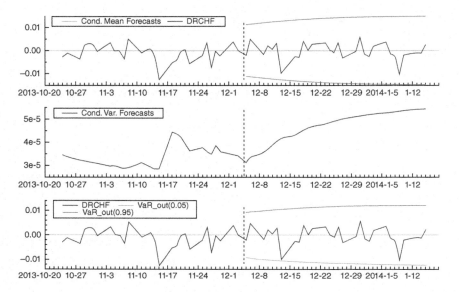

Figure A3.10 Forecasting GARCH (1,1) with normal distribution for MYR/CHF.

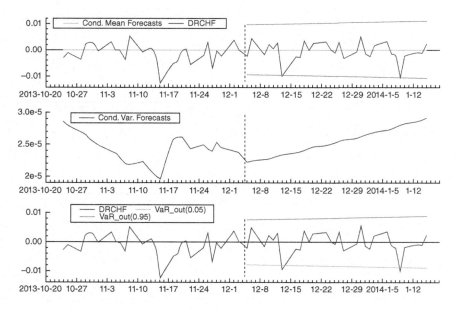

Figure A3.11 Forecasting GARCH (1,1) with normal distribution with no constant term in conditional variance term for MYR/CHF.

Appendix 4
Forecasting diagrams between RiskMetrics and APARCH models

MYR/USD

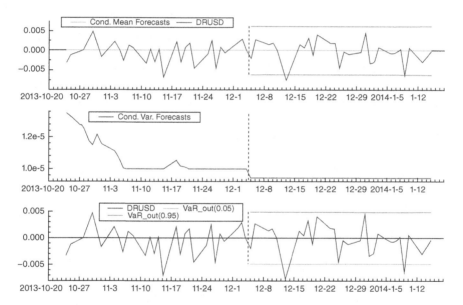

Figure A4.1 Forecasting RiskMetrics with skewed Student distribution for MYR/USD.

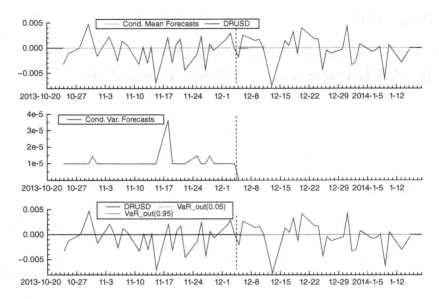

Figure A4.2 Forecasting ARCH(1)-APARCH(1,1) with skewed Student distribution for MYR/USD.

MYR/GBP

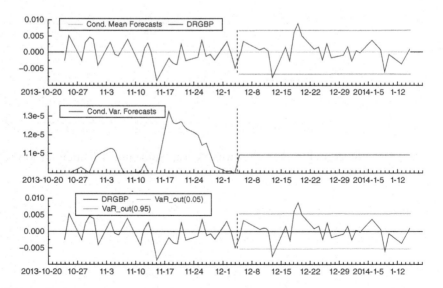

Figure A4.3 Forecasting RiskMetrics with skewed Student distribution for MYR/ GBP.

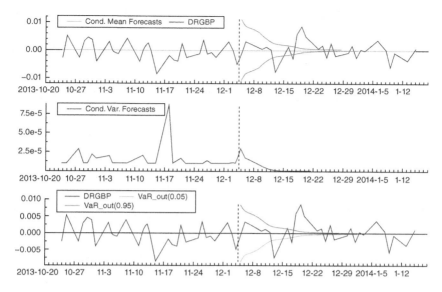

Figure A4.4 Forecasting ARCH(1)-APARCH(1,1) with skewed Student distribution for MYR/GBP.

MYR/EUR

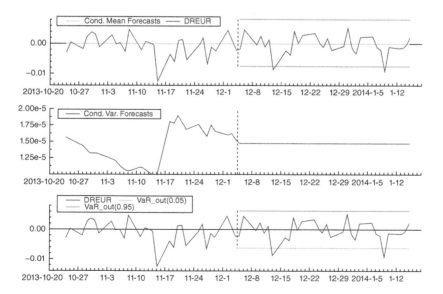

Figure A4.5 Forecasting RiskMetrics with skewed Student distribution for MYR/ EUR.

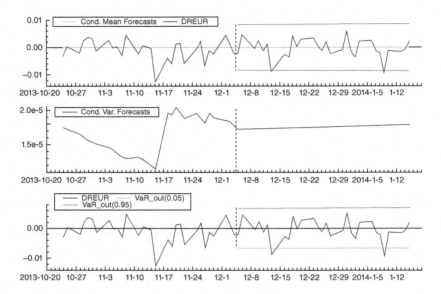

Figure A4.6 Forecasting GARCH(1,1)-APARCH(1,1) with skewed Student distribution for MYR/EUR.

MYR/JPY

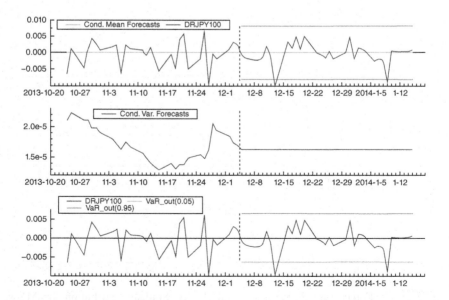

Figure A4.7 Forecasting RiskMetrics with skewed Student distribution for MYR/JPY.

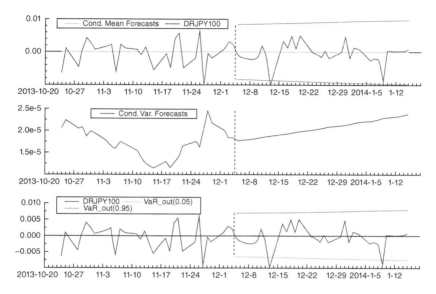

Figure A4.8 Forecasting GARCH(1,1)-APARCH(1,1) with skewed Student distribution for MYR/JPY.

MYR/CHF

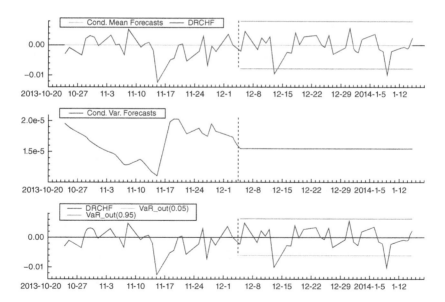

Figure A4.9 Forecasting RiskMetrics with skewed Student distribution for MYR/CHF.

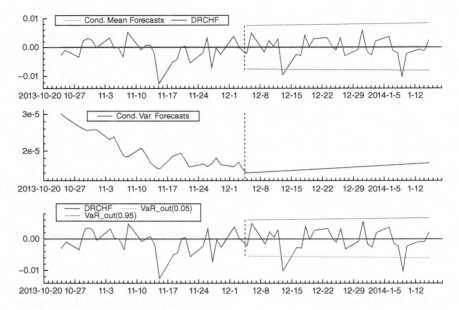

Figure A4.10 Forecasting GARCH(1,1)-APARCH(1,1) with skewed Student distribution for MYR/CHF.

Appendix 5
Empirical results for multivariate GARCH models

Scalar BEKK(1,1) by Engle and Kroner (1995)

Normal distribution for error term

DRUSD	1
DRGBP	2
DREUR	3
DRJPY	4
DRCHF	5

Robust standard errors (Sandwich formula)

	Coefficient	*Std. error*	*t-value*	*t-prob*
C_11	0.000526	5.8266e-005	9.033	0.0000
C_12	0.000258	6.5848e-005	3.913	0.0001
C_13	0.000195	6.0289e-005	3.232	0.0012
C_14	0.000376	9.9273e-005	3.787	0.0002
C_15	0.000166	7.7878e-005	2.127	0.0335
C_22	0.000738	7.1943e-005	10.26	0.0000
C_23	0.000428	6.3369e-005	6.759	0.0000
C_24	0.000177	8.4374e-005	2.099	0.0359
C_25	0.000447	8.2447e-005	5.417	0.0000
C_33	0.00061	6.7553e-005	9.127	0.0000
C_34	0.000226	8.5372e-005	2.648	0.0082
C_35	0.000647	7.7447e-005	8.360	0.0000
C_44	0.000938	0.00012274	7.645	0.0000
C_45	0.000228	5.0889e-005	4.473	0.0000
C_55	0.000876	0.00030364	2.885	0.0040
b_1	0.961572	0.0034765	276.6	0.0000
a_1	0.242062	0.013146	18.41	0.0000

No. of observations: 2,068; No. of parameters: 17
No. of series: 5; Log-likelihood: 41,005.253

TESTS

Information criteria (to be minimised)

Akaike	−39.640477	Shibata	39.640610
Schwarz	−39.594160	Hannan-Quinn	−39.623499

Individual normality tests

Series: DRUSD

	Statistic	t-test	p-value
Skewness	0.21832	4.0562	4.9882e-005
Excess Kurtosis	1.8005	16.733	7.4943e-063
Jarque-Bera	295.76	.NaN	5.9836e-065

Series: DRGBP

	Statistic	t-test	p-value
Skewness	−0.30322	5.6335	1.7661e-008
Excess Kurtosis	1.3258	12.322	6.9331e-035
Jarque-Bera	183.15	.NaN	1.7001e-040

Series: DREUR

	Statistic	t-test	p-value
Skewness	−0.98891	18.373	2.1767e-075
Excess Kurtosis	14.449	134.29	0.00000
Jarque-Bera	18,327	.NaN	0.00000

Series: DRJPY

	Statistic	t-test	p-value
Skewness	−0.28263	5.2510	1.5131e-007
Excess Kurtosis	4.3638	40.557	0.00000
Jarque-Bera	1668.4	.NaN	0.00000

Series: DRCHF

	Statistic	t-test	p-value
Skewness	8.7132	161.88	0.00000
Excess Kurtosis	237.65	2208.7	0.00000
Jarque-Bera	4.8928e+006	.NaN	0.00000

Q-statistics on standardised residuals

Series: DRUSD

Q(5) = 3.97025	[0.5537072]
Q(10) = 9.18814	[0.5143468]
Q(20) = 24.4490	[0.2233303]
Q(50) = 75.4270	[0.0115718]

Series: DRGBP

Q(5) = 3.63881	[0.6024956]
Q(10) = 7.30535	[0.6963373]
Q(20) = 12.3164	[0.9047545]
Q(50) = 52.9286	[0.3617667]

Series: DREUR

Q(5) = 12.8428	[0.0248977]
Q(10) = 22.8395	[0.0113548]
Q(20) = 29.8670	[0.0720378]
Q(50) = 55.2220	[0.2839255]

Series: DRJPY

Q(5) = 4.61471	[0.4646832]
Q(10) = 8.90936	[0.5407266]
Q(20) = 20.9891	[0.3977720]
Q(50) = 56.1492	[0.2554445]

Series: DRCHF

Q(5) = 8.15864	[0.1477068]
Q(10) = 15.4907	[0.1151697]
Q(20) = 22.4363	[0.3173133]
Q(50) = 38.3890	[0.8844297]

Series: DRUSD

Q(5) = 22.1204	[0.0004967]
Q(10) = 23.7807	[0.0082042]
Q(20) = 39.2991	[0.0061189]
Q(50) = 91.2656	[0.0003291]

Series: DRGBP

Q(5) = 2.47145	[0.7807888]
Q(10) = 16.4251	[0.0880932]
Q(20) = 36.7903	[0.0123982]
Q(50) = 71.7870	[0.0233559]

Series: DREUR

Q(5) = 1.17492	[0.9472606]
Q(10) = 1.25593	[0.9995158]
Q(20) = 3.29131	[0.9999909]
Q(50) = 7.12771	[1.0000000]

Series: DRJPY

Q(5) = 9.98135	[0.0757653]
Q(10) = 10.7600	[0.3765155]
Q(20) = 12.1887	[0.9094290]
Q(50) = 26.0779	[0.9979273]

Series: DRCHF

Q(5) = 1.59244	[0.9021617]
Q(10) = 1.62348	[0.9984965]
Q(20) = 1.67739	[1.0000000]
Q(50) = 1.86272	[1.0000000]

Vector Normality test: Chi-square(10) = 5613.3 [0.0000]**

Hosking's Multivariate Portmanteau statistics on standardised residuals

Hosking(5) = 139.700	[0.1742893]
Hosking(10) = 278.220	[0.1061991]
Hosking(20) = 497.420	[0.5241792]
Hosking(50) = 1300.41	[0.1566575]

Hosking's Multivariate Portmanteau statistics on squared standardised residuals

Hosking(5) = 141.460	[0.1220535]
Hosking(10) = 286.465	[0.0469957]
Hosking(20) = 499.626	[0.4710680]
Hosking(50) = 1116.72	[0.9966607]

Li and McLeod's Multivariate Portmanteau statistics on standardised residuals

Li-McLeod(5) = 139.726	[0.1739020]
Li-McLeod(10) = 278.193	[0.1064034]
Li-McLeod(20) = 497.600	[0.5219034]
Li-McLeod(50) = 1299.87	[0.1592254]

Li and McLeod's Multivariate Portmanteau statistics on squared standardised residuals

Li-McLeod(5) = 141.464	[0.1220054]
Li-McLeod(10) = 286.382	[0.0473295]
Li-McLeod(20) = 499.688	[0.4702913]
Li-McLeod(50) = 1119.05	[0.9961182]

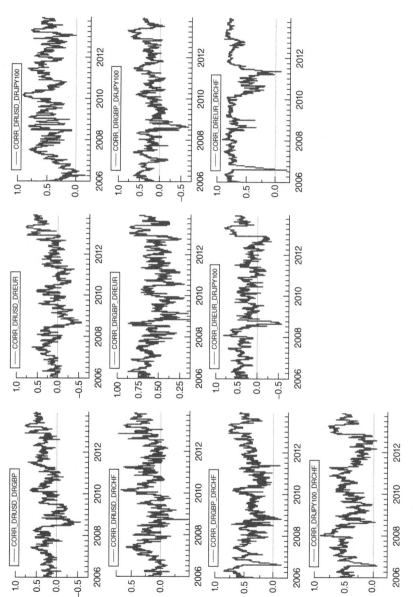

Figure A5.1 Correlations of log difference between five different currency pairs: Scalar BEKK(1,1) by Engle and Kroner (1995) and normal distribution for error terms==

Student distribution for error terms

Robust standard errors (Sandwich formula)

	Coefficient	Std. error	t-value	t-prob
C_11	0.000455	4.2205e-005	10.77	0.0000
C_12	0.000158	5.8581e-005	2.704	0.0069
C_13	0.000118	5.5341e-005	2.132	0.0331
C_14	0.000277	7.2917e-005	3.800	0.0001
C_15	0.000102	6.1368e-005	1.669	0.0952
C_22	0.000684	5.4644e-005	12.51	0.0000
C_23	0.000404	5.3773e-005	7.508	0.0000
C_24	0.000180	6.1417e-005	2.927	0.0035
C_25	0.000408	6.1105e-005	6.684	0.0000
C_33	0.000562	5.3991e-005	10.41	0.0000
C_34	0.000127	6.1173e-005	2.078	0.0378
C_35	0.000559	5.6967e-005	9.821	0.0000
C_44	0.000688	6.0258e-005	11.41	0.0000
C_45	0.000005	2.0595e-005	0.2596	0.7952
C_55	0.000046	0.00011407	0.4057	0.6850
b_1	0.965902	0.0018770	514.6	0.0000
a_1	0.254379	0.0082846	30.71	0.0000
df	5.819146	0.42999	13.53	0.0000

No. of observations: 2,068; No. of parameters: 18
No. of series: 5; Log-likelihood: 4,2234.543

TESTS

Information criteria (to be minimised)			
Akaike	40.828378	Shibata	40.828528
Schwarz	40.779337	Hannan-Quinn	810402

Individual normality tests

Series: DRUSD

	Statistic	t-test	p-value
Skewness	0.18226	3.3862	0.00070871
Excess Kurtosis	1.9691	18.300	8.2795e-075
Jarque-Bera	345.53	.NaN	9.3061e-076

Series: DRGBP

	Statistic	t-test	p-value
Skewness	0.66009	12.264	1.4208e-034
Excess Kurtosis	4.7324	43.982	0.00000
Jarque-Bera	2079.9	.NaN	0.00000

Series: DREUR

	Statistic	*t-test*	*p-value*
Skewness	11.256	209.13	0.00000
Excess Kurtosis	331.21	3078.2	0.00000
Jarque-Bera	9.4964e+006	.NaN	0.00000

Series: DRJPY

	Statistic	*t-test*	*p-value*
Skewness	0.38667	7.1838 6.7805e-013	
Excess Kurtosis	5.2265	48.574	0.00000
Jarque-Bera	2405.2	.NaN	0.00000

Series: DRCHF

	Statistic	*t-test*	*p-value*
Skewness	20.577	382.30	0.00000
Excess Kurtosis	724.16	6730.2	0.00000
Jarque-Bera	4.5333e+007	.NaN	0.00000

Q-statistics on standardised residuals

Series: DRUSD

Q(5) = 4.62471	[0.4633731]
Q(10) = 9.23346	[0.5101003]
Q(20) = 23.8010	[0.2511931]
Q(50) = 74.7045	[0.0133537]

Series: DRGBP

Q(5) = 2.04750	[0.8425348]
Q(10) = 6.26946	[0.7921390]
Q(20) = 9.05780	[0.9822281]
Q(50) = 44.3413	[0.6989444]

Series: DREUR

Q(5) = 6.97485	[0.2225178]
Q(10) = 12.6622	[0.2431770]
Q(20) = 19.2199	[0.5075782]
Q(50) = 38.8492	[0.8734220]

Series: DRJPY

Q(5) = 4.39350	[0.4942586]
Q(10) = 8.59300	[0.5711146]
Q(20) = 21.1016	[0.3911761]
Q(50) = 54.1988	[0.3174135]

Series: DRCHF

Q(5) = 3.95033	[0.5565887]
Q(10) = 7.40637	[0.6866045]
Q(20) = 11.8505	[0.9211268]
Q(50) = 23.1686	[0.9995809]

H0: No serial correlation ==> Accept H0 when prob. is high [Q < Chisq(lag)]

Q-statistics on squared standardised residuals

Series: DRUSD

Q(5) = 23.0462	[0.0003308]
Q(10) = 24.8364	[0.0056644]
Q(20) = 38.6023	[0.0074687]
Q(50) = 85.0060	[0.0014697]

Series: DRGBP

Q(5) = 1.11819	[0.9524810]
Q(10) = 2.74525	[0.9867999]
Q(20) = 8.27281	[0.9899034]
Q(50) = 22.7910	[0.9996684]

Series: DREUR

Q(5) = 0.0156647	[0.9999984]
Q(10) = 0.0330059	[1.0000000]
Q(20) = 0.0820255	[1.0000000]
Q(50) = 0.247125	[1.0000000]

Series: DRJPY

Q(5) = 7.32085	[0.1978507]
Q(10) = 8.20263	[0.6090522]
Q(20) = 9.32656	[0.9788069]
Q(50) = 22.5557	[0.9997143]

Series: DRCHF

Q(5) = 0.0476835	[0.9999740]
Q(10) = 0.0577905	[1.0000000]
Q(20) = 0.0791725	[1.0000000]
Q(50) = 0.144956	[1.0000000]

H0: No serial correlation ==> Accept H0 when prob. is high [Q < Chisq(lag)]

Vector Normality test: Chi-square(10) = 16,691 [0.0000]**

Hosking's Multivariate Portmanteau statistics on standardised residuals

Hosking(5) = 130.058	[0.3602662]
Hosking(10) = 260.631	[0.3090377]
Hosking(20) = 477.604	[0.7573875]
Hosking(50) = 1221.91	[0.7097553]

Hosking's Multivariate Portmanteau statistics on squared standardised residuals

Hosking(5) = 102.571	[0.9097732]
Hosking(10) = 198.245	[0.9911863]
Hosking(20) = 363.979	[0.9999986]
Hosking(50) = 858.284	[1.0000000]

Warning: *P-values* have been corrected by two degrees of freedom

Li and McLeod's Multivariate Portmanteau statistics on standardised residuals

Li-McLeod(5) = 130.092	[0.3594966]
Li-McLeod(10) = 260.643	[0.3088534]
Li-McLeod(20) = 477.858	[0.7547900]
Li-McLeod(50) = 1222.45	[0.7059790]

Li and McLeod's Multivariate Portmanteau statistics on squared standardised residuals

Li-McLeod(5) = 102.615	[0.9092596]
Li-McLeod(10) = 198.399	[0.9909935]
Li-McLeod(20) = 364.660	[0.9999984]
Li-McLeod(50) = 863.206	[1.0000000]

Warning: *P-values* have been corrected by two degrees of freedom

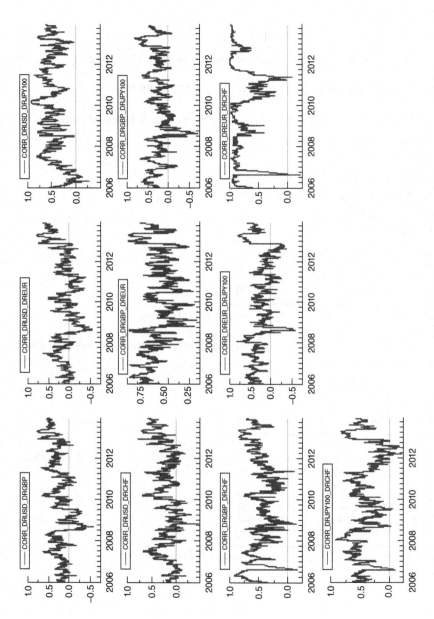

Figure A5.2 Correlations of log difference between five different currency pairs: Scalar **BEKK(1,1)** by Engle and Kroner (1995) and Student distribution for error terms.

Diagonal BEKK

Normal distribution for error terms

DRUSD	1
DRGBP	2
DREUR	3
DRJPY	4
DRCHF	5

Log-likelihood = 41,061.2

Robust standard errors (Sandwich formula)

	Coefficient	*Std. error*	*t-value*	*t-prob*
C_11	0.000488	0.00012208	3.998	0.0001
C_12	0.0001995	4993e-005	3.614	0.0003
C_13	0.0001956	5229e-005	2.983	0.0029
C_14	0.000525	0.00019204	2.734	0.0063
C_15	0.000215	0.00010525	2.047	0.0408
C_22	0.000382	0.00016506	2.313	0.0208
C_23	0.000445	0.00011814	3.770	0.0002
C_24	0.000475	0.00029030	1.636	0.1020
C_25	0.001268	0.00083356	1.521	0.1285
C_33	0.000441	0.00011673	3.782	0.0002
C_34	0.000129	0.00023329	0.5543	0.5795
C_35	0.000529	0.00050592	1.045	0.2962
C_44	0.001141	0.00020212	5.647	0.0000
C_45	0.000103	0.00031574	0.3275	0.7433
C_55	0.000709	0.00034123	2.079	0.0377
b_1.11	0.961188	0.010370	92.69	0.0000
b_1.22	0.982712	0.0046447	211.6	0.0000
b_1.33	0.969143	0.0075994	127.5	0.0000
b_1.44	0.944806	0.010606	89.08	0.0000
b_1.55	0.944554	0.0082228	114.9	0.0000
a_1.11	0.253853	0.030841	8.231	0.0000
a_1.22	0.171958	0.017606	9.767	0.0000
a_1.33	0.223403	0.030001	7.446	0.0000
a_1.44	0.282075	0.025033	11.27	0.0000
a_1.55	0.260409	0.024547	10.61	0.0000

No. of observations: 2,068; No. of parameters: 25
No. of series: 5; Log-likelihood: 41,061.181

TESTS

Information criteria (to be minimised)

Akaike	39.686829	Shibata	39.687116
Schwarz	39.618715	Hannan-Quinn	39.661861

Individual normality tests

Series: DRUSD

	Statistic	t-test	p-value
Skewness	0.19880	3.6935	0.00022117
Excess Kurtosis	1.7747	16.493	4.0979e-061
Jarque-Bera	285.00	.NaN	1.2996e-062

Series: DRGBP

	Statistic	t-test	p-value
Skewness	0.28294	5.2567	1.4665e-007
Excess Kurtosis	1.4197	3.195	9.4371e-040
Jarque-Bera	201.27	.NaN	1.9728e-044

Series: DREUR

	Statistic	t-test	p-value
Skewness	1.1123	20.665	7.1965e-095
Excess Kurtosis	16.520	153.53	0.00000
Jarque-Bera	23,942	.NaN	0.00000

Series: DRJPY

	Statistic	t-test	p-value
Skewness	0.27865	5.1770	2.2549e-007
Excess Kurtosis	4.2258	39.274	0.00000
Jarque-Bera	1565.5	.NaN	0.00000

Series: DRCHF

	Statistic	t-test	p-value
Skewness	7.8392	145.64	0.00000
Excess Kurtosis	208.40	1936.8	0.00000
Jarque-Bera	3.7634e+006	.NaN	0.00000

Q-statistics on standardised residuals

Series: DRUSD

Q(5) = 4.10790	[0.5339879]
Q(10) = 9.09212	[0.5233838]
Q(20) = 24.1158	[0.2373720]
Q(50) = 74.7225	[0.0133064]

Series: DRGBP

Q(5) = 4.49173	[0.4809904]
Q(10) = 7.99829	[0.6290041]
Q(20) = 13.0036	[0.8772305]
Q(50) = 51.2726	[0.4235635]

Series: DREUR

Q(5) = 13.2978	[0.0207420]
Q(10) = 23.4648	[0.0091549]
Q(20) = 30.0567	[0.0689401]
Q(50) = 53.3696	[0.3460388]

Series: DRJPY

Q(5) = 5.11834	[0.4016098]
Q(10) = 9.31349	[0.5026331]
Q(20) = 20.3127	[0.4385252]
Q(50) = 55.4578	[0.2765104]

Series: DRCHF

Q(5) = 6.98207	[0.2219773]
Q(10) = 13.8002	[0.1823026]
Q(20) = 20.1826	[0.4465631]
Q(50) = 37.6245	[0.9013558]

H0: No serial correlation ==> Accept H0 when prob. is high [Q < Chisq(lag)]

Q-statistics on squared standardised residuals

Series: DRUSD

Q(5) = 20.8481	[0.0008654]
Q(10) = 22.7191	[0.0118323]
Q(20) = 39.0120	[0.0066445]
Q(50) = 85.7719	[0.0012310]

Series: DRGBP

Q(5) = 1.39525	[0.9248318]
Q(10) = 27.1875	[0.0024322]
Q(20) = 52.8704	[0.0000849]
Q(50) = 92.4893	[0.0002427]

Series: DREUR

Q(5) = 0.923871	[0.9684695]
Q(10) = 1.01799	[0.9998132]
Q(20) = 2.84990	[0.9999974]
Q(50) = 6.39721	[1.0000000]

Series: DRJPY

Q(5) = 7.02436	[0.2188348]
Q(10) = 7.84163	[0.6443026]
Q(20) = 9.82842	[0.9711776]
Q(50) = 24.7984	[0.9989299]

Series: DRCHF

Q(5) = 1.18942	[0.9458885]
Q(10) = 1.22423	[0.9995684]
Q(20) = 1.28047	[1.0000000]
Q(50) = 1.46180	[1.0000000]

H0: No serial correlation ==> Accept H0 when prob. is high [Q < Chisq(lag)]

Vector Normality test: Chi-square(10) = 6475.0 [0.0000]**

Hosking's Multivariate Portmanteau statistics on standardised residuals

Hosking(5) = 142.115	[0.1404298]
Hosking(10) = 281.937	[0.0805851]
Hosking(20) = 496.829	[0.5316403]
Hosking(50) = 1304.56	[0.1380825]

Hosking's Multivariate Portmanteau statistics on squared standardised residuals

Hosking(5) = 139.875	[0.1417755]
Hosking(10) = 290.761	[0.0322204]
Hosking(20) = 522.115	[0.2197116]
Hosking(50) = 1150.95	[0.9762550]

Warning: *P-values* have been corrected by two degrees of freedom

----

Li and McLeod's Multivariate Portmanteau statistics on standardised residuals

Li-McLeod(5) = 142.135	[0.1401770]
Li-McLeod(10) = 281.900	[0.0808182]
Li-McLeod(20) = 497.034	[0.5290454]
Li-McLeod(50) = 1303.95	[0.1407030]

Li and McLeod's Multivariate Portmanteau statistics on squared standardised residuals

Li-McLeod(5) = 139.887	[0.1416233]
Li-McLeod(10) = 290.671	[0.0324837]
Li-McLeod(20) = 522.012	[0.2206510]
Li-McLeod(50) = 1152.94	[0.9738019]

Warning: *P-values* have been corrected by two degrees of freedom

----

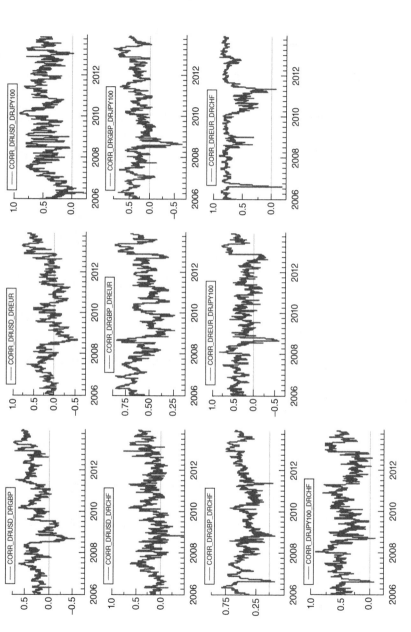

Figure A5.3 Correlations of log difference between five different currency pairs: Diagonal BEKK and normal distribution for error terms.

Student distribution for error terms

Robust standard errors (Sandwich formula)

	Coefficient	Std. error	t-value	t-prob
C_11	0.0005129	9436e-005	5.151	0.0000
C_12	0.0001394	5446e-005	3.061	0.0022
C_13	0.0001425	7379e-005	2.467	0.0137
C_14	0.0003839	5116e-005	4.029	0.0001
C_15	0.0001286	1274e-005	2.093	0.0365
C_22	0.0004218	7433e-005	4.818	0.0000
C_23	0.000646	0.00010500	6.154	0.0000
C_24	0.000334	0.00011747	2.839	0.0046
C_25	0.000646	0.00010164	6.355	0.0000
C_33	0.000449	0.00014551	3.086	0.0021
C_34	0.000009	0.00013608	0.06358	0.9493
C_35	0.0004069	9266e-005	4.093	0.0000
C_44	0.000844	0.00011144	7.574	0.0000
C_45	0.0000112143	3e-005	0.4902	0.6241
C_55	0.0000001.759	4e-009	0.5687	0.5696
b_1.11	0.963389	0.0072535	132.8	0.0000
b_1.22	0.983315	0.0019823	496.0	0.0000
b_1.33	0.959665	0.0038255	250.9	0.0000
b_1.44	0.958374	0.0070674	135.6	0.0000
b_1.55	0.958626	0.0041507	231.0	0.0000
a_1.11	0.251462	0.021609	11.64	0.0000
a_1.22	0.173430	0.010629	16.32	0.0000
a_1.33	0.270009	0.012491	21.62	0.0000
a_1.44	0.264803	0.022036	12.02	0.0000
a_1.55	0.284652	0.015321	18.58	0.0000
df	6.002408	0.43861	13.68	0.0000

No. of observations: 2,068; No. of parameters: 26
No. of series: 5; Log-likelihood: 42,271.794

TESTS

Information criteria (to be minimised)

Akaike	−40.856667	Shibata	−40.856978
Schwarz	−40.785829	Hannan-Quinn	−40.830701

Individual normality tests

Series: DRUSD

	Statistic	t-test	p-value
Skewness	−0.18352	3.4095	0.00065082
Excess Kurtosis	1.9782	18.385	1.7385e-075
Jarque-Bera	348.79	.NaN	1.8206e-076

Series: DRGBP

	Statistic	t-test	p-value
Skewness	−0.63073	11.718	1.0292e-031
Excess Kurtosis	4.7286	43.947	0.00000
Jarque-Bera	2063.8	.NaN	0.00000

Series: DREUR

	Statistic	t-test	p-value
Skewness	−11.866	220.45	0.00000
Excess Kurtosis	352.38	3274.9	0.00000
Jarque-Bera	1.0748e+007	.NaN	0.00000

Series: DRJPY

	Statistic	t-test	p-value
Skewness	−0.35790	6.6493	2.9457e-011
Excess Kurtosis	4.9459	45.966	0.00000
Jarque-Bera	2152.0	.NaN	0.00000

Series: DRCHF

	Statistic	t-test	p-value
Skewness	21.633	401.91	0.00000
Excess Kurtosis	773.27	7186.6	0.00000
Jarque-Bera	5.1684e+007	.NaN	0.00000

Q-statistics on standardised residuals

Series: DRUSD

Q(5) = 4.29132	[0.5082797]
Q(10) = 8.28631	[0.6008931]
Q(20) = 22.7349	[0.3019978]
Q(50) = 73.6509	[0.0164004]

Series: DRGBP

Q(5) = 3.27219	[0.6581017]
Q(10) = 6.28351	[0.7909082]
Q(20) = 9.44018	[0.9772254]
Q(50) = 43.5493	[0.7282839]

Series: DREUR

Q(5) = 7.31724	[0.1980954]
Q(10) = 13.3882	[0.2027681]
Q(20) = 19.5590	[0.4858036]
Q(50) = 39.0334	[0.8688433]

Series: DRJPY

Q(5) = 4.78833	*[0.4422555]*
Q(10) = 8.89556	*[0.5420433]*
Q(20) = 20.7038	*[0.4147478]*
Q(50) = 55.6147	*[0.2716391]*

Series: DRCHF

Q(5) = 3.19307	*[0.6702476]*
Q(10) = 6.24302	*[0.7944495]*
Q(20) = 10.1793	*[0.9648020]*
Q(50) = 21.6228	*[0.9998461]*

H0: No serial correlation ==> Accept H0 when prob. is high [Q < Chisq(lag)]

Q-statistics on squared standardised residuals

Series: DRUSD

Q(5) = 23.2199	*[0.0003064]*
Q(10) = 24.8922	*[0.0055536]*
Q(20) = 38.2465	*[0.0082611]*
Q(50) = 85.2903	*[0.0013764]*

Series: DRGBP

Q(5) = 0.691919	*[0.9834092]*
Q(10) = 5.10053	*[0.8843620]*
Q(20) = 12.8424	*[0.8840440]*
Q(50) = 27.4539	*[0.9960471]*

Series: DREUR

Q(5) = 0.0157139	*[0.9999984]*
Q(10) = 0.0326227	*[1.0000000]*
Q(20) = 0.0747865	*[1.0000000]*
Q(50) = 0.224767	*[1.0000000]*

Series: DRJPY

Q(5) = 7.18533	*[0.2072180]*
Q(10) = 8.11830	*[0.6172822]*
Q(20) = 9.39854	*[0.9778146]*
Q(50) = 22.8649	*[0.9996526]*

Series: DRCHF

Q(5) = 0.0291374	[0.9999924]
Q(10) = 0.0385554	[1.0000000]
Q(20) = 0.0581193	[1.0000000]
Q(50) = 0.118506	[1.0000000]

H0: No serial correlation ==> Accept H0 when prob. is high [Q < Chisq(lag)]

Vector Normality test: Chi-square(10) = 19,562 [0.0000]**

Hosking's Multivariate Portmanteau statistics on standardised residuals

Hosking(5) = 131.781	[0.3215497]
Hosking(10) = 261.115	[0.3016628]
Hosking(20) = 471.426	[0.8159994]
Hosking(50) = 1215.45	[0.7530625]

Hosking's Multivariate Portmanteau statistics on squared standardised residuals

Hosking(5) = 110.905	[0.7749128]
Hosking(10) = 225.466	[0.8447171]
Hosking(20) = 417.410	[0.9963691]
Hosking(50) = 941.657	[1.0000000]

Warning: P-values have been corrected by two degrees of freedom

----

Li and McLeod's Multivariate Portmanteau statistics on standardised residuals

Li-McLeod(5) = 131.812	[0.3208906]
Li-McLeod(10) = 261.129	[0.3014591]
Li-McLeod(20) = 471.730	[0.8133272]
Li-McLeod(50) = 1216.01	[0.7494095]

Li and McLeod's Multivariate Portmanteau statistics on squared standardised residuals

Li-McLeod(5) = 110.940	[0.7741961]
Li-McLeod(10) = 225.546	[0.8437979]
Li-McLeod(20) = 417.806	[0.9962126]
Li-McLeod(50) = 945.842	[1.0000000]

Warning: P-values have been corrected by two degrees of freedom

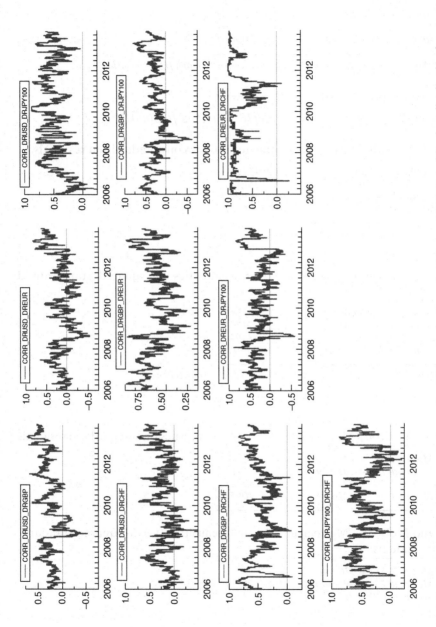

Figure A5.4 Correlations of log difference between five different currency pairs: Diagonal BEKK and Student distribution for error terms.

RiskMetrics

Normal distribution for error terms

Estimation is not needed as lambda is 0.94 for RiskMetrics.

Student distribution for error terms

Robust standard errors (Sandwich formula)

	Coefficient	Std. error	t-value	t-prob
df	7.393250	0.41240	17.93	0.0000

No. of observations: 2,068; No. of parameters: 1
No. of series: 5; Log-likelihood: 42,048.212

TESTS

Information criteria (to be minimised)			
Akaike	−40.664615	Shibata	−40.664616
Schwarz	−40.661891	Hannan-Quinn	−40.663616

Individual normality tests

Series: DRUSD

	Statistic	t-test	p-value
Skewness	−0.068410	1.2710	0.20374
Excess Kurtosis	2.4671	22.929	2.3933e-116
Jarque-Bera	526.08	.NaN	5.7956e-115

Series: DRGBP

	Statistic	t-test	p-value
Skewness	−0.96168	17.867	2.1394e-071
Excess Kurtosis	10.580	98.330	0.00000
Jarque-Bera	9964.2	.NaN	0.00000

Series: DREUR

	Statistic	t-test	p-value
Skewness	−6.3687	118.32	0.00000
Excess Kurtosis	167.95	1560.9	0.00000
Jarque-Bera	2.4445e+006	.NaN	0.00000

Series: DRJPY

	Statistic	*t-test*	*p-value*
Skewness	−0.62046	11.527	9.6094e-031
Excess Kurtosis	7.2765	67.626	0.00000
Jarque-Bera	4695.0	.NaN	0.00000

Series: DRCHF

	Statistic	*t-test*	*p-value*
Skewness	20.318	377.49	0.00000
Excess Kurtosis	715.28	6647.6	0.00000
Jarque-Bera	4.4227e+007	.NaN	0.00000

Q-statistics on standardised residuals

Series: DRUSD

Q(5) = 6.59839	[0.2522620]
Q(10) = 11.1580	[0.3453438]
Q(20) = 24.1564	[0.2356287]
Q(50) = 69.6612	[0.0343932]

Series: DRGBP

Q(5) = 0.743256	[0.9805106]
Q(10) = 7.07913	[0.7179539]
Q(20) = 9.45168	[0.9770607]
Q(50) = 40.9166	[0.8165325]

Series: DREUR

Q(5) = 11.6886	[0.0393136]
Q(10) = 20.9569	[0.0213961]
Q(20) = 27.5993	[0.1192301]
Q(50) = 47.6061	[0.5699802]

Series: DRJPY

Q(5) = 4.26296	[0.5122107]
Q(10) = 9.48018	[0.4872179]
Q(20) = 22.0820	[0.3360795]
Q(50) = 50.6641	[0.4471864]

Series: DRCHF

Q(5) = 3.05286	[0.6918372]
Q(10) = 6.99878	[0.7255606]
Q(20) = 12.5085	[0.8974624]
Q(50) = 25.8912	[0.9981108]

H0: No serial correlation ==> Accept H0 when prob. is high [Q < Chisq(lag)]

Q-statistics on squared standardised residuals

Series: DRUSD

Q(5) = 18.6789	[0.0022055]
Q(10) = 20.4187	[0.0255325]
Q(20) = 31.3031	[0.0513142]
Q(50) = 64.4165	[0.0825963]

Series: DRGBP

Q(5) = 0.844594	[0.9741022]
Q(10) = 1.12476	[0.9997057]
Q(20) = 3.19326	[0.9999930]
Q(50) = 25.3048	[0.9985996]

Series: DREUR

Q(5) = 0.0500324	[0.9999707]
Q(10) = 0.0787828	[1.0000000]
Q(20) = 0.217936	[1.0000000]
Q(50) = 0.658588	[1.0000000]

Series: DRJPY

Q(5) = 4.18621	[0.5229299]
Q(10) = 4.98382	[0.8922560]
Q(20) = 6.06676	[0.9988043]
Q(50) = 17.5697	[0.9999942]

Series: DRCHF

Q(5) = 0.0463732	[0.9999758]
Q(10) = 0.0553197	[1.0000000]
Q(20) = 0.0768622	[1.0000000]
Q(50) = 0.173739	[1.0000000]

H0: No serial correlation ==> Accept H0 when prob. is high [Q < Chisq(lag)]

Vector Normality test: Chi-square(10) = 25,919 [0.0000]**

Hosking's Multivariate Portmanteau statistics on standardised residuals

Hosking(5) = 128.548	[0.3957382]
Hosking(10) = 271.992	[0.1621502]
Hosking(20) = 506.818	[0.4068337]
Hosking(50) = 1239.52	[0.5780149]

Hosking's Multivariate Portmanteau statistics on squared standardised residuals

Hosking(5) = 78.6522	*[0.9993584]*
Hosking(10) = 157.469	*[0.9999985]*
Hosking(20) = 281.806	*[1.0000000]*
Hosking(50) = 787.441	*[1.0000000]*

Warning: P-values have been corrected by two degrees of freedom

----

Li and McLeod's Multivariate Portmanteau statistics on standardised residuals

Li-McLeod(5) = 128.581	*[0.3949417]*
Li-McLeod(10) = 271.957	*[0.1625107]*
Li-McLeod(20) = 506.902	*[0.4058132]*
Li-McLeod(50) = 1240.08	*[0.5736116]*

Li and McLeod's Multivariate Portmanteau statistics on squared standardised residuals

Li-McLeod(5) = 78.7323	*[0.9993427]*
Li-McLeod(10) = 157.729	*[0.9999984]*
Li-McLeod(20) = 282.968	*[1.0000000]*
Li-McLeod(50) = 792.972	*[1.0000000]*

Warning: P-values have been corrected by two degrees of freedom

----

Constant conditional correlations by Bollerslev (1990)

Normal distribution for error terms

Robust standard errors (Sandwich formula)

	Coefficient	*Std. error*	*t-value*	*t-prob*
rho_21	0.254038	0.025835	9.833	0.0000
rho_31	0.112873	0.031859	3.543	0.0004
rho_41	0.495533	0.019288	25.69	0.0000
rho_51	0.204186	0.045799	4.458	0.0000
rho_32	0.563079	0.015835	35.56	0.0000
rho_42	0.249703	0.030152	8.282	0.0000
rho_52	0.402880	0.068646	5.869	0.0000
rho_43	0.248128	0.039109	6.345	0.0000
rho_53	0.643950	0.11144	5.779	0.0000
rho_54	0.397252	0.080490	4.935	0.0000

No. of observations: 2,068; No. of parameters: 20
No. of series: 5; Log-likelihood: 40,370.727

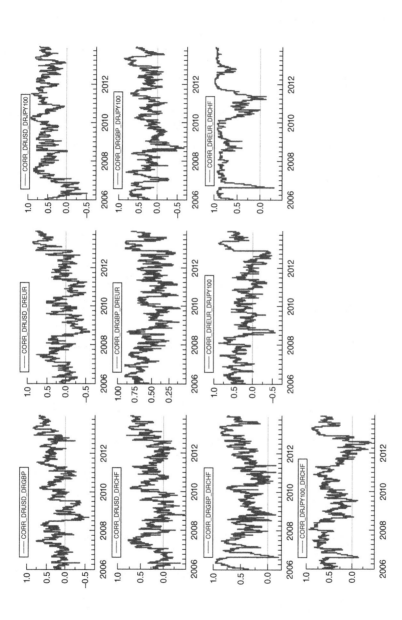

Figure A5..5   Correlations of log difference between five different currency pairs: RiskMetrics and Student distribution for error terms.

TESTS

Information criteria (to be minimised)

Akaike	39.023914	Shibata	−39.024098
Schwarz	−38.969423	Hannan-Quinn	−39.003940

Individual normality tests

Series: DRUSD

	Statistic	*t-test*	*p-value*
Skewness	−0.25857	4.8039	1.5560e-006
Excess Kurtosis	2.1912	20.365	3.4270e-092
Jarque-Bera	436.77	.NaN	1.4320e-095

Series: DRGBP

	Statistic	*t-test*	*p-value*
Skewness	−0.25005	4.6456	3.3903e-006
Excess Kurtosis	1.3477	12.525	5.4235e-036
Jarque-Bera	178.06	.NaN	2.1641e-039

Series: DREUR

	Statistic	*t-test*	*p-value*
Skewness	−0.76588	14.229	6.0549e-046
Excess Kurtosis	10.178	94.595	0.00000
Jarque-Bera	9128.8	.NaN	0.00000

Series: DRJPY

	Statistic	*t-test*	*p-value*
Skewness	−0.18152	3.3723	0.00074541
Excess Kurtosis	3.0090	27.965	4.3056e-172
Jarque-Bera	791.52	.NaN	1.3260e-172

Series: DRCHF

	Statistic	*t-test*	*p-value*
Skewness	9.5180	176.83	0.00000
Excess Kurtosis	264.41	2457.4	0.00000
Jarque-Bera	6.0555e+006	.NaN	0.00000

Q-statistics on standardised residuals

Series: DRUSD

Q(5) = 5.26328	[0.3846017]
Q(10) = 9.28752	[0.5050521]
Q(20) = 23.1873	[0.2796909]
Q(50) = 79.0201	[0.0055252]

Series: DRGBP

Q(5) = 2.55059	[0.7688581]
Q(10) = 7.22285	[0.7042524]
Q(20) = 13.3971	[0.8597052]
Q(50) = 43.5837	[0.7270323]

Series: DREUR

Q(5) = 10.3872	[0.0649778]
Q(10) = 19.6063	[0.0332046]
Q(20) = 26.8172	[0.1404852]
Q(50) = 54.6470	[0.3024840]

Series: DRJPY

Q(5) = 5.10229	[0.4035245]
Q(10) = 10.0521	[0.4359373]
Q(20) = 26.7537	[0.1423362]
Q(50) = 58.7668	[0.1851453]

Series: DRCHF

Q(5) = 11.1078	[0.0492845]
Q(10) = 16.4180	[0.0882755]
Q(20) = 23.1125	[0.2833031]
Q(50) = 38.1132	[0.8907326]

H0: No serial correlation ==> Accept H0 when prob. is high [Q < Chisq(lag)]

Q-statistics on squared Standardised residuals

Series: DRUSD

Q(5) = 4.49224	[0.4809221]
Q(10) = 7.69726	[0.6583806]
Q(20) = 22.4915	[0.3144470]
Q(50) = 77.0599	[0.0083150]

Series: DRGBP

Q(5) = 3.10845	[0.6832696]
Q(10) = 13.9319	[0.1761191]
Q(20) = 25.1430	[0.1960160]
Q(50) = 49.9506	[0.4753654]

Series: DREUR

Q(5) = 7.77378	[0.1691514]
Q(10) = 7.84282	[0.6441866]
Q(20) = 14.7474	[0.7906758]
Q(50) = 22.4727	[0.9997291]

Series: DRJPY

Q(5) = 8.50470	[0.1305270]
Q(10) = 10.0234	[0.4384428]
Q(20) = 12.6470	[0.8920093]
Q(50) = 42.4250	[0.7678952]

Series: DRCHF

Q(5) = 3.66993	[0.5978450]
Q(10) = 3.69565	[0.9600340]
Q(20) = 3.74558	[0.9999730]
Q(50) = 3.96444	[1.0000000]

H0: No serial correlation ==> Accept H0 when prob. is high [Q < Chisq(lag)]

Vector Normality test: Chi-square(10) = 4,882.9 [0.0000]**

Hosking's Multivariate Portmanteau statistics on standardised residuals

Hosking(5) = 143.130	[0.1277341]
Hosking(10) = 289.215	[0.0446533]
Hosking(20) = 514.968	[0.3121664]
Hosking(50) = 1300.75	[0.1550725]

Hosking's Multivariate Portmanteau statistics on squared standardised residuals

Hosking(5) = 108.546	[0.8205275]
Hosking(10) = 217.612	[0.9183886]
Hosking(20) = 479.049	[0.7214216]
Hosking(50) = 1124.78	[0.9944434]

Warning: *P-values* have been corrected by two degrees of freedom

----

Li and McLeod's Multivariate Portmanteau statistics on standardised residuals

Li-McLeod(5) = 143.149	[0.1275072]
Li-McLeod(10) = 289.144	[0.0449263]
Li-McLeod(20) = 515.084	[0.3108970]
Li-McLeod(50) = 1300.37	[0.1568380]

Li and McLeod's Multivariate Portmanteau statistics on squared standardised residuals

Li-McLeod(5) = 108.584	[0.8198377]
Li-McLeod(10) = 217.708	[0.9176701]
Li-McLeod(20) = 478.862	[0.7234671]
Li-McLeod(50) = 1126.19	[0.9939454]

Warning: *P-values* have been corrected by two degrees of freedom

----

Student distribution for error terms

Robust standard errors (Sandwich formula)

	Coefficient	Std. error	t-value	t-prob
rho_21	0.240007	0.021124	11.36	0.0000
rho_31	0.112407	0.023336	4.817	0.0000
rho_41	0.498145	0.017706	28.13	0.0000
rho_51	0.203585	0.024302	8.377	0.0000
rho_32	0.536224	0.015316	35.01	0.0000
rho_42	0.288677	0.020362	14.18	0.0000
rho_52	0.480405	0.018870	25.46	0.0000
rho_43	0.300421	0.019956	15.05	0.0000
rho_53	0.796998	0.0098794	80.67	0.0000
rho_54	0.495433	0.017745	27.92	0.0000
df	5.626915	0.25190	22.34	0.0000

No. of observations: 2,068; No. of parameters: 26
No. of series: 5; Log-likelihood: 41,514.610

TESTS

Information criteria (to be minimised)

Akaike	−40.124381	Shibata	−40.124692
Schwarz	−40.053543	Hannan-Quinn	−40.098415

Individual normality tests

Series: DRUSD

	Statistic	t-test	p-value
Skewness	−0.21812	4.0524	5.0688e-005
Excess Kurtosis	1.6563	15.393	1.8200e-053
Jarque-Bera	252.78	.NaN	1.2894e-055

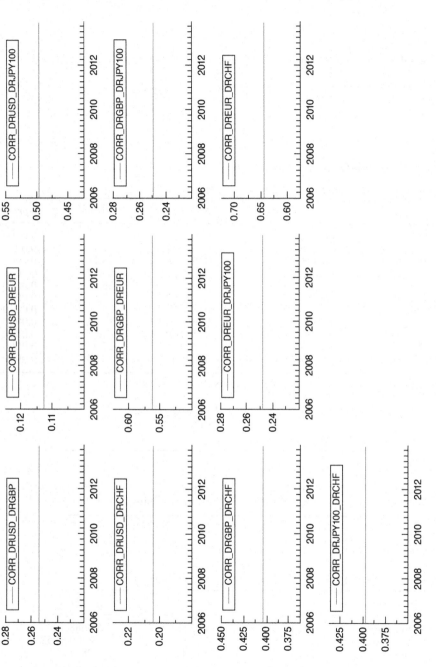

Figure A5.6 Correlations of log difference between five different currency pairs: Constant conditional correlations by Bollerslev (1990) and normal distribution for error terms.

Series: DRGBP

	Statistic	t-test	p-value
Skewness	−0.27687	5.1438	2.6918e-007
Excess Kurtosis	1.4626	13.593	4.4039e-042
Jarque-Bera	210.75	.NaN	1.7259e-046

Series: DREUR

	Statistic	t-test	p-value
Skewness	−1.6167	30.036	3.2769e-198
Excess Kurtosis	26.720	248.33	0.00000
Jarque-Bera	62,421	.NaN	0.00000

Series: DRJPY

	Statistic	t-test	p-value
Skewness	−0.24464	4.5451	5.4907e-006
Excess Kurtosis	3.6459	33.885	1.1193e-251
Jarque-Bera	1166.0	.NaN	6.2925e-254

Series: DRCHF

	Statistic	t-test	p-value
Skewness	6.5125	120.99	0.00000
Excess Kurtosis	176.78	1643.0	0.00000
Jarque-Bera	2.7075e+006	.NaN	0.00000

Q-statistics on standardised residuals

Series: DRUSD

Q(5) = 3.86480	[0.5690406]
Q(10) = 7.64264	[0.6636977]
Q(20) = 21.4434	[0.3714585]
Q(50) = 76.1258	[0.0100570]

Series: DRGBP

Q(5) = 2.29352	[0.8072179]
Q(10) = 6.56299	[0.7659560]
Q(20) = 11.5458	[0.9308241]
Q(50) = 42.1127	[0.7784155]

Series: DREUR

Q(5) = 12.1729	[0.0324945]
Q(10) = 23.6608	[0.0085535]
Q(20) = 37.3377	[0.0106571]
Q(50) = 71.1867	[0.0260992]

Series: DRJPY

Q(5) = 4.48506	[0.4818849]
Q(10) = 8.46835	[0.5831883]
Q(20) = 23.8994	[0.2468139]
Q(50) = 54.3442	[0.3125280]

Series: DRCHF

Q(5) = 8.36711	[0.1371305]
Q(10) = 15.4213	[0.1174404]
Q(20) = 24.1985	[0.2338300]
Q(50) = 54.4727	[0.3082431]

H0: No serial correlation ==> Accept H0 when prob. is high [Q < Chisq(lag)]

Q-statistics on squared standardised residuals

Series: DRUSD

Q(5) = 7.57397	[0.1813309]
Q(10) = 11.7495	[0.3021717]
Q(20) = 31.2725	[0.0516936]
Q(50) = 94.5904	[0.0001426]

Series: DRGBP

Q(5) = 3.24332	[0.6625301]
Q(10) = 15.4769	[0.1156179]
Q(20) = 30.1851	[0.0669100]
Q(50) = 58.9212	[0.1814717]

Series: DREUR

Q(5) = 8.43521	[0.1338257]
Q(10) = 8.67983	[0.5627344]
Q(20) = 12.8285	[0.8846217]
Q(50) = 15.6174	[0.9999992]

Series: DRJPY

Q(5) = 8.79697	[0.1174414]
Q(10) = 9.42881	[0.4919474]
Q(20) = 12.4422	[0.9000169]
Q(50) = 34.5793	[0.9523940]

Series: DRCHF

Q(5) = 0.679001	[0.9841013]
Q(10) = 0.699872	[0.9999673]
Q(20) = 0.728985	[1.0000000]
Q(50) = 0.942554	[1.0000000]

H0: No serial correlation ==> Accept H0 when prob. is high [Q < Chisq(lag)]

Vector Normality test: Chi-square(10) = 8,892.1 [0.0000]**

Hosking's Multivariate Portmanteau statistics on standardised residuals

Hosking(5) = 140.487	[0.1626816]
Hosking(10) = 287.125	[0.0532616]
Hosking(20) = 508.697	[0.3841840]
Hosking(50) = 1319.32	[0.0846034]

Hosking's Multivariate Portmanteau statistics on squared standardised residuals

Hosking(5) = 153.887	[0.0309682]
Hosking(10) = 274.357	[0.1202653]
Hosking(20) = 574.690	[0.0097385]
Hosking(50) = 1255.68	[0.4337779]

Warning: *P-values* have been corrected by two degrees of freedom

----

Li and McLeod's Multivariate Portmanteau statistics on standardised residuals

Li-McLeod(5) = 140.499	[0.1625171]
Li-McLeod(10) = 287.047	[0.0536074]
Li-McLeod(20) = 508.828	[0.3826222]
Li-McLeod(50) = 1318.51	[0.0870397]

Li and McLeod's Multivariate Portmanteau statistics on squared standardised residuals

Li-McLeod(5) = 153.881	[0.0309927]
Li-McLeod(10) = 274.371	[0.1201504]
Li-McLeod(20) = 574.086	[0.0102011]
Li-McLeod(50) = 1255.89	[0.4321479]

Warning: *P-values* have been corrected by two degrees of freedom

----

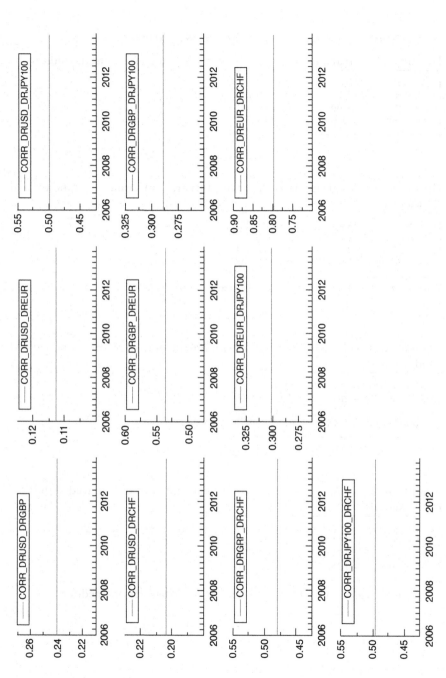

Figure A5.7 Correlations of log difference between five different currency pairs: Constant conditional correlations by Bollerslev (1990) and Student distribution for error terms.

Dynamic conditional correlations by Tse and Tsui (2002)

Normal distribution for error terms
Robust standard errors (Sandwich formula)

	Coefficient	Std. error	t-value	t-prob
rho_21	0.360049	0.066438	5.419	0.0000
rho_31	0.297305	0.096537	3.080	0.0021
rho_41	0.530639	0.054117	9.805	0.0000
rho_51	0.311720	0.070581	4.416	0.0000
rho_32	0.622974	0.037746	16.50	0.0000
rho_42	0.233025	0.056423	4.130	0.0000
rho_52	0.219141	0.15478	1.416	0.1570
rho_43	0.356847	0.10182	3.505	0.0005
rho_53	0.495700	0.27466	1.805	0.0713
rho_54	0.448010	0.18128	2.471	0.0135
alpha	0.039736	0.0050436	7.878	0.0000
beta	0.933642	0.010625	87.87	0.0000

No. of observations: 2,068; No. of parameters: 22
No. of series: 5; Log-likelihood: 40,663.693

TESTS

Information criteria (to be minimised)

Akaike	−39.305312	Shibata	−39.305535
Schwarz	−39.245372	Hannan-Quinn	−39.283341

Individual normality tests

Series: DRUSD

	Statistic	t-test	p-value
Skewness	−0.24891	4.6245	3.7555e-006
Excess Kurtosis	2.1381	19.872	7.1819e-088
Jarque-Bera	415.28	.NaN	6.6545e-091

Series: DRGBP

	Statistic	t-test	p-value
Skewness	−0.26551	4.9328	8.1040e-007
Excess Kurtosis	1.2578	11.690	1.4312e-031
Jarque-Bera	160.63	.NaN	1.3183e-035

Series: DREUR

	Statistic	t-test	p-value
Skewness	−1.2049	22.386	5.3929e-111
Excess Kurtosis	18.463	171.59	0.00000
Jarque-Bera	29873	.NaN	0.00000

Series: DRJPY

	Statistic	t-test	p-value
Skewness	−0.23653	4.3944	1.1110e-005
Excess Kurtosis	3.5894	33.359	5.3971e-244
Jarque-Bera	1129.4	.NaN	5.6100e-246

Series: DRCHF

	Statistic	t-test	p-value
Skewness	12.277	228.10	0.00000
Excess Kurtosis	368.12	3421.2	0.00000
Jarque-Bera	1.1729e+007	.NaN	0.00000

Q-statistics on standardised residuals

Series: DRUSD

Q(5) = 7.36066	[0.1951696]
Q(10) = 12.4663	[0.2550574]
Q(20) = 27.3322	[0.1261748]
Q(50) = 89.3145	[0.0005308]

Series: DRGBP

Q(5) = 2.14055	[0.8293752]
Q(10) = 7.02978	[0.7226306]
Q(20) = 12.4237	[0.9007211]
Q(50) = 43.4007	[0.7336659]

Series: DREUR

Q(5) = 10.8029	[0.0554313]
Q(10) = 19.2285	[0.0374546]
Q(20) = 26.5414	[0.1486655]
Q(50) = 51.0110	[0.4336681]

Series: DRJPY

Q(5) = 5.38492	[0.3707294]
Q(10) = 10.4710	[0.4001880]
Q(20) = 24.7111	[0.2127063]
Q(50) = 56.9546	[0.2322080]

Series: DRCHF

Q(5) = 11.7854	[0.0378491]
Q(10) = 16.6730	[0.0819197]
Q(20) = 21.8527	[0.3485571]
Q(50) = 34.4842	[0.9535925]

H0: No serial correlation ==> Accept H0 when prob. is high [Q < Chisq(lag)]

Q-statistics on squared standardised residuals

Series: DRUSD

Q(5) = 5.43203	[0.3654563]
Q(10) = 8.93802	[0.5379953]
Q(20) = 20.6213	[0.4197143]
Q(50) = 71.8156	[0.0232316]

Series: DRGBP

Q(5) = 3.71541	[0.5910725]
Q(10) = 11.5930	[0.3132170]
Q(20) = 22.4523	[0.3164821]
Q(50) = 46.5657	[0.6119890]

Series: DREUR

Q(5) = 2.60699	[0.7603028]
Q(10) = 2.72944	[0.9870940]
Q(20) = 5.72841	[0.9992177]
Q(50) = 12.1200	[1.0000000]

Series: DRJPY

Q(5) = 8.15712	[0.1477863]
Q(10) = 10.0752	[0.4339172]
Q(20) = 11.6951	[0.9261694]
Q(50) = 32.7605	[0.9716807]

Series: DRCHF

Q(5) = 2.56872	[0.7661117]
Q(10) = 2.58963	[0.9895042]
Q(20) = 2.63216	[0.9999987]
Q(50) = 2.79068	[1.0000000]

H0: No serial correlation ==> Accept H0 when prob. is high [Q < Chisq(lag)]

----

*Vector Normality test: Chi-square(10) = 11,292 [0.0000]***
Hosking's Multivariate Portmanteau statistics on standardised residuals

Hosking(5) = 149.750	[0.0650052]
Hosking(10) = 284.054	[0.0683332]
Hosking(20) = 507.849	[0.3943638]
Hosking(50) = 1286.63	[0.2299699]

Hosking's Multivariate Portmanteau statistics on squared standardised residuals

Hosking(5) = 110.389	[0.7853505]
Hosking(10) = 220.052	[0.8988793]
Hosking(20) = 425.356	[0.9918684]
Hosking(50) = 1022.55	[0.9999992]

Warning: *P-values* have been corrected by two degrees of freedom

----

Li and McLeod's Multivariate Portmanteau statistics on standardised residuals

Li-McLeod(5) = 149.765	[0.0649012]
Li-McLeod(10) = 284.029	[0.0684717]
Li-McLeod(20) = 508.030	[0.3921757]
Li-McLeod(50) = 1286.41	[0.2313369]

Li and McLeod's Multivariate Portmanteau statistics on squared standardised residuals

Li-McLeod(5) = 110.429	[0.7845508]
Li-McLeod(10) = 220.146	[0.8980676]
Li-McLeod(20) = 425.670	[0.9916189]
Li-McLeod(50) = 1025.43	[0.9999989]

Warning: *P-values* have been corrected by two degrees of freedom

----

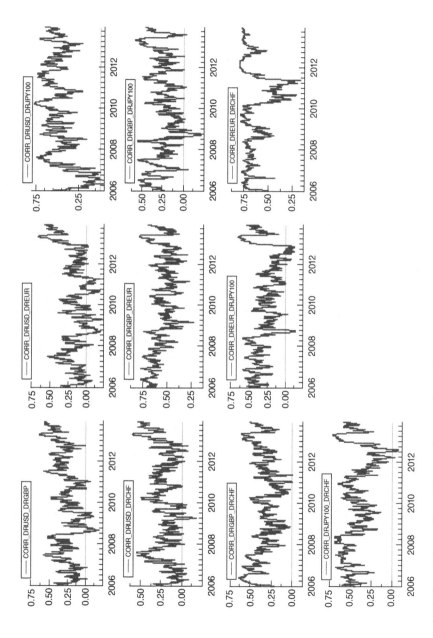

Figure A5.8 Correlations of log difference between five different currency pairs: Dynamic conditional correlations by Tse and Tsui (2002) and normal distribution for error terms.

Student distribution for error terms

Robust standard errors (Sandwich formula)

	Coefficient	*Std. error*	*t-value*	*t-prob*
rho_21	0.342907	0.055703	6.156	0.0000
rho_31	0.281355	0.061191	4.598	0.0000
rho_41	0.536654	0.048675	11.03	0.0000
rho_51	0.290316	0.068670	4.228	0.0000
rho_32	0.595464	0.042612	13.97	0.0000
rho_42	0.360087	0.055560	6.481	0.0000
rho_52	0.584448	0.052963	11.03	0.0000
rho_43	0.474277	0.047197	10.05	0.0000
rho_53	0.895654	0.012286	72.90	0.0000
rho_54	0.607579	0.044184	13.75	0.0000
alpha	0.036422	0.0036522	9.973	0.0000
beta	0.947230	0.0058363	162.3	0.0000
df	6.245787	0.33030	18.91	0.0000

No. of observations: 2,068; No. of parameters: 28
No. of series: 5; Log-likelihood: 42,035.981

TESTS

Information criteria (to be minimised)

Akaike	−40.626674	Shibata	−40.627034
Schwarz	−40.550387	Hannan-Quinn	−40.598710

Individual normality tests

Series: DRUSD

	Statistic	*t-test*	*p-value*
Skewness	−0.20824	3.8687	0.00010940
Excess Kurtosis	1.7594	16.351	4.2452e-060
Jarque-Bera	281.67	.NaN	6.8493e-062

Series: DRGBP

	Statistic	*t-test*	*p-value*
Skewness	−0.62004	11.520	1.0521e-030
Excess Kurtosis	4.6790	43.486	0.00000
Jarque-Bera	2019.0	.NaN	0.00000

Series: DREUR

	Statistic	t-test	p-value
Skewness	−4.0891	75.970	0.00000
Excess Kurtosis	86.296	802.02	0.00000
Jarque-Bera	6.4745e+005	.NaN	0.00000

Series: DRJPY

	Statistic	t-test	p-value
Skewness	−0.25103	4.6638	3.1048e-006
Excess Kurtosis	3.8125	35.433	5.3038e-275
Jarque-Bera	1274.2	.NaN	2.0562e-277

Series: DRCHF

	Statistic	t-test	p-value
Skewness	13.328	247.62	0.00000
Excess Kurtosis	413.78	3845.6	0.00000
Jarque-Bera	1.4814e+007	.NaN	0.00000

Q-statistics on Standardised Residuals

Series: DRUSD

Q(5) = 6.19040	[0.2881309]
Q(10) = 11.9210	[0.2903753]
Q(20) = 27.1781	[0.1303275]
Q(50) = 90.5274	[0.0003948]

Series: DRGBP

Q(5) = 1.67004	[0.8926519]
Q(10) = 5.27358	[0.8721695]
Q(20) = 7.88885	[0.9925779]
Q(50) = 36.3022	[0.9266505]

Series: DREUR

Q(5) = 7.97614	[0.1575556]
Q(10) = 15.1537	[0.1265561]
Q(20) = 24.2645	[0.2310305]
Q(50) = 45.0239	[0.6728691]

Series: DRJPY

Q(5) = 4.40167	[0.4931465]
Q(10) = 7.89629	[0.6389661]
Q(20) = 20.4833	[0.4280822]
Q(50) = 54.0569	[0.3222207]

Series: DRCHF

Q(5) = 8.72789	[0.1204225]
Q(10) = 12.6671	[0.2428865]
Q(20) = 16.1501	[0.7072667]
Q(50) = 32.3824	[0.9748031]

H0: No serial correlation ==> Accept H0 when prob. is high [Q < Chisq(lag)]

Q-statistics on squared standardised residuals

Series: DRUSD

Q(5) = 9.87986	[0.0787117]
Q(10) = 12.9551	[0.2261909]
Q(20) = 28.5277	[0.0974841]
Q(50) = 93.9630	[0.0001673]

Series: DRGBP

Q(5) = 8.80924	[0.1169190]
Q(10) = 10.2661	[0.4174670]
Q(20) = 16.0509	[0.7134603]
Q(50) = 30.8172	[0.9850042]

Series: DREUR

Q(5) = 0.864516	[0.9727371]
Q(10) = 0.917616	[0.9998842]
Q(20) = 1.17540	[1.0000000]
Q(50) = 1.92886	[1.0000000]

Series: DRJPY

Q(5) = 8.10215	[0.1506950]
Q(10) = 9.71482	[0.4658591]
Q(20) = 12.3659	[0.9029065]
Q(50) = 28.4651	[0.9938916]

Series: DRCHF

Q(5) = 0.243164	[0.9985776]
Q(10) = 0.263876	[0.9999997]
Q(20) = 0.300130	[1.0000000]
Q(50) = 0.393617	[1.0000000]

H0: No serial correlation ==> Accept H0 when prob. is high [Q < Chisq(lag)]

Vector Normality test: Chi-square(10) = 7,041.3 [0.0000]
Hosking's Multivariate Portmanteau statistics on standardised residuals

Hosking(5) = 139.305	[0.1803158]
Hosking(10) = 261.321	[0.2985527]
Hosking(20) = 474.388	[0.7890099]
Hosking(50) = 1243.89	[0.5433898]

Hosking's Multivariate Portmanteau statistics on squared standardised residuals

Hosking(5) = 137.094	[0.1817981]
Hosking(10) = 249.916	[0.4539339]
Hosking(20) = 449.878	[0.9400948]
Hosking(50) = 1075.91	[0.9998429]

Warning: *P-values* have been corrected by two degrees of freedom

----

Li and McLeod's Multivariate Portmanteau statistics on standardised residuals

Li-McLeod(5) = 139.320	[0.1800825]
Li-McLeod(10) = 261.347	[0.2981603]
Li-McLeod(20) = 474.701	[0.7860381]
Li-McLeod(50) = 1243.98	[0.5426975]

Li and McLeod's Multivariate Portmanteau statistics on squared standardised residuals

Li-McLeod(5) = 137.123	[0.1813476]
Li-McLeod(10) = 249.981	[0.4527788]
Li-McLeod(20) = 450.189	[0.9388335]
Li-McLeod(50) = 1078.30	[0.9998079]

Warning: *P-values* have been corrected by two degrees of freedom

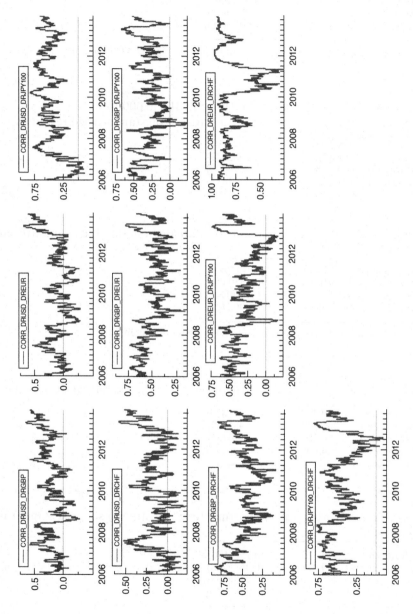

Figure A5.9 Correlations of log difference between five different currency pairs: Dynamic conditional correlations by Tse and Tsui (2002) and Student distribution for error terms.

Dynamic conditional correlations by Engle (2002)

Normal distribution for error terms

Robust standard errors (Sandwich formula)

	Coefficient	Std. error	t-value	t-prob
rho_21	0.310282	0.064545	4.807	0.0000
rho_31	0.207837	0.075765	2.743	0.0061
rho_41	0.442170	0.072159	6.128	0.0000
rho_51	0.141057	0.057737	2.443	0.0146
rho_32	0.549069	0.045467	12.08	0.0000
rho_42	0.214314	0.077551	2.764	0.0058
rho_52	0.210497	0.20869	1.009	0.3133
rho_43	0.309163	0.11622	2.660	0.0079
rho_53	0.502141	0.32585	1.541	0.1235
rho_54	0.398508	0.18074	2.205	0.0276
alpha	0.040355	0.0030213	13.36	0.0000
beta	0.941348	0.0040644	231.6	0.0000

No. of observations: 2,068; No. of parameters: 22
No. of series: 5; Log-likelihood: 40,751.623

TESTS

Information criteria (to be minimised)

Akaike	−39.390351	Shibata	−39.390574
Schwarz	−39.330411	Hannan-Quinn	−39.368380

Individual normality tests

Series: DRUSD

	Statistic	t-test	p-value
Skewness	−0.22057	4.0980	4.1682e-005
Excess Kurtosis	1.9460	18.085	4.1603e-073
Jarque-Bera	343.06	.NaN	3.2037e-075

Series: DRGBP

	Statistic	t-test	p-value
Skewness	−0.27042	5.0241	5.0586e-007
Excess Kurtosis	1.2413	11.536	8.6914e-031
Jarque-Bera	157.96	.NaN	4.9990e-035

Series: DREUR

	Statistic	t-test	p-value
Skewness	−1.1277	20.950	1.8621e-097
Excess Kurtosis	17.002	158.01	0.00000
Jarque-Bera	25,345	.NaN	0.00000

Series: DRJPY

	Statistic	t-test	p-value
Skewness	−0.25901	4.8120	1.4941e-006
Excess Kurtosis	3.8967	36.216	3.4616e-287
Jarque-Bera	1331.5	.NaN	7.2768e-290

Series: DRCHF

	Statistic	t-test	p-value
Skewness	11.620	215.88	0.00000
Excess Kurtosis	341.80	3176.6	0.00000
Jarque-Bera	1.0113e+007	.NaN	0.00000

Q-statistics on standardised residuals

Series: DRUSD

Q(5) = 5.34648	[0.3750734]
Q(10) = 9.36782	[0.4975877]
Q(20) = 24.9214	[0.2044549]
Q(50) = 84.1543	[0.0017863]

Series: DRGBP

Q(5) = 2.05914	[0.8409029]
Q(10) = 7.47299	[0.6801632]
Q(20) = 12.8048	[0.8856007]
Q(50) = 45.6212	[0.6495582]

Series: DREUR

Q(5) = 15.3890	[0.0088234]
Q(10) = 24.0253	[0.0075335]
Q(20) = 31.7667	[0.0458490]
Q(50) = 53.3767	[0.3457879]

Series: DRJPY

Q(5) = 5.04845	[0.4099962]
Q(10) = 10.2628	[0.4177450]
Q(20) = 24.9507	[0.2033248]
Q(50) = 54.4961	[0.3074659]

Series: DRCHF

Q(5) = 9.02200	[0.1081900]
Q(10) = 15.4137	[0.1176925]
Q(20) = 21.6911	[0.3575029]
Q(50) = 35.0229	[0.9465080]

H0: No serial correlation ==> Accept H0 when prob. is high [Q < Chisq(lag)]

Q-statistics on squared standardised residuals

Series: DRUSD

Q(5) = 5.23088	[0.3883586]
Q(10) = 8.10673	[0.6184128]
Q(20) = 24.9276	[0.2042165]
Q(50) = 81.0667	[0.0035576]

Series: DRGBP

Q(5) = 2.70297	[0.7456645]
Q(10) = 10.1945	[0.4235997]
Q(20) = 18.8750	[0.5299672]
Q(50) = 44.8686	[0.6788572]

Series: DREUR

Q(5) = 1.25057	[0.9399349]
Q(10) = 1.37470	[0.9992755]
Q(20) = 3.71880	[0.9999746]
Q(50) = 8.35215	[1.0000000]

Series: DRJPY

Q(5) = 6.54616	[0.2566385]
Q(10) = 8.62066	[0.5684420]
Q(20) = 10.2662	[0.9630838]
Q(50) = 30.5438	[0.9863872]

Series: DRCHF

Q(5) = 1.76446	*[0.8806805]*
Q(10) = 1.78560	*[0.9977349]*
Q(20) = 1.82789	*[1.0000000]*
Q(50) = 1.99159	*[1.0000000]*

H0: No serial correlation ==> Accept H0 when prob. is high [Q < Chisq(lag)]

Vector Normality test: Chi-square(10) = 9,384.2 [0.0000]**

Hosking's Multivariate Portmanteau statistics on standardised residuals

Hosking(5) = 140.577	*[0.1613994]*
Hosking(10) = 279.680	*[0.0954858]*
Hosking(20) = 506.670	*[0.4086357]*
Hosking(50) = 1277.59	*[0.2873962]*

Hosking's Multivariate Portmanteau statistics on squared standardised residuals

Hosking(5) = 110.549	*[0.7821475]*
Hosking(10) = 225.314	*[0.8464391]*
Hosking(20) = 428.322	*[0.9892399]*
Hosking(50) = 1001.84	*[0.9999999]*

Warning: P-values have been corrected by two degrees of freedom

----

Li and McLeod's Multivariate Portmanteau statistics on standardised residuals

Li-McLeod(5) = 140.600	*[0.1610606]*
Li-McLeod(10) = 279.647	*[0.0957208]*
Li-McLeod(20) = 506.811	*[0.4069245]*
Li-McLeod(50) = 1277.51	*[0.2878908]*

Li and McLeod's Multivariate Portmanteau statistics on squared standardised residuals

Li-McLeod(5) = 110.590	*[0.7813046]*
Li-McLeod(10) = 225.390	*[0.8455742]*
Li-McLeod(20) = 428.632	*[0.9889275]*
Li-McLeod(50) = 1005.19	*[0.9999999]*

Warning: *P-values* have been corrected by two degrees of freedom

----

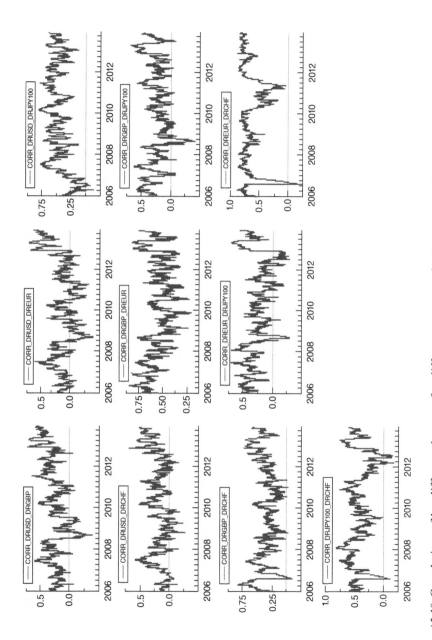

Figure A5.10 Correlations of log difference between five different currency pairs: Dynamic conditional correlations by Engle (2002) and normal distribution for error terms.

Student distribution for error terms

Robust standard errors (Sandwich formula)

	Coefficient	Std. error	t-value	t-prob
rho_21	0.239261	0.056825	4.210	0.0000
rho_31	0.167775	0.063908	2.625	0.0087
rho_41	0.460844	0.051855	8.887	0.0000
rho_51	0.171024	0.069209	2.471	0.0135
rho_32	0.536836	0.042124	12.74	0.0000
rho_42	0.384324	0.054841	7.008	0.0000
rho_52	0.561901	0.047242	11.89	0.0000
rho_43	0.455561	0.048691	9.356	0.0000
rho_53	0.911061	0.011192	81.40	0.0000
rho_54	0.542030	0.044281	12.24	0.0000
alpha	0.040474	0.0028990	13.96	0.0000
beta	0.942911	0.0045841	205.7	0.0000
df	6.358675	0.34450	18.46	0.0000

No. of observations: 2,068; No. of parameters: 28
No. of series: 5; Log-likelihood: 42,041.604

TESTS

Information criteria (to be minimised)

Akaike	−40.632112	Shibata	−40.632472
Schwarz	−40.555825	Hannan−Quinn	−40.604148

Individual normality tests

Series: DRUSD

	Statistic	t-test	p-value
Skewness	−0.19784	3.6756	0.00023728
Excess Kurtosis	1.7369	16.142	1.2859e-058
Jarque-Bera	273.44	.NaN	4.2051e-060

Series: DRGBP

	Statistic	t-test	p-value
Skewness	−0.42746	7.9416	1.9957e-015
Excess Kurtosis	2.3760	22.082	4.6703e-108
Jarque-Bera	549.43	.NaN	4.9207e-120

Series: DREUR

	Statistic	t-test	p-value
Skewness	−4.2526	79.009	0.00000
Excess Kurtosis	89.258	829.54	0.00000
Jarque-Bera	6.9272e+005	.NaN	0.00000

Series: DRJPY

	Statistic	t-test	p-value
Skewness	−0.28203	5.2397	1.6082e-007
Excess Kurtosis	4.1208	38.298	0.00000
Jarque-Bera	1490.6	.NaN	0.00000

Series: DRCHF

	Statistic	t-test	p-value
Skewness	12.243	227.46	0.00000
Excess Kurtosis	370.78	3445.9	0.00000
Jarque-Bera	1.1897e+007	.NaN	0.00000

Q-statistics on standardised residuals

Series: DRUSD

$Q(5)$ = 4.16407	[0.5260443]
$Q(10)$ = 8.42033	[0.5878514]
$Q(20)$ = 24.7460	[0.2113230]
$Q(50)$ = 84.0898	[0.0018127]

Series: DRGBP

$Q(5)$ = 1.60525	[0.9006135]
$Q(10)$ = 5.89094	[0.8243412]
$Q(20)$ = 9.11315	[0.9815593]
$Q(50)$ = 40.3478	[0.8333677]

Series: DREUR

$Q(5)$ = 10.3885	[0.0649460]
$Q(10)$ = 17.9984	[0.0549905]
$Q(20)$ = 25.9528	[0.1673752]
$Q(50)$ = 46.5667	[0.6119504]

Series: DRJPY

Q(5) = 4.28542	[0.5090955]
Q(10) = 8.46495	[0.5835186]
Q(20) = 21.5919	[0.3630585]
Q(50) = 53.6337	[0.3367816]

Series: DRCHF

Q(5) = 6.24500	[0.2831041]
Q(10) = 10.9574	[0.3608498]
Q(20) = 15.2531	[0.7617491]
Q(50) = 33.6783	[0.9628773]

H0: No serial correlation ==> Accept H0 when prob. is high [Q < Chisq(lag)]

Q-statistics on squared standardised residuals

Series: DRUSD

Q(5) = 10.7818	[0.0558826]
Q(10) = 13.4679	[0.1986754]
Q(20) = 34.6731	[0.0219161]
Q(50) = 112.619	[0.0000010]

Series: DRGBP

Q(5) = 2.28553	[0.8083893]
Q(10) = 5.39215	[0.8634916]
Q(20) = 13.4037	[0.8594004]
Q(50) = 33.3288	[0.9664421]

Series: DREUR

Q(5) = 0.0505271	[0.9999700]
Q(10) = 0.113018	[1.0000000]
Q(20) = 0.352236	[1.0000000]
Q(50) = 1.21704	[1.0000000]

Series: DRJPY

Q(5) = 6.76942	[0.2383611]
Q(10) = 8.49123	[0.5809684]
Q(20) = 11.0215	[0.9456624]
Q(50) = 27.8735	[0.9952464]

Series: DRCHF

Q(5) = 0.117060	*[0.9997608]*
Q(10) = 0.140564	*[1.0000000]*
Q(20) = 0.177880	*[1.0000000]*
Q(50) = 0.274771	*[1.0000000]*

H0: No serial correlation ==> Accept H0 when prob. is high [Q < Chisq(lag)]

Vector Normality test: Chi-square(10) = 7120.4 [0.0000]**

Hosking's Multivariate Portmanteau statistics on standardised residuals

Hosking(5) = 133.491	*[0.2852756]*
Hosking(10) = 262.456	*[0.2817150]*
Hosking(20) = 478.955	*[0.7434129]*
Hosking(50) = 1258.70	*[0.4258918]*

Hosking's Multivariate Portmanteau statistics on squared standardised residuals

Hosking(5) = 112.476	*[0.7416090]*
Hosking(10) = 220.780	*[0.8924790]*
Hosking(20) = 431.618	*[0.9855001]*
Hosking(50) = 1089.32	*[0.9995306]*

Warning: P-values have been corrected by two degrees of freedom

----

Li and McLeod's Multivariate Portmanteau statistics on standardised residuals

Li-McLeod(5) = 133.515	*[0.2847814]*
Li-McLeod(10) = 262.465	*[0.2815789]*
Li-McLeod(20) = 479.212	*[0.7407211]*
Li-McLeod(50) = 1258.61	*[0.4265379]*

Li and McLeod's Multivariate Portmanteau statistics on squared standardised residuals

Li-McLeod(5) = 112.511	*[0.7408390]*
Li-McLeod(10) = 220.871	*[0.8916606]*
Li-McLeod(20) = 431.846	*[0.9852060]*
Li-McLeod(50) = 1091.17	*[0.9994579]*

Warning: P-values have been corrected by two degrees of freedom

----

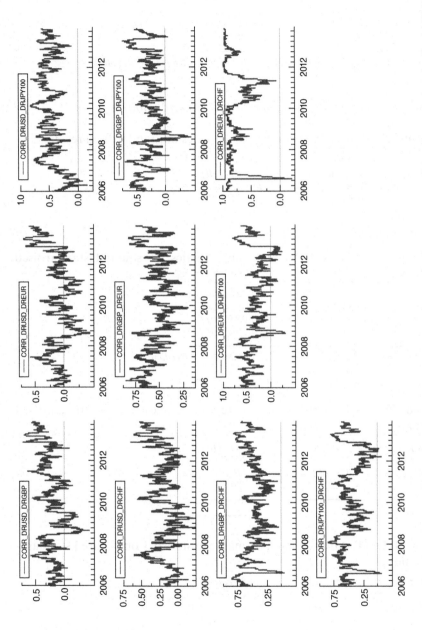

Figure A5.11 Correlations of log difference between five different currency pairs: Dynamic conditional correlations by Engle (2002) and Student distribution for error terms.

Orthogonal GARCH model

Normal distribution

Unconditional mean of the raw series

	Unconditional mean
DRUSD	−7.3263e-005
DREUR	−1.8273e-005
DRJPY	−1.8347e-005
DRCHF	9.4756e-005

STEP 1: PC analysis

Principal components analysis on the correlation matrix

Component	*Eigenvalue*	*Proportion*	*Cumulative*
1.0000	2.3503	0.47006	0.47006
2.0000	1.2509	0.25018	0.72024
3.0000	0.71803	0.14361	0.86384
4.0000	0.37018	0.074036	0.93788
5.0000	0.31060	0.062121	1.0000

Eigenvectors

	PC_1	*PC_2*	*PC_3*	*PC_4*	*PC_5*
DRUSD	0.35299	0.61216	0.39064	0.58974	−0.016550
DRGBP	0.43880	−0.32711	0.67822	−0.38102	−0.30871
DREUR	0.49405	−0.44425	−0.079770	0.23802	0.70395
DRJPY	0.41988	0.54376	−0.26045	−0.63666	0.23423
DRCHF	0.51232	−0.15885	−0.55966	0.21225	−0.59500

Correlation between the PC and the variables

	PC_1	*PC_2*	*PC_3*	*PC_4*	*PC_5*
DRUSD	0.54116	0.68465	0.33101	0.35881	−0.0092236
DRGBP	0.67271	−0.36585	0.57470	−0.23182	−0.17205
DREUR	0.75741	−0.49686	−0.067594	0.14482	0.39232
DRJPY	0.64370	0.60816	−0.22069	−0.38736	0.13054
DRCHF	0.78543	−0.17766	−0.47424	0.12914	−0.33160

O-GARCH rotation matrix

Rotation matrix (Z_m = P_m L_m^1/2 with m=5)

0.54116	0.68465	0.33101	0.35881	−0.0092236
0.67271	−0.36585	0.57470	−0.23182	−0.17205
0.75741	−0.49686	−0.067594	0.14482	0.39232
0.64370	0.60816	−0.22069	−0.38736	0.13054
0.78543	−0.17766	−0.47424	0.12914	−0.33160

STEP 2: ML estimation of the GARCH-type models on the unobserved factors
--------------Estimating the univariate GARCH model for PC(1)--------------

Robust standard errors (Sandwich formula)

	Coefficient	Std. error	t-value	t-prob
ARCH(Alpha1)	0.087019	0.020981	4.148	0.0000
GARCH(Beta1)	0.874149	0.034068	25.66	0.0000
Sigma-square	0.038832			

No. of observations	2,068	No. of parameters	2
Mean (Y):	−0.00000	Variance (Y):	1.00000
Skewness (Y):	0.16319	Kurtosis (Y):	6.04978
Log-likelihood	−2816.620	Alpha[1]+Beta[1]:	0.96117

--------------Estimating the univariate GARCH model for PC(2)--------------

Robust standard errors (Sandwich formula)

	Coefficient	Std. error	t-value	t-prob
ARCH(Alpha1)	0.071489	0.013148	5.437	0.0000
GARCH(Beta1)	0.919784	0.016211	56.74	0.0000
Sigma-square	0.008727			

No. of observations	2,068	No. of parameters	2
Mean (Y):	0.00000	Variance (Y):	1.00000
Skewness (Y):	0.19640	Kurtosis (Y):	6.75266
Log-likelihood:	2659.444	Alpha[1]+Beta[1]:	0.99127

--------------Estimating the univariate GARCH model for PC(3)--------------

Robust standard errors (Sandwich formula)

	Coefficient	*Std. error*	*t-value*	*t-prob*
ARCH(Alpha1)	0.097171	0.018921	5.136	0.0000
GARCH(Beta1)	0.879993	0.030807	28.56	0.0000
Sigma-square	0.022836			

No. of observations:	*2,068*	*No. of parameters:*	*2*
Mean (Y):	0.00000	Variance (Y):	1.00000
Skewness (Y):	−0.08087	Kurtosis (Y):	14.35688
Log-likelihood:	2688.206	Alpha[1]+Beta[1]:	0.97716

--------------Estimating the univariate GARCH model for PC(4)--------------

Robust standard errors (Sandwich formula)

	Coefficient	*Std. error*	*t-value*	*t-prob*
ARCH(Alpha1)	0.033489	0.0070499	4.750	0.0000
GARCH(Beta1)	0.958145	0.0094353	101.5	0.0000
Sigma-square	0.008367			

No. of observations:	*2,068*	*No. of parameters:*	*2*
Mean (Y):	0.00000	Variance (Y):	1.00000
Skewness (Y):	0.15377	Kurtosis (Y):	4.84523
Log-likelihood	−2842.176	Alpha[1]+Beta[1]:	0.99163

--------------Estimating the univariate GARCH model for PC(5)--------------

Robust standard errors (Sandwich formula)

	Coefficient	*Std. error*	*t-value*	*t-prob*
ARCH(Alpha1)	0.205782	0.078392	2.625	0.0087
GARCH(Beta1)	0.721771	0.16528	4.367	0.0000
Sigma-square	0.072447			

No. of observations:	*2,068*	*No. of parameters:*	*2*
Mean (Y):	0.00000	Variance (Y):	1.00000
Skewness (Y):	0.87727	Kurtosis (Y):	57.81050
Log-likelihood	−2543.437	Alpha[1]+Beta[1]:	0.92755

Summary statistics

No. of observations:	2,068	No. of parameters:	15
No. of series:	5	Log-likelihood:	40,661.806

TESTS

Information criteria (to be minimised)

Akaike	−39.310257	Shibata	−39.310361
Schwarz	−39.269389	Hannan-Quinn	−39.295276

Individual normality tests

Series: DRUSD

	Statistic	*t-test*	*p-value*
Skewness	−0.21852	4.0599	4.9101e-005
Excess Kurtosis	1.4769	13.726	7.1116e-043
Jarque-Bera	204.40	.NaN	4.1160e-045

Series: DRGBP

	Statistic	*t-test*	*p-value*
Skewness	−0.29218	5.4283	5.6882e-008
Excess Kurtosis	2.1189	19.693	2.4846e-086
Jarque-Bera	416.30	.NaN	4.0021e-091

Series: DREUR

	Statistic	*t-test*	*p-value*
Skewness	−0.64523	11.988	4.1275e-033
Excess Kurtosis	7.0618	65.631	0.00000
Jarque-Bera	4440.6	.NaN	0.00000

Series: DRJPY

	Statistic	*t-test*	*p-value*
Skewness	−0.076555	1.4223	0.15494
Excess Kurtosis	3.2005	29.744	2.0486e-194
Jarque-Bera	884.62	.NaN	8.0857e-193

Series: DRCHF

	Statistic	*t-test*	*p-value*
Skewness	*6.6356*	*123.28*	*0.00000*
Excess Kurtosis	*177.05*	*1645.5*	*0.00000*
Jarque-Bera	*2.7163e+006*	*.NaN*	*0.00000*

Q-statistics on standardised residuals

Series: DRUSD

Q(5) = 1.88157	*[0.8652778]*
Q(10) = 4.95946	*[0.8938697]*
Q(20) = 16.6470	*[0.6757636]*
Q(50) = 71.3167	*[0.0254823]*

Series: DRGBP

Q(5) = 4.83280	*[0.4366244]*
Q(10) = 9.03904	*[0.5284029]*
Q(20) = 16.3159	*[0.6968438]*
Q(50) = 57.6161	*[0.2141884]*

Series: DREUR

Q(5) = 11.2629	*[0.0464090]*
Q(10) = 21.2320	*[0.0195325]*
Q(20) = 27.0482	*[0.1339142]*
Q(50) = 57.8559	*[0.2078932]*

Series: DRJPY

Q(5) = 6.24403	*[0.2831925]*
Q(10) = 12.9759	*[0.2250203]*
Q(20) = 25.2055	*[0.1936831]*
Q(50) = 67.4898	*[0.0501273]*

Series: DRCHF

Q(5) = 15.0448	*[0.0101727]*
Q(10) = 23.1644	*[0.0101559]*
Q(20) = 33.3179	*[0.0311265]*
Q(50) = 60.5606	*[0.1456342]*

H0: No serial correlation ==> Accept H0 when prob. is high [Q < Chisq(lag)]

Q-statistics on squared standardised residuals

Series: DRUSD

Q(5) = 40.5884	*[0.0000001]*
Q(10) = 68.7762	*[0.0000000]*
Q(20) = 102.129	*[0.0000000]*
Q(50) = 182.336	*[0.0000000]*

Series: DRGBP

Q(5) = 4.77597	*[0.4438289]*
Q(10) = 39.2020	*[0.0000234]*
Q(20) = 98.6008	*[0.0000000]*
Q(50) = 211.168	*[0.0000000]*

Series: DREUR

Q(5) = 16.4633	*[0.0056386]*
Q(10) = 16.7884	*[0.0791796]*
Q(20) = 23.8763	*[0.2478358]*
Q(50) = 37.5264	*[0.9034045]*

Series: DRJPY

Q(5) = 36.8912	*[0.0000006]*
Q(10) = 46.6480	*[0.0000011]*
Q(20) = 55.8023	*[0.0000311]*
Q(50) = 87.1140	*[0.0008987]*

Series: DRCHF

Q(5) = 8.89995	*[0.1131221]*
Q(10) = 8.92381	*[0.5393493]*
Q(20) = 8.98054	*[0.9831316]*
Q(50) = 9.22976	*[1.0000000]*

H0: No serial correlation ==> Accept H0 when prob. is high [Q < Chisq(lag)]

Vector Normality test: Chi-square(10) = 6749.3 [0.0000]

Hosking's Multivariate Portmanteau statistics on standardised residuals

Hosking(5) = 123.338	*[0.5252614]*
Hosking(10) = 254.530	*[0.4086038]*
Hosking(20) = 451.573	*[0.9409250]*
Hosking(50) = 1245.81	*[0.5281511]*

Hosking's Multivariate Portmanteau statistics on squared standardised residuals

Hosking(5) = 181.341	*[0.0004908]*
Hosking(10) = 373.973	*[0.0000004]*
Hosking(20) = 701.601	*[0.0000000]*
Hosking(50) = 1604.26	*[0.0000000]*

Warning: *P-values* have been corrected by two degrees of freedom

----

Li and McLeod's Multivariate Portmanteau statistics on standardised residuals

Li-McLeod(5) = 123.388	*[0.5239973]*
Li-McLeod(10) = 254.549	*[0.4082718]*
Li-McLeod(20) = 451.978	*[0.9392943]*
Li-McLeod(50) = 1245.61	*[0.5297433]*

Li and McLeod's Multivariate Portmanteau statistics on squared standardised residuals

Li-McLeod(5) = 181.302	*[0.0004942]*
Li-McLeod(10) = 373.656	*[0.0000004]*
Li-McLeod(20) = 700.680	*[0.0000000]*
Li-McLeod(50) = 1600.65	*[0.0000000]*

Warning: P-values have been corrected by two degrees of freedom

----

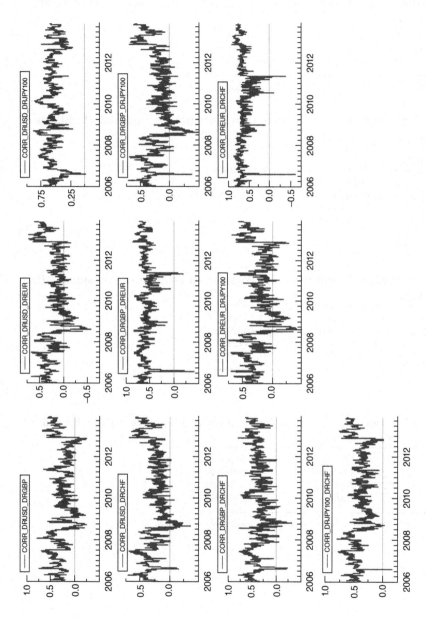

Figure A5.12 Correlations of log difference between five different currency pairs: Orthogonal GARCH and normal distribution for error terms.

Student distribution for error terms

	Coefficient	Std. error	t-value	t-prob
ARCH(Alpha1)	0.205782	0.078392	2.625	0.0087
GARCH(Beta1)	0.721771	0.16528	4.367	0.0000
Sigma-square	0.072447			

No. of observations:	2,068	No. of parameters:	2
Mean (Y):	0.00000	Variance (Y):	1.00000
Skewness (Y):	0.87727	Kurtosis (Y):	57.81050
Log-likelihood	−2543.437	Alpha[1]+Beta[1]:	0.92755

Summary statistics

No. of observations:	2,068	No. of parameters:	15
No. of series:	5	Log-likelihood:	40,661.806

TESTS

Information criteria (to be minimised)

Akaike	−39.310257	Shibata	−39.310361
Schwarz	−39.269389	Hannan-Quinn	−39.295276

Individual normality tests

Series: DRUSD

	Statistic	t-test	p-value
Skewness	−0.21852	4.0599	4.9101e-005
Excess Kurtosis	1.4769	13.726	7.1116e-043
Jarque-Bera	204.40	.NaN	4.1160e-045

Series: DRGBP

	Statistic	t-test	p-value
Skewness	−0.29218	5.4283	5.6882e-008
Excess Kurtosis	2.1189	19.693	2.4846e-086
Jarque-Bera	416.30	.NaN	4.0021e-091

Series: DREUR

	Statistic	t–test	p–value
Skewness	−0.64523	11.988	4.1275e-033
Excess Kurtosis	7.0618	65.631	0.00000
Jarque-Bera	4440.6	.NaN	0.00000

Series: DRJPY

	Statistic	t-test	p-value
Skewness	0.076555	1.4223	0.15494
Excess Kurtosis	3.2005	29.744	2.0486e-194
Jarque-Bera	884.62	.NaN	8.0857e-193

Series: DRCHF

	Statistic	t-test	p-value
Skewness	6.6356	123.28	0.00000
Excess Kurtosis	177.05	1645.5	0.00000
Jarque-Bera	2.7163e+006	.NaN	0.00000

Q-statistics on standardised residuals

Series: DRUSD

Q(5) = 1.88157	[0.8652778]
Q(10) = 4.95946	[0.8938697]
Q(20) = 16.6470	[0.6757636]
Q(50) = 71.3167	[0.0254823]

Series: DRGBP

Q(5) = 4.83280	[0.4366244]
Q(10) = 9.03904	[0.5284029]
Q(20) = 16.3159	[0.6968438]
Q(50) = 57.6161	[0.2141884]

Series: DREUR

Q(5) = 11.2629	[0.0464090]
Q(10) = 21.2320	[0.0195325]
Q(20) = 27.0482	[0.1339142]
Q(50) = 57.8559	[0.2078932]

Series: DRJPY

Q(5) = 6.24403	[0.2831925]
Q(10) = 12.9759	[0.2250203]
Q(20) = 25.2055	[0.1936831]
Q(50) = 67.4898	[0.0501273]

Series: DRCHF

Q(5) = 15.0448	[0.0101727]
Q(10) = 23.1644	[0.0101559]
Q(20) = 33.3179	[0.0311265]
Q(50) = 60.5606	[0.1456342]

H0: No serial correlation ==> Accept H0 when prob. is high [Q < Chisq(lag)]

Q-statistics on squared standardised residuals

Series: DRUSD

Q(5) = 40.5884	[0.0000001]
Q(10) = 68.7762	[0.0000000]
Q(20) = 102.129	[0.0000000]
Q(50) = 182.336	[0.0000000]

Series: DRGBP

Q(5) = 4.77597	[0.4438289]
Q(10) = 39.2020	[0.0000234]
Q(20) = 98.6008	[0.0000000]
Q(50) = 211.168	[0.0000000]

Series: DREUR

Q(5) = 16.4633	[0.0056386]
Q(10) = 16.7884	[0.0791796]
Q(20) = 23.8763	[0.2478358]
Q(50) = 37.5264	[0.9034045]

Series: DRJPY

Q(5) = 36.8912	[0.0000006]
Q(10) = 46.6480	[0.0000011]
Q(20) = 55.8023	[0.0000311]
Q(50) = 87.1140	[0.0008987]

Series: DRCHF

Q(5) = 8.89995	[0.1131221]
Q(10) = 8.92381	[0.5393493]
Q(20) = 8.98054	[0.9831316]
Q(50) = 9.22976	[1.0000000]

H0: No serial correlation ==> Accept H0 when prob. is high [Q < Chisq(lag)]

Vector Normality test: Chi-square (10) = 6749.3 [0.0000]**

Hosking's Multivariate Portmanteau statistics on standardised residuals

Hosking(5) = 123.338	[0.5252614]
Hosking(10) = 254.530	[0.4086038]
Hosking(20) = 451.573	[0.9409250]
Hosking(50) = 1245.81	[0.5281511]

Hosking's Multivariate Portmanteau statistics on squared standardised residuals

Hosking(5) = 181.341	[0.0004908]
Hosking(10) = 373.973	[0.0000004]
Hosking(20) = 701.601	[0.0000000]
Hosking(50) = 1604.26	[0.0000000]

Warning: *P-values* have been corrected by two degrees of freedom

----

Li and McLeod's Multivariate Portmanteau statistics on standardised residuals

Li-McLeod(5) = 123.388	[0.5239973]
Li-McLeod(10) = 254.549	[0.4082718]
Li-McLeod(20) = 451.978	[0.9392943]
Li-McLeod(50) = 1245.61	[0.5297433]

Li and McLeod's Multivariate Portmanteau statistics on squared standardised residuals

Li-McLeod(5) = 181.302	[0.0004942]
Li-McLeod(10) = 373.656	[0.0000004]
Li-McLeod(20) = 700.680	[0.0000000]
Li-McLeod(50) = 1600.65	[0.0000000]

Warning: *P-values* have been corrected by two degrees of freedom

----

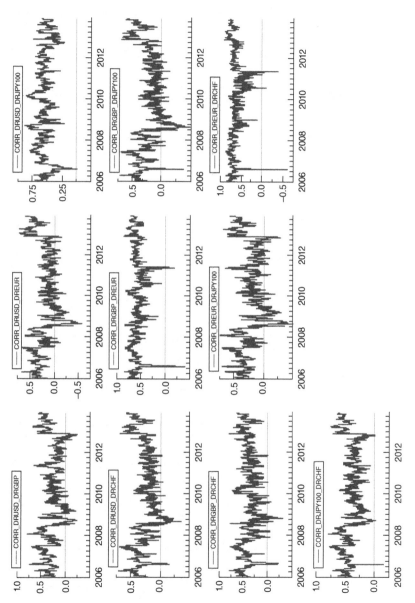

Figure A5.13 Correlations of log difference between five different currency pairs: Orthogonal GARCH and Student distribution for error terms.

GO-GARCH model (by Van der Wedie (2002))

Normal distribution for error terms

delta_1	−0.517615	0.096866	−5.344	0.0000
delta_2	−0.457724	0.071060	−6.441	0.0000
delta_3	−0.409299	0.079237	−5.166	0.0000
delta_4	−0.124049	0.062268	−1.992	0.0465
delta_5	−0.162403	0.52860	−0.3072	0.7587
delta_6	0.710688	0.42546	1.670	0.0950
delta_7	0.308336	0.39626	0.7781	0.4366
delta_8	0.428800	0.23990	1.787	0.0740
delta_9	0.373240	0.17818	2.095	0.0363
delta_10	0.079617	0.11745	0.6779	0.4979

Part: PC_1

ARCH(Alpha1)	0.138439	0.030018	4.612	0.0000
GARCH(Beta1)	0.829607	0.042845	19.36	0.0000

Part: PC_2

ARCH(Alpha1)	0.057592	0.052778	1.091	0.2753
GARCH(Beta1)	0.933455	0.075591	12.35	0.0000

Part: PC_3

ARCH(Alpha1)	0.064389	0.034643	1.859	0.0632
GARCH(Beta1)	0.928144	0.039793	23.32	0.0000

Part: PC_4

ARCH(Alpha1)	0.039999	0.011949	3.348	0.0008
GARCH(Beta1)	0.951200	0.018954	50.19	0.0000

Part: PC_5

ARCH(Alpha1)	0.344733	0.56219	0.6132	0.5398
GARCH(Beta1)	0.514381	0.91697	0.5610	0.5749

No. of observations:	*2,068*	*No. of parameters:*	20

No. of series:	5	Log-likelihood:	−13241.389
Elapsed time	23.167 seconds (or 0.386117 minutes)		

Summary statistics

| No. of observations: | 2,068 | No. of parameters: | 25 |
| No. of series: | 5 | Log-likelihood: | 40,970.300 |

TESTS

Information criteria (to be minimised)

| Akaike | −39.598936 | Shibata | −39.599223 |
| Schwarz | −39.530822 | Hannan-Quinn | −39.573968 |

Individual normality tests

Series: DRUSD

	Statistic	*t-test*	*p-value*
Skewness	−0.083218	1.5461	0.12209
Excess Kurtosis	1.3478	12.526	5.3647e-036
Jarque-Bera	158.92	.NaN	3.1041e-035

Series: DRGBP

	Statistic	*t-test*	*p-value*
Skewness	−0.16997	3.1579	0.0015893
Excess Kurtosis	1.3146	12.218	2.4954e-034
Jarque-Bera	158.87	.NaN	3.1687e-035

Series: DREUR

	Statistic	*t-test*	*p-value*
Skewness	−0.64683	12.017	2.8840e-033
Excess Kurtosis	7.6823	71.398	0.00000
Jarque-Bera	5229.6	.NaN	0.00000

Series: DRJPY

	Statistic	*t-test*	*p-value*
Skewness	−0.24095	4.4766	7.5851e-006
Excess Kurtosis	3.9285	36.511	0.00000
Jarque-Bera	1349.9	.NaN	7.6362e-294

Series: DRCHF

	Statistic	*t-test*	*p-value*
Skewness	6.7483	125.37	0.00000
Excess Kurtosis	168.69	1567.8	0.00000
Jarque-Bera	2.4676e+006	.NaN	0.00000

Q-statistics on standardised residuals

Series: DRUSD

Q(5) = 4.60268	[0.4662643]
Q(10) = 9.66699	[0.4701789]
Q(20) = 23.7351	[0.2541543]
Q(50) = 75.9563	[0.0104067]

Series: DRGBP

Q(5) = 4.06119	[0.5406402]
Q(10) = 7.40317	[0.6869135]
Q(20) = 13.8185	[0.8395793]
Q(50) = 44.5178	[0.6922684]

Series: DREUR

Q(5) = 17.1369	[0.0042473]
Q(10) = 27.4861	[0.0021805]
Q(20) = 38.2175	[0.0083291]
Q(50) = 69.2578	[0.0369397]

Series: DRJPY

Q(5) = 6.65593	[0.2475120]
Q(10) = 13.4329	[0.2004648]
Q(20) = 24.0580	[0.2398691]
Q(50) = 64.5428	[0.0809840]

Series: DRCHF

Q(5) = 4.58192	[0.4689986]
Q(10) = 9.59348	[0.4768527]
Q(20) = 19.7621	[0.4728948]
Q(50) = 44.7847	[0.6820830]

H0: No serial correlation ==> Accept H0 when prob. is high [Q < Chisq(lag)]

Q-statistics on squared standardised residuals

Series: DRUSD

Q(5) = 12.3251	[0.0305951]
Q(10) = 14.8939	[0.1359775]
Q(20) = 26.8933	[0.1382937]
Q(50) = 60.8967	[0.1389908]

Series: DRGBP

Q(5) = 3.86952	[0.5683513]
Q(10) = 16.0126	[0.0992736]
Q(20) = 30.9962	[0.0552405]
Q(50) = 53.4372	[0.3436569]

Series: DREUR

Q(5) = 31.0201	[0.0000093]
Q(10) = 31.2862	[0.0005262]
Q(20) = 39.7590	[0.0053577]
Q(50) = 55.5305	[0.2742458]

Series: DRJPY

Q(5) = 18.4779	[0.0024034]
Q(10) = 24.3596	[0.0067010]
Q(20) = 28.4068	[0.1001132]
Q(50) = 53.0658	[0.3568355]

Series: DRCHF

Q(5) = 0.265028	[0.9982496]
Q(10) = 0.295234	[0.9999995]
Q(20) = 0.356119	[1.0000000]
Q(50) = 0.637818	[1.0000000]

H0: No serial correlation ==> Accept H0 when prob. is high [Q < Chisq(lag)]

Vector Normality test: Chi-square (10) = 5540.1 [0.0000]**

Hosking's Multivariate Portmanteau statistics on standardised residuals

Hosking(5) = 148.267	[0.0762738]
Hosking(10) = 282.792	[0.0754486]
Hosking(20) = 491.895	[0.5935164]
Hosking(50) = 1281.90	[0.2591438]

Hosking's Multivariate Portmanteau statistics on squared standardised residuals

Hosking(5) = 219.191	[0.0000002]
Hosking(10) = 359.648	[0.0000045]
Hosking(20) = 615.288	[0.0002508]
Hosking(50) = 1302.97	[0.1361418]

Warning: *P-values* have been corrected by two degrees of freedom

----

Li and McLeod's Multivariate Portmanteau statistics on standardised residuals

Li-McLeod(5) = 148.283	[0.0761452]
Li-McLeod(10) = 282.766	[0.0756006]
Li-McLeod(20) = 492.151	[0.5903302]
Li-McLeod(50) = 1281.62	[0.2609624]

Li and McLeod's Multivariate Portmanteau statistics on squared standardised residuals

Li-McLeod(5) = 219.171	[0.0000002]
Li-McLeod(10) = 359.561	[0.0000045]
Li-McLeod(20) = 615.108	[0.0002555]
Li-McLeod(50) = 1303.83	[0.1325114]

Warning: *P-values* have been corrected by two degrees of freedom

----

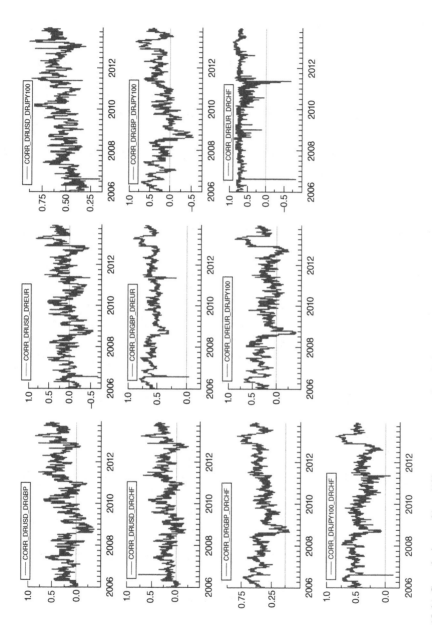

Figure A5.14 Correlations of log difference between five different currency pairs: Generalisation of Orthogonal GARCH model (by Van der Wedie (2002)) and normal distribution for error terms.

Student distribution for error terms

Part: U Matrix

	Coefficient	Std. error	t-value	t-prob
delta_1	−0.517615	0.096866	−5.344	0.0000
delta_2	−0.457724	0.071060	−6.441	0.0000
delta_3	−0.409299	0.079237	−5.166	0.0000
delta_4	−0.124049	0.062268	−1.992	0.0465
delta_5	−0.162403	0.52860	−0.3072	0.7587
delta_6	0.710688	0.42546	1.670	0.0950
delta_7	0.308336	0.39626	0.7781	0.4366
delta_8	0.428800	0.23990	1.787	0.0740
delta_9	0.373240	0.17818	2.095	0.0363
delta_10	0.079617	0.11745	0.6779	0.4979

Part: PC_1

ARCH(Alpha1)	0.138439	0.030018	4.612	0.0000
GARCH(Beta1)	0.829607	0.042845	19.36	0.0000

Part: PC_2

ARCH(Alpha1)	0.057592	0.052778	1.091	0.2753
GARCH(Beta1)	0.933455	0.075591	12.35	0.0000

Part: PC_3

ARCH(Alpha1)	0.064389	0.034643	1.859	0.0632
GARCH(Beta1)	0.928144	0.039793	23.32	0.0000

Part: PC_4

ARCH(Alpha1)	0.039999	0.011949	3.348	0.0008
GARCH(Beta1)	0.951200	0.018954	50.19	0.0000

Part: PC_5

ARCH(Alpha1)	0.344733	0.56219	0.6132	0.5398
GARCH(Beta1)	0.514381	0.91697	0.5610	0.5749

No. of observations:	2,068	No. of parameters:	20
No. of series:	5	Log-likelihood:	−13241.389

Summary statistics

| No. of observations: | 2,068 | No. of parameters: | 25 |
| No. of series: | 5 | Log-likelihood: | 40,970.300 |

TESTS

Information criteria (to be minimised)

| *Akaike* | −39.598936 | *Shibata* | −39.599223 |
| *Schwarz* | −39.530822 | *Hannan-Quinn* | −39.573968 |

Individual normality tests

Series: DRUSD

	Statistic	*t-test*	*p-value*
Skewness	−0.083218	1.5461	0.12209
Excess Kurtosis	1.3478	12.526	5.3647e-036
Jarque-Bera	158.92	*.NaN*	3.1041e-035

Series: DRGBP

	Statistic	*t-test*	*p-value*
Skewness	−0.16997	3.1579	0.0015893
Excess Kurtosis	1.3146	12.218	2.4954e-034
Jarque-Bera	158.87	*.NaN*	3.1687e-035

Series: DREUR

	Statistic	*t-test*	*p-value*
Skewness	−0.64683	12.017	2.8840e-033
Excess Kurtosis	7.6823	71.398	0.00000
Jarque-Bera	5229.6	*.NaN*	0.00000

Series: DRJPY

	Statistic	*t-test*	*p-value*
Skewness	−0.24095	4.4766	7.5851e-006
Excess Kurtosis	3.9285	36.511	0.00000
Jarque-Bera	1349.9	*.NaN*	7.6362e-294

Series: DRCHF

	Statistic	*t-test*	*p-value*
Skewness	*6.7483*	*125.37*	*0.00000*
Excess Kurtosis	*168.69*	*1567.8*	*0.00000*
Jarque-Bera	*2.4676e+006*	*.NaN*	*0.00000*

Q-statistics on standardised residuals

Series: DRUSD

$Q(5)$ = 4.60268	[0.4662643]
$Q(10)$ = 9.66699	[0.4701789]
$Q(20)$ = 23.7351	[0.2541543]
$Q(50)$ = 75.9563	[0.0104067]

Series: DRGBP

$Q(5)$ = 4.06119	[0.5406402]
$Q(10)$ = 7.40317	[0.6869135]
$Q(20)$ = 13.8185	[0.8395793]
$Q(50)$ = 44.5178	[0.6922684]

Series: DREUR

$Q(5)$ = 17.1369	[0.0042473]
$Q(10)$ = 27.4861	[0.0021805]
$Q(20)$ = 38.2175	[0.0083291]
$Q(50)$ = 69.2578	[0.0369397]

Series: DRJPY

$Q(5)$ = 6.65593	[0.2475120]
$Q(10)$ = 13.4329	[0.2004648]
$Q(20)$ = 24.0580	[0.2398691]
$Q(50)$ = 64.5428	[0.0809840]

Series: DRCHF

$Q(5)$ = 4.58192	[0.4689986]
$Q(10)$ = 9.59348	[0.4768527]
$Q(20)$ = 19.7621	[0.4728948]
$Q(50)$ = 44.7847	[0.6820830]

H0: No serial correlation ==> Accept H0 when prob. is high [Q < Chisq(lag)]

Q-statistics on squared standardised residuals

Series: DRUSD

Q(5) = 12.3251	[0.0305951]
Q(10) = 14.8939	[0.1359775]
Q(20) = 26.8933	[0.1382937]
Q(50) = 60.8967	[0.1389908]

Series: DRGBP

Q(5) = 3.86952	[0.5683513]
Q(10) = 16.0126	[0.0992736]
Q(20) = 30.9962	[0.0552405]
Q(50) = 53.4372	[0.3436569]

Series: DREUR

Q(5) = 31.0201	[0.0000093]
Q(10) = 31.2862	[0.0005262]
Q(20) = 39.7590	[0.0053577]
Q(50) = 55.5305	[0.2742458]

Series: DRJPY

Q(5) = 18.4779	[0.0024034]
Q(10) = 24.3596	[0.0067010]
Q(20) = 28.4068	[0.1001132]
Q(50) = 53.0658	[0.3568355]

Series: DRCHF

Q(5) = 0.265028	[0.9982496]
Q(10) = 0.295234	[0.9999995]
Q(20) = 0.356119	[1.0000000]
Q(50) = 0.637818	[1.0000000]

H0: No serial correlation ==> Accept H0 when prob. is high [Q < Chisq(lag)]

Vector Normality test: Chi-square(10) = 5540.1 [0.0000]**

Hosking's Multivariate Portmanteau statistics on standardised residuals

Hosking(5) = 148.267	[0.0762738]
Hosking(10) = 282.792	[0.0754486]
Hosking(20) = 491.895	[0.5935164]
Hosking(50) = 1281.90	[0.2591438]

Hosking's Multivariate Portmanteau statistics on squared standardised residuals

Hosking(5)	*= 219.191*	*[0.0000002]*
Hosking(10)	*= 359.648*	*[0.0000045]*
Hosking(20)	*= 615.288*	*[0.0002508]*
Hosking(50)	*= 1302.97*	*[0.1361418]*

Warning: *P-values* have been corrected by two degrees of freedom

----

Li and McLeod's Multivariate Portmanteau statistics on standardised residuals

Li-McLeod(5)	*= 148.283*	*[0.0761452]*
Li-McLeod(10)	*= 282.766*	*[0.0756006]*
Li-McLeod(20)	*= 492.151*	*[0.5903302]*
Li-McLeod(50)	*= 1281.62*	*[0.2609624]*

Li and McLeod's Multivariate Portmanteau statistics on squared standardised residuals

Li-McLeod(5)	*= 219.171*	*[0.0000002]*
Li-McLeod(10)	*= 359.561*	*[0.0000045]*
Li-McLeod(20)	*= 615.108*	*[0.0002555]*
Li-McLeod(50)	*= 1303.83*	*[0.1325114]*

Warning: *P-values* have been corrected by two degrees of freedom

----

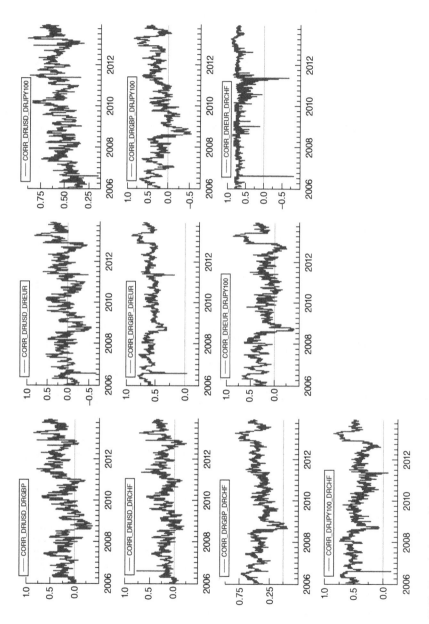

Figure A5.15 Correlations of log difference between five different currency pairs: Generalisation of orthogonal GARCH model (by Van der Wedie (2002)) and Student distribution for error terms.

NLS GO-GARCH model (by Boswijk and Van der Wedie (2006))

Normal distribution for error terms

Summary statistics

No. of observations:	2,068	No. of parameters:	25
No. of series:	5	Log-likelihood:	40,970.300

Unconditional mean of the raw series

Unconditional mean	
DRUSD	−7.3263e-005
DRGBP	−0.00010052
DREUR	−1.8273e-005
DRJPY	−1.8347e-005
DRCHF	9.4756e-005

STEP 1: PC analysis

Principal components analysis on the correlation matrix

Component	*Eigenvalue*	*Proportion*	*Cumulative*
1.0000	2.3503	0.47006	0.47006
2.0000	1.2509	0.25018	0.72024
3.0000	0.71803	0.14361	0.86384
4.0000	0.37018	0.074036	0.93788
5.0000	0.31060	0.062121	1.0000

Eigenvectors

	PC_1	*PC_2*	*PC_3*	*PC_4*	*PC_5*
DRUSD	0.35299	0.61216	0.39064	0.58974	−0.016550
DRGBP	0.43880	−0.32711	0.67822	−0.38102	−0.30871
DREUR	0.49405	−0.44425	−0.079770	0.23802	0.70395
DRJPY	0.41988	0.54376	−0.26045	−0.63666	0.23423
DRCHF	0.51232	−0.15885	−0.55966	0.21225	−0.59500

Correlation between the PC and the variables

	PC_1	PC_2	PC_3	PC_4	PC_5
DRUSD	0.54116	0.68465	0.33101	0.35881	−0.0092236
DRGBP	0.67271	−0.36585	0.57470	−0.23182	−0.17205
DREUR	0.75741	−0.49686	−0.067594	0.14482	0.39232
DRJPY	0.64370	0.60816	−0.22069	−0.38736	0.13054
DRCHF	0.78543	−0.17766	−0.47424	0.12914	−0.33160

STEP 2: NLS estimation of the rotation matrix

NLS function value: −168.418
Estimated Q matrix (symmetric)

0.23818	−0.042920	−0.026811	0.099996	−0.038455
−0.042920	0.51791	−0.14155	−0.12363	0.038462
−0.026811	−0.14155	0.23753	0.034451	0.26602
0.099996	−0.12363	0.034451	0.19998	−0.12907
−0.038455	0.038462	0.26602	−0.12907	0.40813

Estimated U matrix

0.065465	0.44546	−0.60074	0.036532	−0.65959
0.23962	−0.75325	−0.013378	0.41564	−0.44973
−0.83521	−0.33166	−0.11776	−0.36099	−0.21963
0.46009	−0.32426	−0.37841	−0.72301	0.13128
0.17040	0.13797	0.69417	−0.41575	−0.54517

Non-singular matrix (Z = P L^1/2 U)

0.16075	−0.23719	−0.84554	−0.35892	0.27230
−0.35917	0.41010	−0.38672	0.35568	0.65327
−0.38463	0.44040	−0.59829	0.48197	−0.26050
0.34538	−0.52061	−0.60218	0.47968	0.13027
0.48061	0.53118	−0.51502	0.46153	−0.092787

STEP 3: ML estimation of the GARCH-type models on the unobserved factors
--------------Estimating the univariate GARCH model for PC(1)--------------

Log-likelihood = −2460.85

Robust standard errors (Sandwich formula)

	Coefficient	Std. error	t-value	t-prob
ARCH(Alpha1)	0.126802	0.027471	4.616	0.0000
GARCH(Beta1)	0.813129	0.068239	11.92	0.0000
Sigma-square	0.060069			

No. of observations:	2,068	No. of parameters:	2
Mean (Y):	−0.00000	Variance (Y):	1.00000
Skewness (Y):	−0.76988	Kurtosis (Y):	60.95483
Log-likelihood	−2460.845	Alpha[1]+Beta[1]:	0.93993

--------------Estimating the univariate GARCH model for PC(2)--------------

Log-likelihood = −2712.49

Robust standard errors (Sandwich formula)

	Coefficient	Std. error	t-value	t-prob
ARCH(Alpha1)	0.119986	0.023249	5.161	0.0000
GARCH(Beta1)	0.812395	0.058939	13.78	0.0000
Sigma-square	0.067619			

No. of observations:	2,068	No. of parameters:	2
Mean (Y):	0.00000	Variance (Y):	1.00000
Skewness (Y):	−0.56796	Kurtosis (Y):	21.82242
Log-likelihood	−2712.495	Alpha[1]+Beta[1]	0.93238

--------------Estimating the univariate GARCH model for PC(3)--------------

Log-likelihood = −2756.11

Robust standard errors (Sandwich formula)

	Coefficient	Std. error	t-value	t-prob
ARCH(Alpha1)	0.126182	0.028005	4.506	0.0000
GARCH(Beta1)	0.833325	0.040838	20.41	0.0000
Sigma-square	0.040492			

No. of observations:	2,068	No. of parameters:	2
Mean (Y):	−0.00000	Variance (Y):	1.00000
Skewness (Y):	0.04291	Kurtosis (Y):	6.82148
Log-likelihood:	−2756.114	Alpha[1]+Beta[1]:	0.95951

--------------Estimating the univariate GARCH model for PC(4)--------------

Log-likelihood = −2840.08

Robust standard errors (Sandwich formula)

	Coefficient	*Std. error*	*t-value*	*t-prob*
ARCH(Alpha1)	0.039516	0.0084435	4.680	0.0000
GARCH(Beta1)	0.952204	0.012024	79.19	0.0000
Sigma-square	0.008280			

No. of observations:	*2,068*	*No. of parameters:*	*2*
Mean (Y):	−0.00000	Variance (Y):	1.00000
Skewness (Y):	0.24377	Kurtosis (Y):	5.35902
Log-likelihood	−2840.081	Alpha[1]+Beta[1]:	0.99172

--------------Estimating the univariate GARCH model for PC(5)--------------

Log-likelihood = −2671.45

Robust standard errors (Sandwich formula)

	Coefficient	*Std. error*	*t-value*	*t-prob*
ARCH(Alpha1)	0.052366	0.0073858	7.090	0.0000
GARCH(Beta1)	0.943303	0.0085597	110.2	0.0000
Sigma-square	0.004332			

No. of observations:	*2,068*	*No. of parameters:*	*2*
Mean (Y):	0.00000	Variance (Y):	1.00000
Skewness (Y):	−0.21983	Kurtosis (Y):	6.67725
Log-likelihood	−2671.450	Alpha[1]+Beta[1]:	0.99567

Summary statistics

No. of observations:	2,068	No. of parameters:	25
No. of series:	5	Log-likelihood:	40,770.704

TESTS

Information criteria (to be minimised)

Akaike	−39.598936	Shibata	−39.599223
Schwarz	−39.530822	Hannan-Quinn	−39.573968

Individual normality tests

Series: DRUSD

	Statistic	t-test	p-value
Skewness	0.083218	1.5461	0.12209
Excess Kurtosis	1.3478	12.526	5.3647e-036
Jarque-Bera	158.92	.NaN	3.1041e-035

Series: DRGBP

	Statistic	t-test	p-value
Skewness	−0.16997	3.1579	0.0015893
Excess Kurtosis	1.3146	12.218	2.4954e-034
Jarque-Bera	158.87	.NaN	3.1687e-035

Series: DREUR

	Statistic	t-test	p-value
Skewness	−0.64683	12.017	2.8840e-033
Excess Kurtosis	7.6823	71.398	0.00000
Jarque-Bera	5229.6	.NaN	0.00000

Series: DRJPY

	Statistic	t-test	p-value
Skewness	−0.24095	4.4766	7.5851e-006
Excess Kurtosis	3.9285	36.511	0.00000
Jarque-Bera	1349.9	.NaN	7.6362e-294

Series: DRCHF

	Statistic	*t-test*	*p-value*
Skewness	6.7483	125.37	0.00000
Excess Kurtosis	168.69	1567.8	0.00000
Jarque-Bera	2.4676e+006	.NaN	0.00000

Q-statistics on standardised residuals

Series: DRUSD

Q(5) = 4.60268	[0.4662643]
Q(10) = 9.66699	[0.4701789]
Q(20) = 23.7351	[0.2541543]
Q(50) = 75.9563	[0.0104067]

Series: DRGBP

Q(5) = 4.06119	[0.5406402]
Q(10) = 7.40317	[0.6869135]
Q(20) = 13.8185	[0.8395793]
Q(50) = 44.5178	[0.6922684]

Series: DREUR

Q(5) = 17.1369	[0.0042473]
Q(10) = 27.4861	[0.0021805]
Q(20) = 38.2175	[0.0083291]
Q(50) = 69.2578	[0.0369397]

Series: DRJPY

Q(5) = 6.65593	[0.2475120]
Q(10) = 13.4329	[0.2004648]
Q(20) = 24.0580	[0.2398691]
Q(50) = 64.5428	[0.0809840]

Series: DRCHF

Q(5) = 4.58192	[0.4689986]
Q(10) = 9.59348	[0.4768527]
Q(20) = 19.7621	[0.4728948]
Q(50) = 44.7847	[0.6820830]

H0: No serial correlation ==> Accept H0 when prob. is high [Q < Chisq(lag)]

Q-statistics on squared standardised residuals

Series: DRUSD

Q(5) = 12.3251	[0.0305951]
Q(10) = 14.8939	[0.1359775]
Q(20) = 26.8933	[0.1382937]
Q(50) = 60.8967	[0.1389908]

Series: DRGBP

Q(5) = 3.86952	[0.5683513]
Q(10) = 16.0126	[0.0992736]
Q(20) = 30.9962	[0.0552405]
Q(50) = 53.4372	[0.3436569]

Series: DREUR

Q(5) = 31.0201	[0.0000093]
Q(10) = 31.2862	[0.0005262]
Q(20) = 39.7590	[0.0053577]
Q(50) = 55.5305	[0.2742458]

Series: DRJPY

Q(5) = 18.4779	[0.0024034]
Q(10) = 24.3596	[0.0067010]
Q(20) = 28.4068	[0.1001132]
Q(50) = 53.0658	[0.3568355]

Series: DRCHF

Q(5) = 0.265028	[0.9982496]
Q(10) = 0.295234	[0.9999995]
Q(20) = 0.356119	[1.0000000]
Q(50) = 0.637818	[1.0000000]

H0: No serial correlation ==> Accept H0 when prob. is high [Q < Chisq(lag)]

Vector Normality test: Chi-square(10) = 5540.1 [0.0000]**
Hosking's Multivariate Portmanteau statistics on standardised residuals

Hosking(5) = 148.267	[0.0762738]
Hosking(10) = 282.792	[0.0754486]
Hosking(20) = 491.895	[0.5935164]
Hosking(50) = 1281.90	[0.2591438]

Hosking's Multivariate Portmanteau statistics on squared standardised residuals

Hosking(5) = 219.191	[0.0000002]
Hosking(10) = 359.648	[0.0000045]
Hosking(20) = 615.288	[0.0002508]
Hosking(50) = 1302.97	[0.1361418]

Warning: *P-values* have been corrected by two degrees of freedom

----

Li and McLeod's Multivariate Portmanteau statistics on standardised residuals

Li-McLeod(5) = 148.283	[0.0761452]
Li-McLeod(10) = 282.766	[0.0756006]
Li-McLeod(20) = 492.151	[0.5903302]
Li-McLeod(50) = 1281.62	[0.2609624]

Li and McLeod's Multivariate Portmanteau statistics on squared standardised residuals

Li-McLeod(5) = 219.171	[0.0000002]
Li-McLeod(10) = 359.561	[0.0000045]
Li-McLeod(20) = 615.108	[0.0002555]
Li-McLeod(50) = 1303.83	[0.1325114]

Warning: *P-values* have been corrected by two degrees of freedom

----

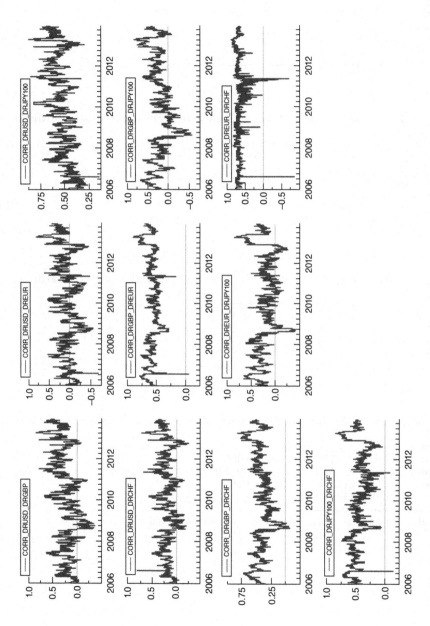

Figure A5.16 Correlations of log difference between five different currency pairs: NLS generalisation of orthogonal GARCH model (by Boswijk and Van der Wedie (2006)) and normal distribution for error terms.

Student distribution for error terms

Unconditional mean of the raw series

Unconditional mean	
DRUSD	-7.3263e-005
DRGBP	-0.00010052
DREUR	-1.8273e-005
DRJPY	-1.8347e-005
DRCHF	9.4756e-005

STEP 1: PC analysis

Principal components analysis on the correlation matrix

Component	Eigenvalue	Proportion	Cumulative
1.0000	2.3503	0.47006	0.47006
2.0000	1.2509	0.25018	0.72024
3.0000	0.71803	0.14361	0.86384
4.0000	0.37018	0.074036	0.93788
5.0000	0.31060	0.062121	1.0000

Eigenvectors

	PC_1	PC_2	PC_3	PC_4	PC_5
DRUSD	0.35299	0.61216	0.39064	0.58974	-0.016550
DRGBP	0.43880	-0.32711	0.67822	-0.38102	-0.30871
DREUR	0.49405	-0.44425	-0.079770	0.23802	0.70395
DRJPY	0.41988	0.54376	-0.26045	-0.63666	0.23423
DRCHF	0.51232	-0.15885	-0.55966	0.21225	-0.59500

Correlation between the PC and the variables

	PC_1	PC_2	PC_3	PC_4	PC_5
DRUSD	0.54116	0.68465	0.33101	0.35881	-0.0092236
DRGBP	0.67271	-0.36585	0.57470	-0.23182	-0.17205
DREUR	0.75741	-0.49686	-0.067594	0.14482	0.39232
DRJPY	0.64370	0.60816	-0.22069	-0.38736	0.13054
DRCHF	0.78543	-0.17766	-0.47424	0.12914	-0.33160

STEP 2: NLS estimation of the rotation matrix

NLS function value: −168.418
Estimated Q matrix (symmetric)

0.23818	−0.042920	−0.026811	0.099996	−0.038455
−0.042920	0.51791	−0.14155	−0.12363	0.038462
−0.026811	−0.14155	0.23753	0.034451	0.26602
0.099996	−0.12363	0.034451	0.19998	−0.12907
−0.038455	0.038462	0.26602	−0.12907	0.40813

Estimated U matrix

0.065465	0.44546	−0.60074	0.036532	−0.65959
0.23962	−0.75325	−0.013378	0.41564	−0.44973
−0.83521	−0.33166	−0.11776	−0.36099	−0.21963
0.46009	−0.32426	−0.37841	−0.72301	0.13128
0.17040	0.13797	0.69417	−0.41575	−0.54517

Non-singular matrix (Z = P L^1/2 U)

0.16075	−0.23719	−0.84554	−0.35892	0.27230
−0.35917	0.41010	−0.38672	0.35568	0.65327
−0.38463	0.44040	−0.59829	0.48197	−0.26050
0.34538	−0.52061	−0.60218	0.47968	0.13027
0.48061	0.53118	−0.51502	0.46153	−0.092787

STEP 3: ML estimation of the GARCH-type models on the unobserved factors
-------------Estimating the univariate GARCH model for PC(1)--------------

SPECIFICATIONS

Dependent variable: PC(1)
Mean equation: ARMA (0, 0) model
No regressor in the conditional mean
Variance equation: GARCH (1, 1) model
Variance targeting
No regressor in the conditional variance
Normal distribution
Strong convergence using numerical derivatives
Log-likelihood = −2460.85

Robust standard errors (Sandwich formula)

	Coefficient	*Std. error*	*t-value*	*t-prob*
ARCH(Alpha1)	0.126802	0.027471	4.616	0.0000
GARCH(Beta1)	0.813129	0.068239	11.92	0.0000
Sigma-square	0.060069			

No. of observations:	2,068	No. of parameters:	2
Mean (Y):	−0.00000	Variance (Y):	1.00000
Skewness (Y):	−0.76988	Kurtosis (Y):	60.95483
Log-likelihood	−2460.845	Alpha[1]+Beta[1]:	0.93993

-------------Estimating the univariate GARCH model for PC(2)-------------

SPECIFICATIONS

Dependent variable: PC(2)
Mean equation: ARMA(0, 0) model
No regressor in the conditional mean
Variance equation: GARCH(1, 1) model
Variance targeting
No regressor in the conditional variance
Normal distribution
Strong convergence using numerical derivatives
Log-likelihood = −2712.49

Robust standard errors (Sandwich formula)

	Coefficient	*Std. error*	*t-value*	*t-prob*
ARCH(Alpha1)	0.119986	0.023249	5.161	0.0000
GARCH(Beta1)	0.812395	0.058939	13.78	0.0000
Sigma-square	0.067619			

No. of observations:	*2,068*	*No. of parameters:*	*2*
Mean (Y):	0.00000	Variance (Y):	1.00000
Skewness (Y):	−0.56796	Kurtosis (Y):	21.82242
Log-likelihood	2,712.495	Alpha[1]+Beta[1]:	0.93238

------------Estimating the univariate GARCH model for PC(3)------------

SPECIFICATIONS

Dependent variable: PC(3)
Mean equation: ARMA(0, 0) model
No regressor in the conditional mean
Variance equation: GARCH(1, 1) modelVariance targeting
No regressor in the conditional variance
Normal distribution
Strong convergence using numerical derivatives
Log-likelihood = −2756.11

Robust standard errors (Sandwich formula)

	Coefficient	Std. error	t-value	t-prob
ARCH(Alpha1)	0.126182	0.028005	4.506	0.0000
GARCH(Beta1)	0.833325	0.040838	20.41	0.0000
Sigma-square	0.040492			

No. of observations:	2,068	No. of parameters:	2
Mean (Y):	−0.00000	Variance (Y):	1.00000
Skewness (Y):	0.04291	Kurtosis (Y):	6.82148
Log-likelihood	−2756.114	Alpha[1]+Beta[1]:	0.95951

-------------Estimating the univariate GARCH model for PC(4)---------------

SPECIFICATIONS

Dependent variable: PC(4)
Mean equation: ARMA(0, 0) model
No regressor in the conditional mean
Variance equation: GARCH(1, 1) model
Variance targeting
No regressor in the conditional variance
Normal distribution
Strong convergence using numerical derivatives
Log-likelihood = −2840.08

Robust standard errors (Sandwich formula)

	Coefficient	Std. error	t-value	t-prob
ARCH(Alpha1)	0.039516	0.0084435	4.680	0.0000
GARCH(Beta1)	0.952204	0.012024	79.19	0.0000
Sigma-square	0.008280			

No. of observations:	2,068	No. of parameters:	2
Mean (Y):	−0.00000	Variance (Y):	1.00000
Skewness (Y):	0.24377	Kurtosis (Y):	5.35902
Log-likelihood:	−2840.081	Alpha[1]+Beta[1]:	0.99172

------------Estimating the univariate GARCH model for PC(5)--------------

SPECIFICATIONS

Dependent variable: PC(5)
Mean equation: ARMA(0, 0) model
No regressor in the conditional mean
Variance equation: GARCH(1, 1) model
Variance targeting
No regressor in the conditional variance
Normal distribution
Strong convergence using numerical derivatives
Log-likelihood = −2671.45

Robust standard errors (Sandwich formula)

	Coefficient	Std. error	t-value	t-prob
ARCH(Alpha1)	0.052366	0.0073858	7.090	0.0000
GARCH(Beta1)	0.943303	0.0085597	110.2	0.0000
Sigma-square	0.004332			

No. of observations:	2,068	No. of parameters:	2
Mean (Y):	0.00000	Variance (Y):	1.00000
Skewness (Y):	−0.21983	Kurtosis (Y):	6.67725
Log-likelihood	2,671.450	Alpha[1]+Beta[1]:	0.99567

Summary statistics

No. of observations:	2,068	No. of parameters:	25
No. of series:	5	Log-likelihood:	40,770.704

TESTS

Information criteria (to be minimised)

Akaike	−39.405903	Shibata	−39.406191
Schwarz	−39.337790	Hannan-Quinn	−39.380936

Individual normality tests

Series: DRUSD

	Statistic	t-test	p-value
Skewness	−0.12463	2.3155	0.020583
Excess Kurtosis	1.2585	11.697	1.3278e-031
Jarque-Bera	141.83	.NaN	1.5899e-031

Series: DRGBP

	Statistic	t-test	p-value
Skewness	−0.25141	4.6709	2.9988e-006
Excess Kurtosis	1.6175	15.032	4.5035e-051
Jarque-Bera	247.21	.NaN	2.0800e-054

Series: DREUR

	Statistic	t-test	p-value
Skewness	−0.89596	16.646	3.2533e-062
Excess Kurtosis	12.283	114.16	0.00000
Jarque-Bera	13,278	.NaN	0.00000

Series: DRJPY

	Statistic	t-test	p-value
Skewness	−0.12037	2.2363	0.025329
Excess Kurtosis	3.2939	30.613	8.1640e-206
Jarque-Bera	939.90	.NaN	7.9849e-205

Series: DRCHF

	Statistic	*t-test*	*p-value*
Skewness	7.7715	144.38	0.00000
Excess Kurtosis	209.38	1945.9	0.00000
Jarque-Bera	3.7983e+006	.NaN	0.00000

Q-statistics on standardised residuals

Series: DRUSD

Q(5) = 2.77959	[0.7339205]
Q(10) = 7.94239	[0.6344645]
Q(20) = 21.7152	[0.3561649]
Q(50) = 65.8470	[0.0657956]

Series: DRGBP

Q(5) = 3.68451	[0.5956711]
Q(10) = 7.70136	[0.6579813]
Q(20) = 14.1321	[0.8237361]
Q(50) = 44.5831	[0.6897858]

Series: DREUR

Q(5) = 13.9524	[0.0159145]
Q(10) = 27.0666	[0.0025419]
Q(20) = 35.2184	[0.0189713]
Q(50) = 61.6818	[0.1243707]

Series: DRJPY

Q(5) = 4.85208	[0.4341982]
Q(10) = 10.9801	[0.3590677]
Q(20) = 24.4726	[0.2223572]
Q(50) = 63.9971	[0.0881395]

Series: DRCHF

Q(5) = 6.54261	[0.2569387]
Q(10) = 15.3245	[0.1206714]
Q(20) = 22.5838	[0.3096873]
Q(50) = 43.4674	[0.7312557]

H0: No serial correlation ==> Accept H0 when prob. is high [Q < Chisq(lag)]

Q-statistics on squared standardised residuals

Series: DRUSD

Q(5) = 27.8157	[0.0000395]
Q(10) = 32.4558	[0.0003361]
Q(20) = 47.2626	[0.0005393]
Q(50) = 89.4451	[0.0005142]

Series: DRGBP

Q(5) = 0.908104	[0.9696322]
Q(10) = 35.5435	[0.0001008]
Q(20) = 73.4857	[0.0000000]
Q(50) = 127.959	[0.0000000]

Series: DREUR

Q(5) = 1.51242	[0.9116324]
Q(10) = 1.70818	[0.9981270]
Q(20) = 5.08629	[0.9996833]
Q(50) = 9.34318	[1.0000000]

Series: DRJPY

Q(5) = 17.3309	[0.0039131]
Q(10) = 29.9634	[0.0008685]
Q(20) = 50.4474	[0.0001911]
Q(50) = 98.2118	[0.0000556]

Series: DRCHF

Q(5) = 1.46200	[0.9174134]
Q(10) = 1.48472	[0.9989821]
Q(20) = 1.52678	[1.0000000]
Q(50) = 1.71531	[1.0000000]

H0: No serial correlation ==> Accept H0 when prob. is high [Q < Chisq(lag)]

Vector Normality test: Chi-square(10) = 5998.9 [0.0000]**
Hosking's Multivariate Portmanteau Statistics on standardised residuals

Hosking(5) = 127.509	[0.4208393]
Hosking(10) = 271.817	[0.1639729]
Hosking(20) = 472.581	[0.8057251]
Hosking(50) = 1230.22	[0.6496527]

Hosking's Multivariate Portmanteau statistics on squared standardised residuals

Hosking(5) = 162.661	[0.0096347]
Hosking(10) = 338.850	[0.0001097]
Hosking(20) = 611.417	[0.0003717]
Hosking(50) = 1368.82	[0.0091954]

Warning: *P-values* have been corrected by two degrees of freedom

----

Li and McLeod's Multivariate Portmanteau statistics on standardised residuals

Li-McLeod(5) = 127.539	[0.4201168]
Li-McLeod(10) = 271.768	[0.1644810]
Li-McLeod(20) = 472.891	[0.8029155]
Li-McLeod(50) = 1230.53	[0.6473018]

Li and McLeod's Multivariate Portmanteau statistics on squared standardised residuals

Li-McLeod(5) = 162.642	[0.0096600]
Li-McLeod(10) = 338.630	[0.0001133]
Li-McLeod(20) = 611.010	[0.0003872]
Li-McLeod(50) = 1368.34	[0.0094233]

Warning: *P-values* have been corrected by two degrees of freedom

----

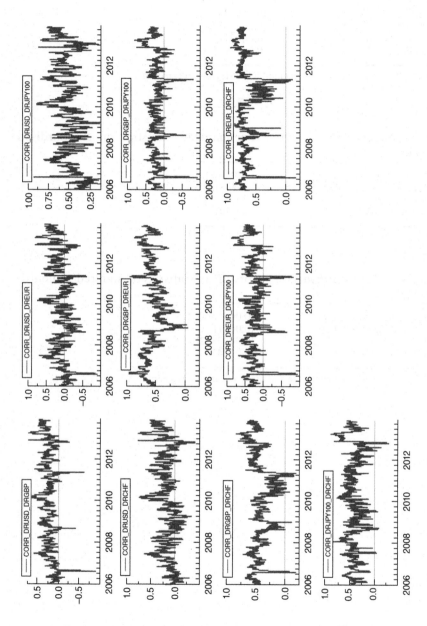

Figure A5.17 Correlations of log difference between five different currency pairs: NLS generalisation of orthogonal GARCH model (by Boswijk and Van der Wedie (2006)) and normal distribution for error terms.

References

Abbott, A., Cushman, D. O. and De Vita, G. (2012). Exchange-rate regimes and foreign direct investment flows to developing countries. *Review of International Economics, 20*(1), 95–107.

Abdalla, S. Z. S. (2012). Modelling exchange rate volatility using GARCH models: Empirical evidence from Arab countries. *International Journal of Economics and Finance, 4*(3), 216–229.

Aghion, P., Bacchetta, P., Ranciere, R. and Rogoff, K. (2009). Exchange-rate volatility and productivity growth: The role of financial development. *Journal of Monetary Economics, 56*(4), 494–513.

Aielli, G. (2009). *Dynamic conditional correlations: On properties and estimation*, Department of Statistics, University of Florence, Florence, Unpublished paper.

Alexander, C. (2001). Orthogonal GARCH. *Mastering Risk, 2*, 21–38.

Alexander, C. (2002). Principal component models for generating large GARCH covariance matrices. *Economic Notes, 31*(2), 337–359.

Alexander, C. and Chibumba, A. (1997). Multivariate orthogonal factor GARCH. University of Sussex, *Mimeo*.

Allayannis, G., Ihrig, J. and Weston, J. P. (2001). Exchange-rate hedging: Financial versus operational strategies. *American Economic Review, 91*(2), 391–395.

Antonakakis, N. and Darby, J. (2013). Forecasting volatility in developing countries' nominal exchange returns. *Applied Financial Economics, 23*(21), 1675–1691.

Arize, A. C., Osang, T. and Slottje, D. J. (2000). Exchange-rate volatility and foreign trade: Evidence from thirteen LDC's. *Journal of Business and Economic Statistics, 18*(1), 10–17.

AuYong, H. H., Gan, C. and Treepongkaruna, S. (2004). Cointegration and causality in the Asian and emerging foreign exchange markets: Evidence from the 1990s financial crises. *International Review of Financial Analysis, 13*, 479–515.

Aydemir, A. B. (2002). Volatility modeling in finance, in J. Knight and S. Satchell (eds.), *Forecasting volatility in the financial markets*, Elsevier, Amsterdam, 1–46.

Baba, Y., Engle, R. F., Kraft, R. D. and Kroner, K. F. (1991). *Multivariate simultaneous generalised ARCH*, Department of Economics, University of California, San Diego (No. 89-57). Discussion Paper.

Baba, Y. E., Kraft, R. D. and Kroner, K. (1987). Multivariate simultaneous generalised ARCH, University of California, San Diego, Unpublished Manuscript.

Baillie, R. T. (1996). Long memory processes and fractional integration in econometrics. *Journal of Econometrics, 73*(1), 5–59.

Baillie, R. T. and Bollerslev, T. (1989). Common stochastic trends in a system of exchange-rates. *Journal of Finance, 44*(1), 167–181.

Baillie, R. T. and McMahon, P. (1989). *The foreign exchange market: Theory and econometric evidence*, Cambridge University Press, Cambridge.

Bakker, A. and Chapple, B. (eds.), (2003). *Capital liberalisation in transition countries: Lessons from the past and for the future*, Edward Elgar Publishing, Cheltenham/ Northampton MA.

Bala, D. A. and Asemota, J. O. (2013). Exchange-rates volatility in Nigeria: Application of GARCH models with exogenous break. *CBN Journal of Applied Statistics, 4*(1), 89–116.

Bali, T. G. (2003). An extreme value approach to estimating volatility and value at risk. *The Journal of Business, 76*(1), 83–108.

Ball, R., Brown, P., Finn, F. J. and Officer, R. R. (1979). Dividends and the value of the firm: Evidence from the Australian equity market. *Australian Journal of Management, 4*(1), 13–26.

Barkoulas, J. T., Baum, C. F. and Caglayan, M. (2002). Exchange-rate effects on the volume and variability of trade flows. *Journal of International Money and Finance, 21*(4), 481–496.

Barton, T. L., Shenkir, W. G. and Walker, P. L. (2002). *Making enterprise risk management pay off*. FT Press, New Jersey.

Bartram, S. M. and Bodnar, G. M. (2012). Crossing the lines: The conditional relation between exchange-rate exposure and stock returns in emerging and developed markets. *Journal of International Money and Finance, 31*(4), 766–792.

Bartram, S. M., Brown, G. W. and Minton, B. A. (2010). Resolving the exposure puzzle: The many facets of exchange rate exposure. *Journal of Financial Economics, 95*(2), 148–173.

Bautista, C. C. (2006). The exchange rate–interest differential relationship in six East Asian countries. *Economics Letters, 92*(1), 137–142.

Bauwens, L., Hafner, C. M. and Laurent, S. (2012). *Handbook of volatility models and their applications, 3*. John Wiley & Sons, New Jersey.

Bauwens, L., Laurent, S. and Rombouts, J. V. (2006). Multivariate GARCH models: A survey. *Journal of Applied Econometrics, 21*(1), 79–109.

Bera, A. K. and Higgins M. (1995). On ARCH models: Properties, estimating and testing, in L. Exley, D. A. R. George, C. J. Roberts and S. Sawyer (eds.), *Surveys in econometrics*, Basil Blackwell, Oxford, reprinted from *Journal of Economic Surveys*.

Billingsley, P. (1995). *Probability and measure*, John Wiley & Sons, Inc, New York.

Black, F. (1976). Studies of stock market volatility changes. *Proceedings of the American Statistical Association*, Business and Economic Statistics Section, 177–181.

Black, F. and Scholes, M. (1974). The effects of dividend yield and dividend policy on common stock prices and returns. *Journal of Financial Economics, 1*(1), 1–22.

Bleaney, M. and Fielding, D. (2002). Exchange rate regimes, inflation and output volatility in developing countries. *Journal of Development Economics, 68*(1), 233–245.

Bollerslev, T. (1986). Generalized autoregressive conditional heteroscedasticity. *Journal of Econometrics, 31*, 307–328.

Bollerslev, T. (1987). A conditional heteroskedastic time series model for speculative prices and rates of return. *Review of Economics and Statistics, 69*, 542–547.

Bollerslev, T. (1990). Modelling the coherence in short-run nominal exchange-rates: Multivariate generalized ARCH approach. *Review of Economics and Statistics, 72*, 498–505.

Bollerslev, T., Chou, R. Y. and Kroner, K. F. (1992). ARCH modeling in finance: A review of the theory and empirical evidence. *Journal of Econometrics, 52*, 5–59.

Bollerslev, T., Engle, R. F. and Nelson, D. B. (1994). ARCH models. *Handbook of econometrics, 4*, 2959–3038.

Bollerslev, T., Engle, R. F. and Wooldridge, J. M. (1988). A capital asset pricing model with time-varying covariances. *Journal of Political Economy, 96*(1), 116–131.

Bollerslev, T. and Mikkelsen, H. O. (1996). Modeling and pricing long memory in stock market volatility. *Journal of Econometrics, 73*(1), 151–184.

Bollerslev, T. and Wooldridge, J. M. (1992). Quasi-maximum likelihood estimation and inference in dynamic models with time-varying covariances. *Econometric Reviews, 11*(2), 143–172.

Bond, C. A. and Najand, M. (2002). Volatility changes in European currency exchange-rates due to EMS announcements. *Global Finance Journal, 13*(1), 93–108.

Boswijk, H. P., & Van Der Weide, R. (2006). *Wake me up before you GO-GARCH* (No. 06-079/4). Tinbergen Institute Discussion Paper.

Box, G. E., and Jenkins, G. M. (1970). *Statistical models for forecasting and control*, Holden Day, San Francisco.

Brailsford, T. J. and Faff, R. W. (1996). An evaluation of volatility forecasting techniques. *Journal of Banking & Finance, 20*(3), 419–438.

Buffie, E. F. (1984). Financial repression, the new structuralists, and stabilization policy in semi-industrialized economies. *Journal of Development Economics, 14*(3), 305–322.

Calvo, G. A., Goldstein, M. and Hochreiter, E. (1996). *Private capital flows to emerging markets after the Mexican crisis*. Institute for International Economics, Washington.

Calvo, G. A., Leiderman, L. and Reinhart, C. M. (1996). Inflows of capital to developing countries in the 1990s. *Journal of Economic Perspectives, 10*(2), 123–139.

Calvo, G. A. and Mishkin, F. S. (2003). The mirage of exchange rate regimes for emerging market countries. *Journal of Economic Perspectives, 17*(4), 99–118.

Calvo, G. A. and Reinhart, C. M. (2002). Fear of floating. *The Quarterly Journal of Economics, 117*(2), 379–408.

Campbell, J. Y. (1990). Measuring the persistence of expected returns. *American Economic Review Papers and Proceedings, 80*, 43–47.

Campbell, J. Y. (1991). A variance decomposition for stock returns. *The Economic Journal, 101*(405), 157–179.

Campbell, J. Y. and Ammer, J. (1993). What moves the stock and bond markets? A variance decomposition for long-term asset returns. *Journal of Finance, XLVIII*(1), 3–37.

Campbell, J. Y. and Hentschel, L. (1992). No news is good news: An asymmetric model of changing volatility in stock returns. *Journal of financial Economics, 31*(3), 281–318.

Campbell, J. Y., Lo, A. W. and MacKinlay, A. C. (1997). *The econometrics of financial markets*, Princeton University Press, Princeton, NJ.

Campbell, J. Y., Shiller, R. J. and Viceira, L. M. (2009). *Understanding inflation-indexed bond markets* (No. w15014). National Bureau of Economic Research, Cambridge, MA.

Caporin, M. and McAleer, M. (2012). Do we really need both BEKK and DCC? A tale of two multivariate GARCH models. *Journal of Economic Surveys, 26*(4), 736–751.

Cera, G., Cera, E. and Lito, G. (2013). A GARCH model approach to calculate the value at risk of Albanian LEK exchange-rate. *European Scientific Journal, 9*(25), 250–260.

Chang, R. and Velasco, A. (2000). Exchange-rate policy for developing countries. *American Economic Review, 90*(2), 71–75.

Chong, L. L. and Tan, H. B. (2007). Macroeconomic factors of exchange-rate volatility: Evidence from four neighbouring ASEAN economies. *Studies in Economics and Finance, 24*(4), 266–285.

Chou, R. Y. (1988). Volatility persistence and stock valuations: Some empirical evidence using GARCH. *Journal of Applied Econometrics, 3*(4), 279–294.

Christie, A. A. (1982). The stochastic behavior of common stock variances: Value, leverage and interest rate effects. *Journal of financial Economics, 10*(4), 407–432.

Christoffersen, P. F. (2012). *Elements of financial risk management*, Academic Press, New York.

Christoffersen, P. F. and Diebold, F. X. (2000). How relevant is volatility forecasting for financial risk management? *Review of Economics and Statistics, 82*(1), 12–22.

Comte, F. and Lieberman, O. (2003). Asymptotic theory for multivariate GARCH processes. *Journal of Multivariate Analysis, 84*(1), 61–84.

Cornell, W. B. and Dietrich, J. K. (1978). The efficiency of the foreign exchange market under floating exchange-rates. *Review of Economics and Statistics, 60*, 111–120.

Cowles 3rd, A. (1933). Can stock market forecasters forecast? *Econometrica: Journal of the Econometric Society, 1*(3), 309–324.

Cowles 3rd, A. and Jones, H. E. (1937). Some a posteriori probabilities in stock market action. *Econometrica, Journal of the Econometric Society, 5*(3), 280–294.

Crosby, M. and Voss, G. (1999). Theoretical issues in exchange-rate determination. *Australian Economic Review, 32*(2), 175–179.

Dale, W. B. (1983). Financing and adjustment of payments imbalances. *IMF Conditionality*, Institute for International Economics, Washington, DC.

Day, T. E. and Lewis, C. M. (1992). Stock market volatility and the information content of stock index options. *Journal of Econometrics, 52*(1), 267–287.

De Santis, G. and Gerard, B. (1998). How big is the premium for currency risk? *Journal of Financial Economics, 49*(3), 375–412.

Devereux, M. (2003). A tale of two currencies: The Asian financial crisis and the exchange-rate regimes of Hong Kong and Singapore. *Review of International Economics, 11*(1), 38–54.

Devereux, M. B. and Lane, P. R. (2003). Understanding bilateral exchange rate volatility. *Journal of International Economics, 60*(1), 109–132.

Dickey, D. A. and Fuller, W. A. (1981). Likelihood ratio statistics for autoregressive time series with a unit root. *Econometrica, 50*, 1057–1072.

Diebold, F. X. (1986). Testing for serial correlation in the presence of ARCH. *Proceedings of the American Statistical Association, Business and Economic Statistics Section, 323*, 328.

Diebold, F. X., Gunther, T. and Tay, A. S. (1998). Evaluating density forecasts with applications to finance and management. *International Economic Review, 39*, 863–883.

Diebold, F. X., Hahn, J. and Tay, A. S. (1999). Multivariate density forecast evaluation and calibration in financial risk management: High frequency returns on foreign exchange. *Review of Economics and Statistics, 81*, 661–673.

Diebold, F. and Lopez, J. A. (1995). Modelling volatility dynamics, in K. Hoover (ed.), *Macroeconometrics: Developments, tensions and prospects, 46.* Springer Science & Business Media, Berlin, 427–466.

Diebold, F. and Nason, J. A. (1990). Nonparametric exchange-rate prediction? *Journal of International Economics, 28,* 315–332.

Ding, Z. and Engle, R. F. (2001). Large scale conditional covariance matrix modeling, estimation and testing. *Academic Economics Papers, 29,* 157–184.

Ding, Z. and Granger, C. W. (1996). Modeling volatility persistence of speculative returns: A new approach. *Journal of Econometrics, 73*(1), 185–215.

Ding, Z., Granger, C. W. and Engle, R. F. (1993). A long memory property of stock market returns and a new model. *Journal of Empirical Finance, 1*(1), 83–106.

Dixon, H. (1999). Controversy: Exchange-rates and fundamentals. *The Economic Journal, 109*(November), 652–654.

Doornik, J. A. (2007a). *An introduction to OxMetrics 5 – A software system for data analysis and forecasting,* 1st edition, Timberlake Consultant Ltd., New York.

Doornik, J. A. (2007b). *Ox 5.0 – An object-oriented matrix programming language,* 1st edition, Timberlake Consultant Ltd., New York.

Doornik, J. A. (2009). *An introduction to OxMetrics 6 – A software system for data analysis and forecasting,* 1st edition, Timberlake Consultant Ltd., New York.

Doornik, J. A. and Ooms, M. (1999). A package for estimating, forecasting and simulating Arfima models: Arfima package 1.0 for Ox. *Preprint,* Erasmus University.

Doraisami, A. (2004). From crisis to recovery: The motivations for and effects of Malaysian capital controls. *Journal of International Development, 16*(2), 241–254.

Dornbusch, R. (1976). Expectations and exchange-rate dynamics. *Journal of Political Economy, 84,* 1161–1176.

Dubas, J. M. (2009). The importance of the exchange-rate regime in limiting misalignment. *World Development, 37*(10), 1612–1622.

Duchesne, P. and Lalancette, S. (2003). On testing for multivariate ARCH effects in vector time series models. *Canadian Journal of Statistics, 31*(3), 275–292.

Dufour, J. M., Khalaf, L. and Beaulieu, M. C. (2003). Exact Skewness–Kurtosis tests for multivariate normality and goodness-of-fit in multivariate regressions with application to asset pricing models. *Oxford Bulletin of Economics and Statistics, 65*(s1), 891–906.

Edmonds, R. G. and So, J. Y. (2004). Is exchange-rate volatility excessive? An ARCH and AR approach. *The Quarterly Review of Economics and Finance, 44*(1), 122–154.

Edwards, S. (1989). *Real exchange-rates, devaluation and adjustment: Exchange-rate policy in developing countries,* MIT Press, Cambridge, MA.

Edwards, S. and Yeyati, E. L. (2005). Flexible exchange rates as shock absorbers. *European Economic Review, 49*(8), 2079–2105.

Eichengreen, B. and Hausmann, R. (1999). *Exchange rates and financial fragility* (No. w7418). National Bureau of Economic Research, Cambridge, MA.

Eichengreen, B. and Hausmann, R. (2003a). *Original sin: The road to redemption,* University of California, Berkeley CA, and Harvard University, Cambridge, MA, Unpublished paper, June.

Eichengreen, B. and Hausmann, R. (2003b). *Debt denomination and financial instability in emerging market economies: Editors' introduction,* University of California, Berkeley, CA, and Harvard University, Cambridge, MA, Unpublished paper.

Eichengreen, B. and Hausmann, R. (2003c). *Original sin: The road to redemption*, University of California, Berkeley, CA, and Harvard University, Cambridge, MA, Unpublished paper.

Eichengreen, B., Hausmann, R. and Panizza, U. (2002). Paper presented at a conference on currency *Original Sin: The Pain, the mystery, and the road to redemption* and maturity matchmaking: Redeeming debt from original sin, Inter-American Development Bank, November 21–22, Washington, DC.

Eichengreen, B., Hausmann, R. and Panizza, U. (2003a). *The mystery of original sin*, University of California, Berkely, CA, Harvard University, Cambridge, MA, and Inter-American Development Bank, Washington, DC, Unpublished paper.

Eichengreen, B., Hausmann, R. and Panizza, U. (2003b). The pain of original sin, in *Other people's money: Debt denomination and financial instability in emerging market economies*, University of Chicago Press, Chicago, IL, 1–49.

Eichengreen, B., Hausmann, R. and Panizza, U. (2003c). *The mystery of original sin*, University of California, Berkely, CA, Harvard University, Cambridge, MA, and Inter-American Development Bank, Washington, DC, Unpublished paper.

Eichengreen, B., Hausmann, R. and Panizza, U. (2003e). "Currency mismatches, debt intolerance, and original sin: Why they are not the same and why it matters", *NBER Working paper 10036*, National Bureau of Economic Research, Cambridge, MA.

Engle, R. F. (1982). Autoregressive conditional heteroscedasticity with estimates of the variance of United Kingdom inflations. *Econometrica, 50*(4), 987–1008.

Engle, R. F. (1987). On the theory of cointegrated economic time series. Paper presented at Econometric Society European Meeting 87, Copenhagen.

Engle, R. F. (2002). Dynamic conditional correlation-a simple class of multivariate GARCH models. *Journal of Business and Economic Statistics, 20*, 339–350.

Engle, R. F. (2009). *Anticipating correlations: A new paradigm for risk management*, Princeton University Press, Princeton, NJ.

Engle, R. F. and Bollerslev, T. (1986). Modelling the persistence of conditional variances. *Econometric Reviews, 5*(1), 1–50.

Engle, R. F. and González-Rivera, G. (1991). Semiparametric ARCH models. *Journal of Business and Economic Statistics, 9*, 345–359.

Engle, R. F., Granger, C. W. and Kraft, D. (1984). Combining competing forecasts of inflation using a bivariate ARCH model. *Journal of Economic Dynamics and Control, 8*(2), 151–165.

Engle, R. F., Hong, C. H., Kane, A. and Noh, J. (1993), Arbitrage valuation of variance forecasts with simulated options. *Advances in Futures and Options Research,* JIA Press, Greenwich, USA.

Engle, R. F., Ito, T. and Lin, W. L. (1990). Meteour showers of heat waves? Heteroskedastic intra-daily volatility in the foreign exchange market. *Econometrica, 58*, 525–542.

Engle, R. F. and Kelly, B. (2012). Dynamic equicorrelation. *Journal of Business & Economic Statistics, 30*(2), 212–228.

Engle, R. F. and Kroner, K. F. (1995). Multivariate simultaneous generalized ARCH. *Econometric Theory, 11*(1), 122–150.

Engle, R. F., Lilien, D. M. and Robins, R. P. (1987). Estimating time varying risk premia in the term structure: The ARCH-M model. *Econometrica: Journal of the Econometric Society*, 391–407.

Engle, R. F. and Manganelli, S. (2004). CAViaR: Conditional autoregressive value at risk by regression quantiles. *Journal of Business & Economic Statistics, 22*(4), 367–381.

Engle, R. and Mezrich, J. (1996). Garch for groups: A round-up of recent developments in GARCH techniques for estimating correlation. *Risk-London-Risk Magazine Limited, 9*, 36–40.

Engle, R. F. and Ng, V. K. (1993). Measuring and testing the impact of news on volatility. *The Journal of Finance, 48*(5), 1749–1778.

Engle, R. F. and Rangel J. G. (2008). The Spline-GARCH model for low-frequency volatility and its global macroeconomic causes. *Review of Financial Studies, 21*, 1187–1222.

Engle, R. F. and Sheppard, K. (2001). *Theoretical and empirical properties of dynamic conditional correlation multivariate GARCH* (No. w8554), National Bureau of Economic Research, Cambridge, MA.

Epaphra, M. (2017). Modeling exchange rate volatility: Application of the GARCH and EGARCH models. *Journal of Mathematical Finance, 7*(1), 121–143.

Fama, E. F. (1965). The behavior of stock market prices. *Journal of Business, 38*, 34–105.

Fama, E. F. (1970). Efficient capital markets: A review of theory and empirical work. *The Journal of Finance, 25*(2), 383–417.

Fama, E. F. (1991). Efficient capital markets: II. *The Journal of Finance, 46*(5), 1575–1617.

Fernández, C. and Steel, M. F. (1998). On Bayesian modeling of fat tails and skewness. *Journal of the American Statistical Association, 93*(441), 359–371.

Financial Stability Forum. (2000). *Report of the working group on capital flows* (Mario Draghi, Chair), Basel, April.

Finnerty, J. D. and Leistikow, D. (1993). The behavior of equity and debt risk premiums. *Journal of Portfolio Management, 19*(4), 73.

Fiorentini, G., Sentana, E. and Calzolari, G. (2003). Maximum likelihood estimation and inference in multivariate conditionally heteroscedastic dynamic regression models with Student t innovations. *Journal of Business & Economic Statistics, 21*(4), 532–546.

Fischer, S. (1999). On the need for an international lender of last resort. *Journal of economic perspectives, 13*(4), 85–104.

Fischer, S. (2001). Exchange rate regimes: Is the bipolar view correct? *Journal of Economic Perspectives, 15*(2), 3–24.

Fischer, S. (2008). Mundell-Fleming lecture: Exchange-rate systems, surveillance, and advice. *International Monetary Fund Staff Papers*, Washington, DC, *55*(3), 367–383.

Fraga, A., Goldfajn, I. and Minella, A. (2003). Inflation targeting in emerging market economies. *NBER Macroeconomics Annual, 18*, 365–400.

Francq, C. and Zakoian, J. M. (2019). *GARCH models: Structure, statistical inference and financial applications.* John Wiley & Sons, Hoboken, New Jersey.

Frankel, J. A. (1999). *No single currency regime is right for all countries or at all times* (No. w7338), National Bureau of Economic Research, Washington, DC.

Frankel, J. A. (2003). *Experience of and lessons from exchange rate regime in emerging economies* (No. w10032), National Bureau of Economic Research, Washington, DC.

Frankel, J. A. (2005). Mundell-Fleming lecture: Contractionary currency crashes in developing countries. *IMF Staff Papers, 52*(2), 149–192.

Frankel, J. (2006). On the Yuan: The choice between adjustment under a fixed exchange-rate and adjustment under a flexible rate. *CESifo Economic Studies, 52*(2), 246–275.

Frankel, J. A. and Rose, A. K. (1996). Currency crashes in emerging markets: An empirical treatment. *Journal of International Economics, 41*(3–4), 351–366.

Franses, P. H. and Van Dijk, D. (2000). *Non-linear time series models in empirical finance*, Cambridge University Press, Cambridge.

Gan, W. B. and Soon, L. Y. (2003, August). Current account reversal during a currency crisis: The Malaysian experience. *ASEAN Economic Bulletin, 20*(2), 128–144.

Gencay, R. and Selcuk, F. (2004). Extreme value theory and value-at-risk: Relative performance in emerging markets. *International Journal of Forecasting, 20*(2), 287–303.

Geweke, J. (1986). Exact inference in the inequality constrained normal linear regulation model. *Journal of Applied Econometrics, 1*, 127–141.

Ghazali, M. F. and Lean, H. H. (2015). Asymmetric volatility of local gold prices in Malaysia, in V. N. Huynh, V. Kreinovich, S. Sriboonchitta, and K. Suriya (eds.), *Econometrics of Risk*, Springer, Cham, 203–218.

Ghysels, E., Harvey, A. C. and Renault, E. (1996). Stochastic volatility, in G. S. Maddala and C. R. Rao (eds.), *Statistical methods in finance*, Elsevier Science Publishers, Amsterdam, 119–192.

Gilli, M. (2006). An application of extreme value theory for measuring financial risk. *Computational Economics, 27*(2–3), 207–228.

Giot, P. and Laurent, S. (2003). Value-at-risk for long and short trading positions. *Journal of Applied Econometrics, 18*(6), 641–663.

Glosten, L. R., Jagannathan, R. and Runkle, D. E. (1993). On the relation between the expected value and the volatility of the nominal excess return on stocks. *The Journal of Finance, 48*(5), 1779–1801.

Goldstein, M. (1998). *The Asian financial crisis: Causes, cures, and systemic implications, 55*, Peterson Institute, Washington, DC.

Goldstein, M., Kaminsky, G. L. and Reinhart, C. M. (2000). *Assessing financial vulnerability: An early warning system for emerging markets*. Peterson Institute, Washington, DC.

Goldstein, M. and Turner, P. (2004). *Controlling currency mismatches in emerging markets*. Columbia University Press, New York.

Gouriéroux, C. (1997). *ARCH models and financial applications*, Springer Science & Business Media, Berlin.

Granger, C. W. J. (1980). Testing for causality: A personal viewpoint. *Journal of Economic Dynamics and Control, 2*, 329–352.

Granger, C. W. J. and Joyeux, R. (1980). An introduction to long-memory time series models and fractional differencing. *Journal of Time Series Analysis, 1*(1), 15–29.

Granger, C. W. J. and Newbold, P. (1977). *Forecasting economic time series*, Academic Press, New York.

Gregory, A. W. (1994). Testing for cointegration in linear quadratic models. *Journal of Business & Economic Statistics, 12*(3), 347–360.

Guittan, M. (1976). The balance of payments as a monetary phenomenon: Empirical evidence, Spain 1955-71, in H. G. Johnson and J.A. Frenkel (Eds.), *The monetary approach to the balance of payments*, Allen and Unwin, London, 672.

Habermeier, M. K. F., Kokenyne, A. and Baba, C. (2011). *The effectiveness of capital controls and prudential policies in managing large inflows* (No. 11-14). International Monetary Fund, Washington, DC.

Hafner, C. and Franses, P. H. (2003). *A generalized dynamic conditional correlation model for many asset returns* (No. EI 2003-18), Econometric Institute Research Papers, Rotterdam.

Hafner, C. M. and Herwartz, H. (1998). Structural analysis of portfolio risk using beta impulse response functions. *Statistica Neerlandica, 52*(3), 336–355.

Hallwood, C. P. and MacDonald, R. (2000). *International money and finance*, 3rd edition, Blackwell Publishing, Hoboken, NJ.

Hamilton-Hart, N. (2002). *Asian states, Asian bankers: Central banking in Southeast Asia*, Cornell University Press, Ithaca, NY.

Hansanti, S., Islam, S. M. and Sheehan, P. (2008). Overview of Thailand's approach to financial liberalisation, in *International finance in emerging markets: Issues, welfare economics analyses and policy implications, 47–65, Heidelberg: Physica-Verlag.*

Hansen, B. E. (1994). Autoregressive conditional density estimation. *International Economic Review, 35*(3), 705–730.

Hansen, P. R. and Lunde, A. (2005). A forecast comparison of volatility models: Does anything beat a GARCH (1, 1)? *Journal of Applied Econometrics, 20*(7), 873–889.

Harvey, A., Ruiz, E. and Shephard, N. (1994). Multivariate stochastic variance models. *The Review of Economic Studies, 61*(2), 247–264.

Hasanti, S., Islam, S. M. N. and Sheehan, P. (2007). *International finance in emerging markets: Issues, welfare economics analyses and policy implications*, Contributions to Economics, Springer, Heidelberg.

Hausmann, R. and Panizza, U. (2003). On the determinants of original sin: An empirical investigation. *Journal of International Money and Finance, 22*, 957–990.

He, C. and Teräsvirta, T. (1999). Properties of moments of a family of GARCH processes. *Journal of Econometrics, 92*(1), 173–192.

He, C. and Teräsvirta, T. H. M. (2002). Fourth moment structure of a family of first order exponential GARCH models. *Econometric Theory, 18*, 868–885.

Hellar, H. R. (1976). International reserves and worldwide inflation. *IMF Staff Papers*, 61–87.

Higgins, M. L. and Bera, A. K. (1992). A class of nonlinear ARCH models. *International Economic Review, 33*(1), 137–158.

Hinkle, L. E. and Monteil, P. J. (1999). *Exchange-rate misalignment: Concepts and measurement for developing countries*, Oxford University Press, New York.

Ho, C. S. and Ariff, M. (2009). Examining foreign exchange behaviour in Asia Pacific and Eastern European emerging countries. *Global Economy and Finance Journal, 2*(1), 1.

Honkapohja, S. and Pikkarainen, P. (1992). Country characteristics and choice of exchange-rate regime. *CERP Discussion Paper*, 744.

Hosking, J. R. (1980). The multivariate portmanteau statistic. *Journal of the American Statistical Association, 75*(371), 602–608.

Hossain, A. A. (2009). *Central banking and monetary policy in the Asia-Pacific*, Edward Elgar Publishing, Cheltenham.

Hsieh, D. A. (1989). Modeling heteroscedasticity in daily foreign-exchange-rates. *Journal of Business & Economic Statistics, 7*(3), 307–317.

Hurley, D. T. and Santos, R. A. (2001). Exchange-rate volatility and the role of regional currency linkages: The ASEAN case. *Applied Economics, 33*, 1991–1999.

Husain, A. M., Mody, A. and Rogoff, K. S. (2005). Exchange rate regime durability and performance in developing versus advanced economies. *Journal of Monetary Economics, 52*(1), 35–64.

Hussin, M. Y. M., Muhammad, F., Abu, M. F. and Razak, A. A. (2012). The relationship between oil price, exchange-rate and Islamic stock market in Malaysia. *Research Journal of Finance and Accounting, 3*(5), 83–92.

Islam, S. M. N., Watanapalachaikul, S. and Clark, C. (2007). Some tests of the efficiency of the emerging financial markets an analysis of the Thai stock market. *Journal of Emerging Market Finance, 6*(3), 291–302.

Ito, T., Engle, R. F. and Lin, W. L. (1992). Where does the meteor shower come from?: The role of stochastic policy coordination. *Journal of International Economics, 32*(3), 221–240.

Jarque, C. M. and Bera, A. K. (1987). A test for normality of observations and regression residuals. *International Statistical Review/Revue Internationale de Statistique, 55*(2), 163–172.

Jeantheau, T. (1998). Strong consistency of estimators for multivariate ARCH models. *Econometric Theory, 14*(01), 70–86.

Jensen, M. C. (1978). Some anomalous evidence regarding market efficiency. *Journal of Financial Economics, 6*(2/3), 95–101.

Jondeau, E., Poon, S. H. and Rockinger, M. (2007). *Financial modeling under non-Gaussian distributions*. Springer Science & Business Media, Berlin.

Jonston, R. B. and Brekk, O. P. (1989). Monetary control procedures and financial reform: Approaches, issues and recent experience in developing countries. *IMF working papers*, WP/89/48.

Jorgenson, D. (1966). Rational distributed lag functions. *Econometrica, 34*, 135–149.

Jorion, P. (2000). *Value-at-Risk: The new benchmark for managing financial risk*, McGraw-Hill, New York.

Kamal, Y., Ghani, U. and Khan, M. M. (2012). Modeling the exchange rate volatility, using generalized autoregressive conditionally heteroscedastic (GARCH) type models: Evidence from Pakistan. *African Journal of Business Management, 6*(8), 2830–2838.

Kariya, T. (1988). MTV model and its application to the prediction of stock prices, in T. Pullila and S Puntanen (eds.), *Proceedings of the Second International Tampere Conference in Statistics*, University of Tampere, Finland.

Karolyi, G. A. (1995). A multivariate GARCH model of international transmissions of stock returns and volatility: The case of the United States and Canada. *Journal of Business & Economic Statistics, 13*(1), 11–25.

Kawakatsu, H. (2006). Matrix exponential GARCH. *Journal of Econometrics, 134*(1), 95–128.

Kearney, C. and Patton, A. J. (2000). Multivariate GARCH modeling of exchange rate volatility transmission in the European monetary system. *Financial Review, 35*(1), 29–48.

Kendall, M. G. (1953). The analysis of economic time series – Part I: Prices. *Journal of the Royal Statistical Society (Series A), 96*, 11–25.

Kettell, B. (2001). *Financial economics: Making sense of information in financial markets*, Financial Times Prentice Hall, London.

Kim, S. J. (1998). Do Australian and the US macroeconomic news announcements affect the USD/AUD exchange-rate? Some evidence from E-GARCH estimations. *Journal of Multinational Financial Management, 8*(2), 233–248.

Knight, J. and Satchell, S. (eds.). (2002). *Forecasting volatility in the financial markets*, Butterworth Heinemann, Oxford.

Knoop, T. A. (2008). *Modern financial macroeconomics: Panics, crashes, and crises.* Blackwell Pub., Hoboken, NJ.

Kohsaka, A. (1984). High interest rate policy under financial repression. *Developing Economies*, 22(4), 419–452.

König, H. and Gaab, W. (1982). The advanced theory of statistics, Vol. 2 of *Inference and Relationships*, Haffner, New York, 504.

Koske, I. (2008). Assessing the equilibrium exchange-rate of the Malaysian ringgit: A comparison of alternative approaches. *Asian Economic Journal*, 22(2), 179–208.

Kroner, K. E. and Ng, V. K. (1998). Modeling asymmetric comovements of asset return. *Review of Financial Studies*, 11(4), 817–844.

Lam, J. (2003). Ten predictions for risk management. *RMA JOURNAL*, 85(8), 84–87.

Lambert, P. and Laurent, S. (2002). Modelling skewness dynamics in series of financial data using skewed location-scale distributions. Institut de Statistique, Italy. *Louvain-la-Neuve Discussion Paper*, 119.

Laurent, S. (2006). *Estimating and forecasting ARCH models using G@ RCH 5*, Timberlake Consultants Limited, UK.

Laurent, S. and Peters, J. P. (2006). *G@RCH 4.2, estimating and forecasting ARCH models*, Timberlake Consultants Limited, UK.

Lee, S. W. and Hansen, B. E. (1994). Asymptotic theory for the GARCH (1, 1) quasi-maximum likelihood estimator. *Econometric Theory*, 10(1), 29–52.

Le Fort, G. R. (1988). The relative price of nontraded goods, absorption, and exchange-rate policy in Chile: 1974–82. *IMF Staff Papers*, 32(2), 336–370.

Levy-Yeyati, E. and Sturzenegger, F. (2003). To float or to fix: Evidence on the impact of exchange rate regimes on growth. *American Economic Review*, 93(4), 1173–1193.

Lewis, K. K. (1994). Puzzles in international financial markets. *NBER Working Paper*, No. 4951.

Li, W. K. and McLeod, A. I. (1981). Distribution of the residual autocorrelations in multivariate ARMA time series models. *Journal of the Royal Statistical Society: Series B (Methodological)*, 43(2), 231–239.

Lien, D. and Tse, Y. K. (2002). Some recent developments in futures hedging. *Journal of Economic Surveys*, 16(3), 357–396.

Ling, S. and McAleer, M. (2003). Asymptotic theory for a vector ARMA-GARCH model. *Econometric Theory*, 19(2), 280–310.

Liu, L. G., Noland, M., Robinson, S. and Wang, Z. (1998). *Asian competitive devaluations* (No. 98), Institute for International Economics, Washington, DC.

Longin, F. and Solnik, B. (1995). Is the correlation in international equity returns constant: 1960–1990? *Journal of International Money and Finance*, 14(1), 3–26.

Longmore, R. and Robinson, W. (2004). Modelling and forecasting exchange rate dynamics: An application of asymmetric volatility models. *Bank of Jamaica, Working Paper, WP2004, 3*, 191–217.

Loudon, G. F., Watt, W. H. and Yadav, P. K. (2000). An empirical analysis of alternative parametric ARCH models. *Journal of Applied Econometrics*, 15(2), 117–136.

Low, C. K. (2000). *Financial Markets in Malaysia.* Malayan Law Journal Sdn Bhd, Kuala Lumpur.

Lum, Y. C. and Islam, S. N. (2016a). *The nature and incidents of stochastic volatility in the FOREX market in developing countries: Some new insights*, Victoria University, Melbourne.

Lum, Y. C. and Islam, S. N. (2016b). *Modelling stochastic volatility in the FOREX market in developing countries: An appropriate approach*, Victoria University, Melbourne.

Lum, Y. C. and Islam, S. N. (2016c). *Stochastic volatility and policy responses in developing countries: An information asymmetric perspective*, Victoria University, Melbourne.

Lum, Y. C. and Islam, S. N. (2016d). *Risk management in the FOREX market in developing countries: Measurement, modelling and strategies – some new insights*, Victoria University, Melbourne.

Lumsdaine, R. L. (1996). Consistency and asymptotic normality of the quasi-maximum likelihood estimator in IGARCH (1, 1) and covariance stationary GARCH (1, 1) models. *Econometrica: Journal of the Econometric Society, 64*(3), 575–596.

MacDonald, R. (1999). Exchange-rate behaviour: Are fundamentals important? *The Economic Journal, 109*(459), 673–691.

Madhavi, K. and Malleswaramma, C. (2013). Tools of risk management in banking sector with special reference to India. *Innovative Journal of Business and Management, 2*(5), 95–96.

Madura, J. (2016). *International financial management*, Cengage Learning, Independence, KY.

Mahmood, W. M. W. and Ahmad, S. S. S. (2006). Interrelatedness of Malaysian foreign exchange markets: Comparing two different regimes *The ICFAI Journal of Applied Economics*, (5), 22–36.

Mandelbrot, B. (1963), The variation of certain speculative prices. *Journal of Business, 36*, 394–419.

Markowitz, H. (1952). Portfolio selection. *Journal of Finance, 7*(1), 77–91.

Marsh, I. and McDonald, R. (1999). *Exchange-rate modeling*, Springer, Heidelberg.

McFarland, J. W., Pettit, R. R. and Sung, S. K. (1982). The distribution of foreign exchange price changes: Trading day effects and risk management. *Journal of Finance, 37*, 693–715.

McKenzie, M. D. (1999). The impact of exchange-rate volatility on international trade flows. *Journal of Economic Surveys, 13*(1), 71–106.

McLeod, A. I. and Li, W. K. (1983). Diagnostic checking ARMA time series models using squared-residual autocorrelations. *Journal of Time Series Analysis, 4*(4), 269–273.

McNeil, A. J., Frey, R. and Embrechts, P. (2010). *Quantitative risk management: Concepts, techniques, and tools*, Princeton University Press, Princeton, NJ.

Miletić, S. (2015). Modeling and forecasting exchange rate volatility: Comparison between EEC and developed countries. *Industrija, 43*(1), 7–24.

Mina, J. and Xiao, J. Y. (2001). Return to RiskMetrics: The evolution of a standard. *RiskMetrics Group, 1*, 1–11.

Mishkin, F. S. (1999). Lessons from the Asian crisis. *Journal of International Money and Finance, 18*(4), 709–723.

Mohammed, K. S., Benhabib, A. and Maliki, S. (2014). Foreign exchange market and contagion: The evidence through GARCH model. *International Journal of Innovation and Applied Studies, 7*(1), 283–297.

Montiel, P. J. and Ostry, J. D. (1991). Macroeconomics implications of real exchange-rate targeting in developing countries. *IMF Staff Papers, 37*(1), 872–900.

Montiel, P. J. and Ostry, J. D. (1992). Real exchange-rate targeting under capital controls. *IMF Staff Papers, 39*(1), 58–78.

Morgan, J. P. (1996). *RiskMetrics technical document.* Retrieved from the World Wide Web www.jpmorgan.com.

Mun, K. C. (2007). Volatility and correlation in international stock markets and the role of exchange-rate fluctuations. *Journal of International Financial Markets, Institutions and Money, 17*(1), 25–41.

Murari, K. (2015). Exchange Rate Volatility Estimation Using GARCH Models, with Special Reference to Indian Rupee Against World Currencies. *IUP Journal of Applied Finance, 21*(1), 22–37.

Mussa, M. L. (1979). Empirical regularities in the behaviour of exchange-rates and theories of the foreign exchange markets, in K. Bruner and A. H. Meltzer (eds.), *Policies for employment, prices and exchange-rates, Carnegie-Rochester Conference Series on public policy,* supplement to the *Journal of Monetary Economics,* 9–57.

Nelson, D. B. (1991). Conditional heteroscedasticity in asset returns: A new approach. *Econometrica, 59*(2), 343–370.

Nelson, D. B. and Cao, C. Q. (1992). Inequality constraints in the univariate GARCH model. *Journal of Business & Economic Statistics, 10*(2), 229–235.

Newey, W. K. and Steigerwald, D. G. (1997). Asymptotic bias for quasi-maximum-likelihood estimators in conditional heteroskedasticity models. *Econometrica: Journal of the Econometric Society, 65*(3), 587–599.

Nielsen, L. (2011). *Classifications of countries based on their level of development: How it is done and how it could be done [Electronic resource].* IMF Working Paper. Mode of access: http://www.relooney.fatcow.com/0_NS4053_1504.pdf.

Olowe, R. A. (2009). Modelling naira/dollar exchange rate volatility: Application of GARCH and asymmetric models. *International Review of Business Research Papers, 5*(3), 377–398.

Osborne, M. F. M. (1959). Brownian motion in the stock market. *Operation Research, 7,* 145–173.

Ostry, J. D., Ghosh, A. R., Habermeier, K., Laeven, L., Chamon, M., Qureshi, M. S. and Kokenyne, A. (2011). Managing capital inflows: What tool to use!, *IMF Staff Discussion Note,* SDN/11/06.

Pagan, A. (1996). The econometrics of financial markets. *Journal of Empirical Finance, 3*(1), 15–102.

Pagan, A. R. and Schwert, G. W. (1990). Alternative models for conditional stock volatility. *Journal of Econometrics, 45*(1), 267–290.

Palm, F. C. (1996). GARCH models of volatility, in G. S. Maddala and C. R. Rao (eds.), *Handbook of statistics,* Elsevier Science B. V., Amsterdam, 209–240.

Palm, F. C. and Vlaar, P. J. (1997). *Simple diagnostic procedures for modeling financial time series* (No. urn: nbn: nl: ui: 27-5772). Maastricht University, Maastricht.

Papaioannou, M. M. G. (2006). *Exchange Rate Risk Measurement and Management: Issues and Approaches for Firms (EPub)* (No. 6-255). International Monetary Fund, Washington, DC.

Pentula, S. (1986). Modeling the persistence of conditional variances: A comment. *Econometric Review, 5,* 71–74.

Polak, J. J. (1957). Monetary analysis of income formation and payments problems. *IMF Staff Papers, 4,* 1–50.

Polak, J. J. (1991). The changing nature of IMF conditionality. *OECD Development Centre Working Papers,* No. 41, OECD Publishing, Paris.

Poon, W. C., Choong, C. K. and Habibullah, M. S. (2005). Exchange rate volatility and exports for selected East Asian countries: Evidence from error correction model. *ASEAN Economic Bulletin*, *22*(2), 144–159.

Poterba, J. M. and Summers, L. H. (1988). Mean reversion in stock prices: Evidence and implications. *Journal of Financial Economics*, *22*, 27–59.

Prasad, E., Rogoff, K., Wei, S. J. and Kose, M. A. (2005). Effects of financial globalization on developing countries: Some empirical evidence, in W. Tseng and D. Cowen (eds.), *India's and China's recent experience with reform and growth*, Palgrave Macmillan, London, 201–228.

Radelet, S. and Sachs, J. (1998). *The onset of the East Asian financial crisis*, No. w6680, National Bureau of Economic Research, Cambridge, MA.

Ramzan, S., Ramzan, S. and Zahid, F. M. (2012). Modeling and forecasting exchange rate dynamics in Pakistan using ARCH family of models. *Electronic Journal of Applied Statistical Analysis*, *5*(1), 15–29.

Ranaldo, A. and Söderlind, P. (2010). Safe haven currencies. *Review of finance*, *14*(3), 385–407.

Reinhart, C. M., Rogoff, K. S. and Savastano, M. A. (2003). *Debt intolerance*, No. w9908, National Bureau of Economic Research, Cambridge, MA.

Remillard, B. (2013). *Statistical methods for financial engineering*. CRC Press, Florida.

Rogoff, K. (1999). *International institutions for reducing global financial instability*, No. w7265, National Bureau of Economic Research, Cambridge, MA.

Rusydi, M. and Islam, S. M. N. (2006). *Quantitative exchange-rate economics in developing countries: A new pragmatic decision making approach*, Manuscript of Victoria University, Australia.

Sarno, L. and Taylor, M. P. (2002). *The economics of exchange-rates*, Cambridge University Press, London.

Savvides, A. (1993). Real exchange-rate variability and the choice of exchange-rate regime by developing countries. *Journal of International Money and Finance*, *9*, 440–454.

Schnabl, G. (2008). Exchange rate volatility and growth in small open economies at the EMU periphery. *Economic Systems*, *32*(1), 70–91.

Schwert, G. W. (1990). Stock volatility and the crash of '87. *Review of Financial Studies*, *3*(1), 77–102.

Shiller, R. J. (2003). Social security and individual accounts as elements of overall risk-sharing. *American Economic Review*, *93*(2), 343–347.

Silvennoinen, A. and Teräsvirta, T. (2008). *Multivariate GARCH models*, SSE, No. 669, EFI Working Paper Series in Economics and Finance, Stockholm School of Economics, Stockholm.

Sims, C. (1980). Macroeconomics and reality. *Econometrica*, *48*(1), 1–48.

Spiegel, M. (2002). Argentina's currency crisis: Lessons for Asia, Federal Reserve Bank of San Francisco (July), *Mimeo*.

Spraos, J. (1986). *IMF conditionality: Ineffectual, inefficient, mistargeted*. International Finance Section, Department of Economics, Princeton University, Princeton, NJ.

Stiglitz, J. E. (2002). Capital market liberalisation and exchange-rate regimes: Risk without reward. *The Annals of the American Academy of Political and Social Science*, *579*(1), 219–248.

Stiglitz, J. E. (2003). Democratizing the International Monetary Fund and the World Bank: Governance and accountability. *Governance*, *16*(1), 111–139.

Sun, D. (2006). Asian Currency Unit still a dream. People's Daily Online. http:// english.peopledaily.com.cn/200611/16/eng20061116_322155.html. Accessed on 3 April 2009.

Swanson, N. R. and White, H. (1994). A model-selection approach to assessing the information in the term structure using linear models and artificial neural networks. *Journal of Business and Economic Statistics*, *13*(3), 265–275.

Tai, C. S. (2004). Looking for risk premium and contagion in Asia-Pacific foreign exchange markets. *International Review of Financial Analysis*, *13*, 381–409.

Tan, H. B. and Chong, L. L. (2008). Choice of exchange-rate system and macroeconomic volatility of three Asian emerging economies. *Macroeconomics and Finance in Emerging Market Economies*, *1*(2), 167–179.

Tanzi, V. (1987). Fiscal policy, growth, and stabilization programmes. *Finance and Development*, *87*(2), 15–17.

Taylor, L. (1983). *Structuralist macroeconomics*, Basic Books, New York.

Taylor, S. J. (1986). *Modelling financial time series*, John Wiley & Sons, Ltd, Chichester.

Taylor, S. J. (2005). *Asset price dynamics, volatility and prediction*, Princeton University Press, Princeton, NJ.

Thomas, S. (1995). *An empirical characterization of the Bombay Stock Exchange*. Dissertation in partial fulfillment of Doctor of Philosophy for University of Southern California, Los Angeles, CA.

Thomas, S. and Shah, A. (1999). Risk and the Indian Economy, in K. S. Parikh (ed.), *India development report, 1999–2000*, Oxford University Press, Oxford.

Thorlie, M. A., Song, L., Wang, X. and Amin, M. (2014). Modelling exchange rate volatility using asymmetric GARCH models (evidence from Sierra Leone). *International Journal of Science and Research*, *3*(11), 1206–1214.

Timmermann, A. and Granger, C. W. (2004). Efficient market hypothesis and forecasting. *International Journal of Forecasting*, *20*(1), 15–27.

Titman, S. and Wei, K. J. (1999). Understanding stock market volatility: The case of Korea and Taiwan. *Pacific-Basin Finance Journal*, *7*(1), 41–66.

Tokarick, S. (1995). External shocks, the real exchange-rate, and tax policy. *IMF Staff Papers*, *42*(1), 49–79.

Tse, Y. K. (2002). Residual-based diagnostics for conditional heteroscedasticity models. *The Econometrics Journal*, *5*(2), 358–374.

Tse, Y. K. and Tsui, A. K. C. (1997). Conditional volatility in foreign exchange-rates: Evidence from the Malaysian Ringgit and Singapore Dollar. *Pacific-Basin Finance Journal*, *5*(3), 345–356.

Tse, Y. K. and Tsui, A. K. C. (1999). A note on diagnosing multivariate conditional heteroscedasticity models. *Journal of Time Series Analysis*, *20*(6), 679–691.

Tse, Y. K. and Tsui, A. K. C. (2002). A multivariate generalized autoregressive conditional heteroscedasticity model with time-varying correlations. *Journal of Business and Economic Statistics*, *20*(3), 351–362.

Van den Goorbergh, R. W. and Vlaar, P. J. (1999). *Value-at-Risk analysis of stock returns historical simulation, variance techniques or tail index estimation?* De Nederlandsche Bank, NV, Netherlands.

Van der Weide, R. (2002). GO-GARCH: A multivariate generalized orthogonal GARCH model. *Journal of Applied Econometrics*, *17*(5), 549–564.

Van Wijnbergen, S. (1983a). Credit policy, inflation and growth in a financially repressed economy. *Journal of Development Economics*, *13*(3), 45–65.

Van Wijnbergen, S. (1983b). Interest rate management in Ldcs. *Journal of Monetary Economics*, *12*(3), September, 433–452.

Weil, P. (1987). Confidence and the real value of money in an overlapping generations economy. *The Quarterly Journal of Economics*, 102(1), 1–22.

Weiss, A. A. (1986). ARCH and bilinear time series models: Comparison and combination. *Journal of Business & Economic Statistics*, *4*(1), 59–70.

White, H. (1980). A heteroskedasticity-consistent covariance matrix estimator and a direct test for heteroscedasticity. *Econometrica*, *48*, 817–838.

Whitt Jr, J. A. (1996). The Mexican peso crisis. *Economic Review-Federal Reserve Bank of Atlanta*, *81*(1), 1.

Williamson, J. (1983). *The exchange-rate system*, Institute for International Finance, Washington, DC.

Wong, H. T. (2013). Real exchange-rate misalignment and economic growth in Malaysia, *Journal of Economic Studies*, *40*(3), 298–313.

Working, H. (1934). A random-difference series for use in the analysis of time series. *Journal of the American Statistical Association*, *29*(185), 11–24.

Zakoian, J. M. (1994). Threshold heteroskedastic models. *Journal of Economic Dynamics and Control*, *18*(5), 931–955.

Žiković, S. (2008). Calculating VaR in EU candidate States. *South East European Journal of Economics and Business*, *3*(1), 23–33.

Index

Note: **Bold** page numbers refer to tables and *italic* page numbers refer to figures.

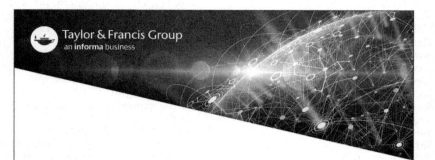

Printed in the United States
by Baker & Taylor Publisher Services